Coaching
Women's
Gymnastics

Bill Sands

Human Kinetics Publishers, Inc.
Champaign, Illinois 61820

Production Director: Kathryn Gollin Marshak
Editorial Staff: Peg Goyette and Mary Glockner
Typesetter: Sandra Meier
Text Layout: Lezli Harris
Cover Design and Layout: Debra Watson
Cover Photo: Dave Black. Photo shows Amy Koopman, 1980 Olympian, 1981
World Championship team member, 1982 National Floor Exercise cham-
pion, member of national team for three years.

ISBN: 0-931250-58-7
Library of Congress Catalog Card Number 83-083163

Printed in the United States of America

10 9 8 7 6 5 4 3 2 1

Human Kinetics Publishers, Inc.
Box 5076 Champaign, IL 61820

To Donna
Always my source of inspiration

Contents

Chapter 12   Psychological Preparation   129

Chapter 13   Technical Preparation   144

Chapter 14   Tactical Preparation   163

Chapter 15   Theoretical Preparation   178

Foreword

One limiting factor to the growth in quantity and quality of gymnastics in our country is the discouraging lack of knowledgeable teachers and coaches. This is not necessarily due to a lack of interest or enthusiasm. More likely, it is due to a lack of readily available up-to-date information. It seems that we make the same mistakes over and over and that the basis for the majority of our decisions are trial and error. If gymnastics in the United States hopes to approach its potential, we must begin to formalize our methods of teaching and coaching based on quantitative evidence.

To present, few have tackled such concerns. One who has is Bill Sands. In his relatively short coaching career Bill has achieved phenomenal success in helping young athletes maximize their potential. Thus Bill has gained great respect as a coach but, more importantly, as a student of gymnastics and of those athletes involved in our sport.

As a result of his intellectual approach, he has gathered, recorded, and analyzed a great deal of information pertinent to both the coach and the aspiring athlete. In the text, *Coaching Women's Gymnastics*, Bill shares much of what he has learned through research and experience.

Coaching Women's Gymnastics is directed toward those interested in maximizing potential yet is relevant to those at all levels. It deals with traditional issues as well as more technical areas on the forefront of analytical training procedures. While this text could not possibly resolve all problems facing the modern-day gymnastics coach, it encourages awareness and challenges all to become involved in the resolution process. It is certainly a major step forward in the evolution of available information within the gymnastics area.

Greg Marsden
Head Gymnastics Coach
University of Utah

Preface

This text attempts to fill a long existing need for a text dedicated to coaching and teaching gymnastics. Most books on gymnastics have been skill- rather than system-oriented—possibly because the skills of gymnastics are relatively easy to define, write about, and illustrate. My purpose in writing this book is to provide a framework around which a gymnastics coach can develop an organized, systematic, consistent training program. As far as possible I will avoid discussing skills and will concentrate instead on analyzing my own system of gymnastics as a demonstration that can help all coaches and teachers to proceed step-by-step through the training process or to evaluate programs already underway.

I have written this book a thousand times in my mind over the last 17 years. When I began coaching I thought I knew all the answers, and I am sure I was rather obnoxious at that stage. Now I realize that I know only a few of the answers, but at least I can ask some of the right questions. I have learned a great deal during my experiences coaching at nearly all levels. Some of my early ideas have proved to be totally worng, but I'm convinced that my philosophy and goals have been right all along. As with all lifelong endeavors, I have found that the more I learn the less I am sure of.

We are living in a fast-paced world and are constantly being bombarded with new information. Some is valid and useful; some is not. Much of it is simply bunk. As a coach, you will always be on the lookout for innovative methods, machinery, and ideas that will give you an edge on the competition. But you will have to learn how to sift through all this information, pull out the trash, and keep what is useful and relevant. I hope to provide you with some guidelines for setting up a framework to screen information, since over the years I have learned how and where to look for useful ideas and to gauge their promise.

I believe that the greatest service I can provide for gymnasts and coaches alike is to assist in the development of a philosophically based, systematically organized training program that (a) can give the gymnast the consistent, competent training she needs to realize her fullest potential, and (b) can give the coach both philosophical and practical guidelines for proceeding step by step through the training process.

The first tool a carpenter uses in beginning construction is not a saw, but a tape measure. Before starting he has to determine the needs of the project and whether the material will support his needs. The tape measure used in gymnastics is made of old-fashioned informed judgment. It is interesting to find out what the nations whose athletes win prestigious competitions are doing with and for their gymnasts; however, this information does not automatically apply to us. American coaches have their own needs and problems which must be identified and measured before coordinated efforts can be made to provide solutions.

Because the needs of each gymnastics coach are different, it is impossible to write a set of guidelines that will fulfill all these needs. Anyway, my real aim is to help you learn to solve your own coaching problems.

In most approaches to coaching the tendency is to use a strictly scientific viewpoint. Although this is the right starting point, it is not the end. Coaching is as much an art as it is a science, and if you deny the artistic aspects of coaching, you will surely invite failure. Some of the coaches I've worked with could not in any sense be called scientists, but they were surely artists and had an amazing ability to motivate young people. These creative coaches represent one end of the continuum, and the scientist-technicians the other. At the center of this continuum is the artist-scientist coach, a type I have seen only rarely. In my opinion the best coaches sit near this midpoint. This approach balances the areas of art and science, supplying gymnasts with the most productive environment for training and competition.

The scientific aspects of training and coaching should not be underrated. Knowledge of scientific and physiological aspects of training is certainly useful and comes in very handy in specific situations. This knowledge is gained from study and experience. The art of coaching comes more slowly. It is sometimes said that experience is measured in the amount of equipment ruined. This may be applicable to the trade arts, but our equipment happens to be children and young adults, and we cannot ruin any of them.

It is my hope that you will find this book useful, no matter how far along you are in your coaching career. My aim is to give young or inexperienced coaches some help in determining the appropriate training for each athlete, to help new coaches gain some "street wisdom" that will enable them to become more professional in a shorter time, and to challenge veteran coaches to examine their training approaches more thoroughly and question some activities that are of dubious value. These coaches may find that they've been doing just fine; then the suggestions I make in this book will simply reinforce their own efforts and perhaps give a little help in one or two areas. I hope that some of the concepts I've discussed can help coaches at any level make better decisions by serving as a measuring stick against which every idea or activity must pass before being implemented in the training program.

One of my fondest hopes is to help bring coaching to the level of a profession in the eyes of other professions as well as our own. Many attributes required for the finest athletes are also required for the finest coaches: honesty, determination, drive, desire, and confidence. Gymnastics is a relatively ungoverned sport in the sense that very few qualifications have been established for coaches. Although the problem of determining the areas of competence for the professional coach is not an easy task, determining fitness for coaching gymnastics is as vital as it is difficult. I hope this book will help give you a foundation on which to build a degree of accountability and professionalism.

We need to take a look at society's attitudes about coaching, athletics, and winning. Coaches must bear some of the responsibility for the negative image of professional and collegiate athletics today. The ideal of "a sound mind in a sound body" should accompany all amateur athletics and physical education. Too often it does not.

Responsible coaches must be ready to practice a philosophy that brings young people to athletics and builds good character. It is time to replace the "win at all costs" attitude in gymnastics, as in all sports. Winning should be seen not as an end in itself, but as a result of learning to do things well.

Athletics teaches young people the satisfaction of learning to do things right. We are not teaching winning first, we are teaching our athletes how to do something right. They should learn this message from us every day: Winning is the byproduct, not the goal. I see athletics as an excellent way to teach this attitude.

ACKNOWLEDGMENTS

I would like to express my appreciation to the following people for their help in making this book possible and for their patience with me during the preparation of the manuscript:

Basil Kane, for his help in getting me this opportunity.

Donna Cozzo, Sharon Valley, Suzie Kinsman, Paula Wagener, Lee Foreman, Rich Kenney, Greg Marsden, Dr. Lowell Weil, and Tom Hawes, for their encouragment.

My gymnasts, for their continued patience and understanding. These young people will always occupy a large place in my heart: Amy Koopman, Lynne Lederer, Sandy Sobotka, Marie Roethlisberger, Ika Lindholm,

Sheryl Kurowski, Phoebe Mills, Nicole Trewitt, Tina Travlos, Paula Schaffner, Jennifer Jakopin, Ginny Kipka, Tammy Labuy, Katie McDivitt, Lorie Leafman, and Gail Hamilton.

Karrie Swanson, Amy Zeitz, Liza Smith, Michelle Brown, Joanna Higgins, Carrie Riley, Erica Lefton, Sharene Shariatzadeh, Michelle Hashiguchi, Susie Margulies, Heather Keller, Renee Marquardt, Sherri Oguss, Nicole Cozzo, Amy Antognoli, Jennifer Cless, Jennifer Laun, Simi Mehta, Jennifer Messineo.

Dave Black, of the U.S. Gymnastics Federation, for taking the cover photo.

Rainer Martens, for encouraging me and helping me prepare the manuscript.

I

PHILOSOPHY

Ideals are like stars. You will not succeed in touching them with your hands;
but like the seafaring man, you choose them as your guide, and,
following them, you will reach your destiny.

Carl Schurz

Philosophy is the foundation upon which all human enterprises are built.
Our goals, value system, determination, and confidence are all outgrowths
of our philosophy. Each of us has a slightly different value system and set
of priorities.

The kind of value system that coaches evolve will, to a considerable
degree, determine which coaches will be successful and contribute to their
sport and to their athletes and which coaches will not; it is important to
remember that we must exhibit the same fine qualities we try so hard to
foster in our athletes as they participate in our programs. Children learn
from example, so we must furnish the example from which the athletes will
build their value systems for sport and many other lifelong activities that require similar personality characteristics. I believe that to deny that coaches
have an impact on their athletes would be a grave error. The coach must accept the responsibility of guiding our young athletes through their short
period of competitive athletics by exemplifying the finest of human qualities
for these athletes to emulate. In my opinion, the worth of every human
endeavor is based on the character of the people involved. A good coach
should display good character.

Gymnastics must be fun. The definition of fun is not simple. For
gymnasts, and perhaps for all athletes, the fun of sport is in accomplish-

ment — the realization that they can do something now that they couldn't do before, or can do it better than before. This realization is the pride, the fun, the motivation behind most participation. Winning is the ultimate realization that new goals have been set and reached, and new skills attempted and mastered. In athletics we do this every day. The kind of dedication we demand from our athletes we hope will filter out from athletics into their lives; the coach too must demonstrate the same qualities. We would be hypocritical to demand quality behavior for its own sake from an athlete and not from the coach. As the athlete must strive to come closer and closer to perfection, so must the coach; we must do it together.

Gymnastics must also be play. Play is a concept that has gotten a little clouded in our thinking. Athletes are supposed to work during training and then work hard to win during the competition. I think we would be better off calling these kinds of activities play. If I have to do something I don't enjoy, it is work to me, whether it is hard or not. When I do something I enjoy, that is play, even though it can be harder to do than any "work." Coaches and gymnasts play purposefully with gymnastics. When the play becomes work, we suffer and the sport suffers.

Actually, this idea is not new at all. Plato wrote in his *Laws*, "Life must be lived as play, playing certain games, singing and dancing" (Sheehan, 1978). Thomas Edison thought that inventing the light bulb was simply the result of playing with some filaments in a vacuum. Since the beginning of the industrial revolution we have gotten caught up in our utilitarianism, and Johan Huizinga wrote, "All Europe donned the boiler suit" (Sheehan, 1978). Regarding gymnastics as play allows the gymnasts to rehearse personality characteristics that will gradually become part of their behavior and enhance their character.

The goals these athletes set for themselves will come from the information and examples furnished to them by their teachers. The gymnast must be involved in the sport to several degrees of depth in order to see the results of their efforts. The athlete must see demonstrations of good character in the ambitions of fine men and women — other athletes. In short, each athlete must come to understand: "You must become something more than 'mere man' on pain of becoming otherwise something less" (A.E. Taylor in Lytle, 1958).

I believe that most people are involved in sport for honor in their own eyes. Honor is a quality in which our world is particularly lacking. Athletes have a clear opportunity to achieve honor by participating in sport. The pursuit of honor is what makes athletes the kind of people that contribute to society, and honor is what you as a coach must teach them. Many other alternatives — goals, life styles, and attitudes — can be developed in children and young adults. Those willing to work and train for honor are the flowers in a meadow that can suffer from a drought of good character. As Herodotus said, "What manner of men are these against whom you have sent us to fight—men who compete in their games not for money, but for honor" (Sheehan, 1978). Every young person who learns honor from or brings honor to sport should receive our utmost gratitude and encouragement. These are the people who represent our nation's finest.

Philosophy forms the foundation for the continuing development of policies and characteristics that permeate the entire program, teaching, interactions, goals, and nearly every facet of the gymnastics experience. The need to build a strong and thorough foundation is nearly self-explanatory and is assuredly difficult to argue with, but in our haste we usually forget the simple and overlook the obvious. A plan to develop gymnastics and coaching with a purpose must originate in foundational philosophy. Without stated goals, limits, and priorities the plan risks failure through internal inertia.

The chapters in Part I explore a few simple but vital questions. (1) *Why do you want to be a coach?* It's important early in your career to take an honest look at your motives for going into coaching and to understand whether you are coaching for the right reasons. (2) *What is the role of the coach?* If you understand this, you can keep in perspective where you belong in relation to the lives of the athletes you coach and to the sport of gymnastics. As you typically examine the athlete's commitment and goal-directedness, you should also examine your own motives and commitment. If the introspection is thorough and honest, it will go a long way to help you channel your energies in the most appropriate directions to enhance the athlete's abilities.

1

Why Coaching?

Why do you want to be a gymnastics coach? I have found that most people who go into coaching have about six characteristics in common: independence, individualism, creativity, leadership, love of young people, and love of teaching. I have often heard the remark that gymnastics is a unique sport and that the people involved in it are a little weird. I agree—why else would you be willing to take a low-paying job, live in a gym, forego your vacations, risk financial failure, and put up with the fickleness of athletics, young people, and parents?

INDEPENDENCE AND INDIVIDUALISM

Some people don't enjoy working for others; they prefer to be directly responsible for something important (in this case the development of a young person) and they want their efforts and their energy to matter. That feeling of importance is missing in a highly mechanized society where most people are simply a small part of a huge corporate machine. This sense that an individual lacks effect on the total picture leads to apathy. The gymnastic coach wants to have an effect, and must be able to see this effect grow on a continual and consistent basis. The typical set-up for gymnastics instruction provides an opportunity to work independently: the coach is generally responsible for one or two events or for a few individual gymnasts. This tradition has evolved not necessarily because it is efficient but because it is understood that every coach must feel important in order to do a good job. In a sense, the coach is like an independent contractor who is directly responsible for a particular job. While not necessarily responsible for all other factors relating to that job, the coach is responsible for some of these, and can take personal pride in the accomplishments of the young people he or she is guiding along the way.

The coach usually has an individualistic approach and feels a certain pride of authorship in developing an athlete and the particular routines she performs. I believe it is this pride (in "my" gymnast, or "my" team) that keeps most of us going. In fact, if it were not for this pride and individual joy in accomplishment, I do not think that gymastics would be as productive as it is.

The rewards system for coaches is small but recognizable. Along with simply being able to earn a living the coach is usually measured by his/her productivity of champion athletes. It is standard procedure among the media and the society to notice who the champion's coach is. Often few accolades are given to this coach, but the notice fuels the fire to keep the coach producing. An American coach who returned from Europe told me an interesting story about a European coach that illustrates this point. This coach had produced many fine gymnasts and had been responsible for producing the entire national team of this small country. Then legislation passed by the governing body of the sport in his country made him ineligible to travel abroad to meets along with his athletes. The coach soon lost interest, and although he is still coaching, he is not producing top gymnasts anywhere near the previous level and rate. For him, the rewards were simply no longer worth the effort. The coach is rarely selfless enough to take pride only in the accomplishments of his or her gymnasts and not in the notice or praise he or she receives as a result.

The possibility of being a good or great coach (and being noticed for that achievement) provides much of the incentive for enticement to getting involved with coaching. The desire to do well and be the best permeates coaching as well as competition. In fact, many psychological studies of great coaches have shown them to be extraordinarily competitive people. The coach is the old-fashioned individual who asks to be able to do the best job possible and to be judged solely by the performance of that job.

CREATIVITY

Good gymnastics coaching requires a fair amount of creativity. Because the sport is constantly evolving (new routines are introduced, old ones refined), a coach has plenty of opportunity to try new ideas. Gymnastics is a unique sport, in that the young gymnast must learn thousands of separate skills and then learn how to combine these separate skills in thousands of ways to produce ever more intricate and more artistic routines. (Most other sports involve the repetition of one or only a few skills and the winner is determined by speed, distance, or accuracy.) The gymnast is also encouraged to develop completely new skills that have never been done and even gets additional bonus points for them. So, if you are a creative coach, you can help your gymnasts win.

You can express your creativity by constructing new skills and routines, by your choice of music, and by the choreography and dance. As a coach you can be an artist, not only in the sense of applying the coaching arts, but also in the sense of creating a beautiful exercise of movement that has form, shape, grace, line, proportion, clarity, and story. Few sports offer as great an opportunity for creativity as gymnastics. But perhaps your biggest challenge as a creative coach is to teach and inspire your gymnasts to create their own art.

LEADERSHIP

Natural leaders often fulfill their potential as coaches. Coaching provides such individuals with an opportunity to lead people from one point to another, keep training moving toward a realistic goal, and provide the perspective needed to reach that goal as quickly and efficiently as possible. The coach must keep an eye on the panoramic picture of the progress toward the goal. The gymnast is usually too involved in the individual skills and activities of the sport to see the picture in totality. The coach provides that perspective.

Gymnastics offers a broad and challenging opportunity for a leader. The coach must guide the gymnasts along a rope above a chasm of failure. The gymnast can work too little and be inadequately prepared or work too hard and be overtrained. The coach must make the important training decisions. The risk and the gamble of leadership are always apparent; and so are the excitement and the pride of real accomplishment.

LOVE OF YOUNG PEOPLE

Young people offer a tremendous lesson for all of us through the energy of their youth. The coach should have a love for young people on a different level than that of a parent. In young people lie hope, unrealized potential, energy, and adventure. It has been said, "Never tell a young person that something cannot be done. God may have been waiting for countless centuries for somebody ignorant of the impossibility to do that thing" (Sheehan, 1978).

Coaching young people is tremendously rewarding. It can offer you a new vista every day, because even though you may have taught the same skill a hundred or a thousand times, for each child there is a first time. Sharing that thrill of the first time with the gymnast provides much of the reward in teaching and developing young people. Young people see the future as an adventure. Any shred of wisdom that we can share with their brief participation in sport that can help serve their journey through life will be a seed well planted, and the prospects of growth through the workings of one child are enormous. A certain admiration often results from association with a gifted athlete, and this admiration is even more compelling when the gifted athlete is a young person. Athletes' energy and vitality allow coaches to live vicariously through them and to make some valuable contributions to their future.

CONCLUSION

Coaching gymnastics is one of the most rewarding experiences you will ever undertake. The rewards are far-reaching, for both athlete and coach. As talent in an athlete must be recognized, supported, and nurtured, so the talent of a coach should be recognized and supported. This talent of leadership, creativity, pride, and love of young people is not shared by everyone, and those few coaches who have it should be given every opportunity to share their skills with young people in gymnastics, to give athletes an opportunity to realize their fullest potential. Like the talented athlete, the talented coach is worth more than money, for his or her work will have lasting effects on our young people and will help to mold the future.

2

The Role
of the Coach

THE COACH AS TEACHER

First and foremost, a coach is a teacher. A teacher can also be called an educator. The word *educate* comes from a Latin word *educare* which means to lead, or to guide forth. This concept of guidance is of primary importance to understand the role of the coach in the training and learning process. The gymnast must begin with the potential to become a gymnast; and your task as coach or teacher is to allow or encourage this potential to manifest itself. You can't do the work for the gymnast — you are simply a guide. The motivation for success must come from both gymnast and coach; the gymnast contributes her best effort in working and striving, and the coach gives his or her best effort in forethought, planning, and good judgment.

The lessons of gymnastics take place during a period commonly called training, competition, workout, practice, or class. Education means that the student will acquire something — knowledge, skill, ideas — that he or she lacked. The gymnast progresses from the state of being uneducated in a given skill, to the new state of education in which the gymnast can now perform a skill that she could not perform before. The elegant simplicity of this type of learning provides much of the enjoyment in gymnastics for young people. The ability to measure learning so concretely and simply is a tremendous advantage to motivation, since the activity motivates itself through continued, measurable success in acquiring one new skill after another. Learning is fun.

One of the objectives of a gymnast's education is competence in the performance of a "routine"—a series of skills with a beginning, a middle, and an end. This routine is then performed for "impartial" observers who score or evaluate the routine on the basis of established standards of excellence and performance.

MENTAL PREPARATION

The education of the gymnast includes many elements besides skills. In addition to learning skills, the gymnast must learn

- to control emotions that inevitably cloud judgment and performance, particularly when being evaluated by a highly respected evaluator;
- to control the amount of effort expended on the various parts and stages of training so that she is neither undertraining nor overtraining;
- to understand the strategies involved in gymnastic competition: choosing what skills to use, deciding when the meet is important and when it is not, complying with line-ups in team situations, and using skills and efforts commensurate with a qualifying score;
- to develop a personal philosophy that she can use to help her establish a gymnast's hierarchy of values and priorities.

One of your important jobs is to guide the gymnast through this learning process, ensuring that it occurs thoroughly and that everything receives its proper emphasis. Nearly every moment and juncture of training and competition provides an opportunity to learn.

Your worth as a coach may be measured better by how well you teach than by a simple trophy count. Champions can be measured as much by their ability to handle life and to become persons of value, as by their accomplishments in competition.

The coach and the gymnast will learn together how to win the real victory. This learning process will take a lifetime, and athletics provides a simple exercise in this lifelong lesson. As Charlie Brown would say, "We do not fail in losing, only in not wanting to win" (Charles M. Schulz, in Sheehan, 1978).

The most valuable lesson you can teach the gymnast is how to win, how to lose, and how to know the difference. It is important to teach the athlete that the ultimate goal, or long-range lesson, is more important than immediate goals, or short-range lesson, but that these immediate goals are important steps in the plan to reach that ultimate goal. The gymnast must learn to help set goals, work toward success, evaluate progress, and ultimately to deal appropriately with success or failure. The coach must be an effective teacher and the gymnast a proficient learner, since the results of the learning process will help form the foundation for the gymnast's future abilities through projects and problems that may not disappear when the scores go up or after the gymnasium lights go out. If learning is not sport's primary objective, the value to young people of any sport and teaching is open to immediate and critical questioning. The short-term battles are important, for they form our curriculum. The long-term objective should always be kept in clear view so that each of the smaller incidents can be measured by that standard concern of appropriateness and relevance.

THE ROLE OF THE COACH

A paragraph from a Russian book on gymnastics training (*The Sport of Gymnastics*, by A.B. Krivenko) changed my approach to coaching more than any other single statement I ever read. The title of the section was "Some Questions about the Preparation of Elite Gymnasts." The translation was done for the United States Elite Coaches Association for Women's Gymnastics. I believe that the concept implied here covers the entire spectrum of gymnastics involvement, not simply the elite athlete.

The author began observing that an athlete and a coach often would work together very profitably for several years, only to come to a parting of the ways and a loss of understanding between the student and the teacher. I have noticed this same phenomenon in the United States—and it has also happened to me and gymnasts I've worked with.

The author then spoke of the time early in the gymnast's career, when the coach is an authoritarian figure, a dictator, commanding all aspects of training. Later, the successful coach stepped out of the authoritarian role and into the role of comrade. This concept seems to me to be one of the most profound ideas ever expressed about the coaching of gymnastics. The description of the coach's role is so simple and so logical that I can't understand now why I didn't recognize years ago what was happening often in my coaching. I was so impressed with Krivenko's simple but logical concept of the stages in coaching that I have expanded on his idea in the following pages.

THE THREE STAGES OF COACHING

Stage 1: The Coach as Dictator

The gymnast begins her career with little knowledge and experience. The coach, necessarily, engages in the role of authoritarian or dictator because much work has to be done as efficiently as possible, and the athlete is not equipped to make the decisions about her own work. The coach acts as a dictator, a role that works very efficiently if the dictator is competent and the subjects are willing to be led or are incapable of leading themselves. The credit for success and the blame for failure at this level sits largely with the coach. The gymnast needs to be led at this point, consents to the dictatorship, and more or less blindly follows the "expert" coach who is quite definite about what projects he or she must undertake. The coach, in effect, stands in front of the gymnasts and forces them to comply with his or her wishes, desires, and plan. This seems rather natural and, in fact, it is.

Stage 2: The Coach as Comrade

In stage 2 the gymnast begins to understand what type of training is necessary to meet her goals and takes responsibility for making some training decisions. At this point, says Krivenko, the coach is becoming a comrade. This wording is particularly appropriate. The coach is not a friend, as this term would imply that no one is in command. The coach is still clearly in command, but slowly begins the process of relinquishing small pieces of this command, allowing the gymnast gradually to assume a more controlling role.

The coach is really a comrade by helping the gymnast move toward the goal they both seek, stepping in when the gymnast's judgment is inappropriate, moving aside when it is on the mark. The credit for success and the blame for failure are now more equally shouldered by the coach and the gymnast.

The rate and amount of control that the coach relinquishes to the gymnast is very important. If too much responsibility is given too fast, the gymnast could be frightened and progress could be retarded. On the other hand, if too little responsibility is given to the gymnast, friction may arise between the coach and the gymnast, especially if the gymnast deserves and desires more control over the training process.

Stage 3: The Coach as Resource Person

In stage 3, the gymnast is now capable of handling most training situations that arise, and the coach has become a resource person. Although the coach's guidance is still important, the gymnast has the primary responsibility of seeing that the training is carried out. The gymnast still probably does not have an overall perspective of the training and its relationship to the goal, so this direction is provided by the coach. But she is well-trained, and knows when and how hard to work to achieve the best results. Credit or blame for the outcome is now more fully shouldered by the gymnast.

The coach is freed from some of the more mundane tasks and decisions, and is responsible for recognizing the small detours in the training plan. These small and large problems may come during training and competition and are handled better by the coach than by the gymnast. The coach makes an effort to scout out the opposition and lay a foolproof plan for attaining success.

This three-stage system is similar to the growth of a child from infancy and childhood, to adolescence or young adulthood, and finally to adulthood. Much of the art of coaching consists of orchestrating the transitions from one stage to another. The major significance of these stages is that the athlete is not always merely a subservient creature who simply follows instructions. As the athlete's experience and knowledge grows, the more responsibility she deserves and should receive. We should not create dependent athletes who cannot function without their coach. The process of training should bring each child to adulthood through the gradual, consistent acquisition of more and more responsibility over matters that they can control, that have relevance to them, and will benefit them. You should enjoy your changing roles as the gymnast proceeds through training and becomes an independently functioning young person capable of handling most or all of the situations presented. The gradual maturity of her role will make the gymnast a better competitor who is more likely to succeed at whatever tasks she undertakes.

RELINQUISHING CONTROL GRACEFULLY

It is sometimes difficult for us to give up our dictator role. Fear of allowing the gymnast to control the training process can be genuine: the gymnast may make mistakes that will embarrass both coach and gymnast. But we have to remember that children will learn a great deal from their mistakes; allowing them to make a few harmless ones will teach more than most successes.

How do you start the process of relinquishing control over a gymnast you work with? One way to begin is to ask the gymnast for her opinion of some training situation or skill (How much time do you think you'll need to combine these skills? Do you think you'll really be able to compete in both these meets?) and then allow the gymnast to act on the basis of her opinion. Of course, you have to decide whether the gymnast's judgment is realistic. If it isn't, explain why and encourage her to amend her opinion. If you discuss the theory behind the decisions you make, you will provide the gymnast with a model of how training decisions are made. And the fact that you take the time to explain the situation or theory indicates that you believe this is important.

Often, in our haste, we overlook the panoramic picture of the development of young people through gymnastics. The immediate situation requires the coach's concentration, but an occasional careful look at the large picture keeps the training in line and keeps any singular situation in its proper perspective.

3

Commitment

Coaches of all sports talk repeatedly about commitment—the understood pledge the athlete makes to the sport or the understood goals the athlete and coach may share. The commitment to excellence is based on the possibility that the athlete can attain competence and that the coach can guide the athlete to this goal. Since this commitment is based on an uncertainty, it requires faith, trust, and risk. Faith is the belief in something, someone, or some idea that has not been proven through a scientific or empirical method. Trust is a confidence or reliance in the certainty of something, someone, or some idea, again without scientific or empirical proof. Risk is chance or the element of chance that affects the outcome of anything, anyone, or any idea. The coach and the athlete operate with this ideal daily, almost minute by minute. The gymnasts must have faith in themselves, in their goal, and in their coach if they are to act on the possibility of success with confidence and enthusiasm.

FAITH

The gymnast's faith comes from a dream and the possibility that this dream can be realized. For some gymnasts the dream may simply involve learning a few skills; for others, the dream extends to Olympic and world proportions. In either case, the dream is valid, representing the target of the gymnast's faith, desire, and determination. The means to this dream is good old-fashioned hard work. If the goal is realistic, the plan appropriate, the desire genuine, and the work accomplished, then the goal should eventually be realized.

Our strong faith in this process is the American ethic behind capital-ism, progress, and success. Theoretically, by following this plan, the athlete who works hardest, has the greatest faith, the best plan, and the most genu-ine and enthusiastic determination, should win every time. This is, in fact, often the case. Pertinent intervening variables include talent, level of train-ing at the time of the contest, partiality of "impartial" officials, politics, in-jury, and illness. These variables, many of which are controllable by suc-cessful coaches and athletes, represent the outer reaches of both the coach's and the athlete's ability to control their environment. Getting control of these nebulous variables is sometimes very difficult, and will involve vast in-vestments of time and energy from a committed coach.

You, as well as the athlete, must believe that the goal is realistic and worth working for. Many times a gifted athlete has been held back by a coach who did not have enough expertise or enough faith in the goal to move the athlete toward it. And on the other hand, many athletes aspire to higher levels than their talents or training situations allow. As a coach, you must have the kind of faith in the abilities of the athlete and in the worth of the goal to remove all obstacles lying in the way of the goal. When an athlete finds a committed coach, she should hang on to him or her. When you find an athlete with the talent and desire to attain a realistic, worthwhile goal, you should hang on to her. A relationship between coach and gymnast based on mutual commitment to excellence is typical of that existing be-tween the finest coaches and athletes. It should be prized and supported.

TRUST

Trust is an outgrowth of the faith shared by both the athlete and coach in the training and competitive process, and the athlete's and the coach's faith in each other. Much of the reliance of the athlete and the coach on the train-ing process usually results from reports that other athletes trained similarly have been successful.

Often the coach's and athlete's trust in the training process is simply the constant evaluation of the progress or lack of progress being made over the time of training. This can be further examined during competitions early in the gymnast's career. It is possible to compare the ability of a particular athlete with that of other athletes of similar ability. If a gymnast wins or does well in the early contests, the training methods and systems will be at least partly justified. If the athlete does poorly, the coach and athlete must evaluate the training system, determine the inadequacies, and attempt to repair them before the important contests. Talking with some of the better athletes and coaches can bring about some beneficial changes in the training program. This can add trust to the training method simply through the sup-port by these "experts" of changes that are implemented.

    The trust between coach and athlete is a simple concept, but extraordinarily sensitive and difficult to maintain and foster from moment to moment. Once lost, it is almost impossible to regain. This trust is built daily as the athlete complies with your demands and suggestions, and as you help the gymnast work toward immediate and long-term goals. You must make decisions quickly and confidently concerning the learning and performance of many athletes, and those decisions must be correct ones. If your decisions bring about failure and frustration, the trust you have established begins to suffer; if the decisions bring progress and success then the athlete will tend to trust you more implicitly.

    Trust is also built from mutual respect between coach and athlete. This respect is built from the civilized and genuine concern that each has for the other. The coach shows respect for the athlete by giving her increasingly more responsibility, in appropriate doses, so that she gains increasingly more and more control over her environment. The athlete shows respect for the coach by following instructions and by participating actively in the training process, accomplishing the tasks assigned by the coach. Trust can be destroyed with sarcasm, uncivilized or inappropriate remarks, and lack of follow-through on the tasks required of both coach and athlete in the training process.

RISK

Risk makes sport fun. Since the outcomes of the training process and of competition are uncertain, anyone can win, given the right circumstances. The concept of risk as used here does not include the risk of injury—only the risk of losing. Risk is what intrigues us, invites us to attempt the unlikely and enjoy the big gamble. Although we are constantly trying to remove the chance element by improving our training methods, playing the "political game," and increasing work loads, the gamble is still always there, and people by nature enjoy gambling.

    Eastern European nations are using scientific techniques to improve the performances of their athletes and reduce the risk factor. This has worked for some sports but definitely not all. If these nations had found the definitive answer for removing risk and guaranteeing winning performance, they would dominate all sports. Not only does the evidence not support this, but some think that the primary effect of such scientific experimentation is psychological, in the perceived inferiority our athletes feel as a result (Jerome, 1980).

    Almost everyone agrees that the eastern European countries are ahead of us in applying scientific knowledge to sports in an attempt to improve their athletes' performance and reduce the risk factor. Evidence seems to indicate that it is not so much what they know and what we don't know that makes the difference, but that they make better use of what they know. To equalize the risk of competition among athletes from all nations we may well have to catch up in the application of science to training. We don't want our athletes with Olympic and world aspirations left out of the running because their coaches have not fulfilled their end. (The 1980 Winter Olympics displayed a medal count that was somewhat lopsided. East Germany 23, Soviet Union 22, U.S.A. 12.) (Gilbert, 1980). If some techniques or scientific methods give a country or a team such an advantage that they cannot be beaten, then the risk is gone and the joy of sport along with it. We must always strive to balance the scientific and political dominance.

APPRAISAL OF POTENTIAL

One of your most important tasks as a coach is to make an honest appraisal of each athlete and set up an appropriate training environment; this is absolutely vital to the athlete's productiveness and enjoyment of the sport. Goals set too high cannot be supported by the talent, training situation, or experience and aspirations of the coach and will be a constant frustration to the athlete; goals set too low will be too easily met, and will result in boredom and loss of trust in the athlete or coach.

It's not always easy to make an objective judgment of how well your athletes are doing and how much potential they really have. You must step out of the situation for a moment to look at what is, or is not, developing. If you can strip away the immediate concerns and focus on the direction of the training, you will be better able to plan and to act on the plan rationally and quickly. This is a difficult skill and becomes even more difficult when you and the gymnast have been working together for some time to obtain this goal.

My plea for honest appraisals does not imply that most coaches underestimate or overestimate the abilities of their athletes or are unrealistic in goal setting. The coach and the athlete should be a little optimistic in goal setting and should set goals a little higher than cold honesty would dictate. Harry Kemp wrote, "The poor man is not he who is without a cent but he who is without a dream" (Lytle, 1958). Part of the real education provided by athletics is that of setting a goal and striving for that goal with a little bit of optimism. The psychological state of optimism is infinitely more productive and pleasurable than pessimism. Simply put by L.P. Jacks, "The pessimist sees the difficulty in every opportunity; the optimist the opportunity in every difficulty" (Lytle, 1958).

It is up to you to see that the gymnast selects a worthwhile, reasonable, slightly optimistic goal, and works hard to obtain this goal, in the proper sequence. Athletics is perhaps one of the few places left where striving is still the only way to get ahead. You can't buy your medals, you can't inherit them, and a lot of hard work is needed to gain them.

THE DEDICATED COACH

One of the goals of gymnastics is to produce good all-around athletes through training, and one of your goals as a coach should be to become a good all-around coach. For example, you should be able to coach all events. This increasingly apparent phenomenon of specialization in gymnastics events limits the coach's ability to deal with the gymnast and her problems. It is a more significant problem in women's gymnastics than in men's. At this time there are probably fewer than 10 coaches in America who can coach all four women's events competently. The typical division is that men coach tumbling, vault, and bars, and that women coach beam, dance, and floor. In my opinion, this prevents efficient teaching of some skills and events by most coaches. Since your gymnasts must strive to conquer four events and eight routines, surely you should become competent at coaching all the events and routines your gymnasts are involved in. The male coach who can't coach beam is not very useful at meets, nor is the female coach who can't coach bars and vault. At nearly any clinic or symposium on gymnastics, the male coaches all flock to the classes on bars, vault, and tumbling. When the beam and dance classes come up, the women coaches are involved and the men all go out for coffee. This scenario exemplifies the hypocrisy demonstrated by coaches who expect athletes to be thoroughly dedicated but do not bother to expand their own education by learning how to teach events their athletes must demonstrate brilliance in.

Excellence in sport is an idea much talked about. Honesty and integrity are the only way to achieve it. You are in charge of a process of training that should provide your gymnasts with a healthy exercise in goal setting, hard work, evaluation of progress, and dealing with success and failure. The athletes will learn that progressing to the goal was the most fun and the most rewarding. Once they've reached the goal, they usually discover that the joy is genuine but short-lived, and that they must now set a new goal and begin the process all over again. This process of cumulative learning and reestablishing goals once former goals are achieved forms a lifelong pattern. In other words, you are teaching them to win the "real game." This long-term game of life is not only more important than the short-lived game of gymnastics, gymnastics cannot be successful on its own without laying a foundation for learning about life and self. "Sometimes a person's mind is stretched by a new idea and never does go back to its old dimensions" (Oliver Wendell Holmes in Wallis, 1965). We should continually stretch minds as far as they will go.

4

Setting
Reasonable Goals

Goal setting demands a certain amount of courage from you and from the athlete. Goal-directed behavior is a little risky, particularly when those involved have publicly announced their goals. If they fail there will be embarrassment—and failure comes more frequently than success. Setting goals and announcing dreams is a practice to be commended in the young athlete and the coach, and, in my opinion, society has not looked kindly on the goal-oriented person. Many young people find that mediocrity is much more comfortable than excellence. After all, once the athlete and coach have established success in something, society expects them to be successful all the time. Living up to this standard is nearly impossible, and involves coping not only with the pressure of being constantly successful but with defeat and failure when it comes. It takes a brave young person to set a goal and work hard to achieve it in spite of the hardships that accumulate through the process. The risk of embarrassment, chance of failure, pressure from family and friends, and the conspicuousness of excelling at a sport face the young athlete with a constant, concrete goal and help provide the desire and determination to reach it.

DETERMINATION

The amount of determination needed by the athlete and the coach varies with the level and accessibility of the goal; the higher the goal and the more constraints upon athlete and coach, the greater the determination required. Determination is often the factor that brings about success or failure. Goal setting for both you and the athlete should be based partly on your determination levels; talent, training, and ability are no guarantees to success if determination is lacking.

You can evaluate the level of determination in a young gymnast by measuring the desire and determination she demonstrates during everyday training. If the child sticks to the task and sees it through to completion — even in the face of frustration, fatigue, and other problems — then this gymnast will be likely to warrant reasonably high goals. If she gives up when training becomes difficult and will not push through fatigue and other deterring factors she can probably handle only the lower goals. Of course, goals should always represent a challenge. A realistic choice of goals in terms of abilities and commitment of athlete and coach will help the gymnast develop rational powers of evaluation and will avoid frustration by all involved.

The athletes and coaches who show high levels of determination are most likely to succeed and should seek each other out so that each complements the other. When the goals set by the coach and the athlete reflect the ability, talent, and determination of both athlete and coach the goal is likely to be reached, frustration avoided, and the price of accomplishment in sport worth paying.

THE PETER PRINCIPLE

The "Peter Principle" is a concept identified and developed by Laurence J. Peter and Raymond Hull in their book, *The Peter Principle* (1969). The concept relates in many ways to gymnastics and to the coach and athlete relationship. The Peter Principle depends on the existence of a hierarchy. In gymnastics, we have a tremendous hierarchy, or pecking order. We begin with classes: as the gymnast progresses to competition she begins with class IV compulsories and routines and moves through class III, class II, class I, Junior Elite, Senior Elite, and then the national team, followed by membership on various world championship, Pan American, and Olympic teams. As she becomes more competent she moves up in this system as far as she can go.

The Peter Principle says that people move up a hierarchy of competence until they are promoted to a final level that is slightly above their abilities. This last promotion puts the person at a hierarchical level that demands more than the person can give, and the unfortunate part is that these people often remain at that level without achieving further competence. The Peter Principle applies to gymnastics in that we often continue to promote our athletes consistently — as they demonstrate ability to handle the competitive environment — to a level at which they can no longer compete with the other athletes. Then we keep them at this level until they retire or leave the sport for some other reason. Elevation or promotion becomes the goal, rather than competence and contention.

The continued elevation of the athlete is usually due to impatience on the part of both the coach and athlete to move up fast. The final elevation to a class level beyond the competence of the athlete is based on poor planning, incorrect evaluation of the ability of the athlete, coach, and training situation, and a bit of inappropriate overzealousness. We tend to leave the athlete at this final level of incompetence because demoting the athlete one level to her point of competence is an admission of a mistake. We don't like to admit mistakes. It is more comfortable for young people in athletics to be at a high level, competing poorly, than to be demoted to a lower level, even though they would have a better chance to win at that level. In my opinion, this is an interesting and sad commentary on our honesty as a society and on our need for headlong progress even if it is progress in name only.

Combatting this tendency toward over-promotion in coaching is not an easy task. Responsibility for promotion rests primarily with the coach. Promotion should be guarded and cautious, since moving up the ladder is easier than moving back down. Consider promotions carefully and evaluate the gymnast thoroughly so that final promotion brings the gymnast to a level where she competes confidently with the other athletes on her level. For the most appropriate competition, athletes should contend for honors relative to their determination, hard work, and desire within their correct levels.

Understanding the Peter Principle will help you keep your athletes and their abilities in perspective. Those athletes who have all that it takes to reach the highest goals will often achieve these goals despite all the careful planning you provide for them. If you and the athlete believe that you can reach this goal (objectively and idealistically), then proceed with all the powers available. Both wisdom and healthy determination are required to come to this conclusion.

DIMINISHING RETURNS

One final consideration related to goal setting concerns the law of diminishing returns. This principle relates most directly to the specific goals of the particular training day or to other short-term goals, and can be described as the lack of commensurate gains from continued effort. You and the gymnast should evaluate the training for a particular skill or routine by this principle as the learning progresses. The gymnast may often reach a point at which continued work may result in some progress, but the small amount of progress made is not worth the large investment of time and energy at this particular point in the training. The learning and health of the athlete can suffer through fatigue during training periods occurring near the end of each day's work. This phenomenon must be weighed along with the factor of overload. Gymnasts *must* overload their physiological systems to gain strength, flexibility, and endurance. (The learning of many gymnastics skills is so highly related to the acquired strength of the athlete that overload is also a very important factor in learning and performance.) But you must be able to choose wisely when to push on for the benefit of overload, and when to save the problem for another day because the gymnast is experiencing diminishing returns. This wisdom comes with experience and open interaction between the athlete and the coach.

The Peter Principle and the law of diminishing returns can be used as guidelines to follow before you incorporate training decisions into the program. This will help give your program consistency.

II

PROGRAM

Expect nothing, be ready for everything.

Samurai

The program—the practical, or sometimes the "business," concerns of gymnastics training—is the part of gymnastics upon which all the nuts and bolts of training is built. The program may have a tremendous influence upon the level of accomplishment the athlete can attain: your ability to manipulate and enhance the program can mean the difference between success and failure. The program concerns itself with three major objectives: obtaining all the finest opportunities for improvement of the athletes; avoiding problems that are obstacles to accomplishment; and solving as quickly as possible any problems that may arise in the training environment.

The potential of the program to produce high-quality athletes consistently is largely determined by the energy that you devote to the business factors of the program, such as facility, training load and schedule, equipment, doctors, rehabilitation, and meet schedule. All these factors must be orchestrated properly to bring about the finest training environment and allow the gymnast to reach her fullest potential.

The program for gymnastics covers six areas: schedule and training load, facility, support staff from the sciences, selection process, talented and motivated coaches, and research. All these facets of the program can be further divided into more specific categories. The following chapters will attempt to define and describe these categories and their relationship to the program.

I really like to put things in categories. By doing this, I can keep better track of the variables that affect training so that none are left out. The use of categories allows us to divide and conquer the problems more easily. Assigning categories that reflect all the needs of a program is not necessarily easy, but it can be extremely helpful to you. Once categories are evolved the distribution of effort can be directed into the categories that need the most help. This saves repetition of effort and provides a gauge of progress.

It is my opinion that the real productivity of a gymnastics program is determined by the depth and breadth of the activities and benefits offered by the program. Therefore, along with the actual coaching you must provide, either directly or indirectly, for the physical, psychological, rest, educational, conditioning, and other needs of the athlete.

The destiny of gymnastics as a sport is controlled by the program aspect (gymnastics cannot be a sandlot sport). The size, cost, and danger of the equipment and of the skills forces gymnastics to be controlled by the coaches and administrators and by their energy and character. As we attempt to compete with the rest of the world in gymnastics we must remember that the reason others beat us is not because of talent but because of program. Their program is better than ours. They make better use of time; they have more and better-equipped facilities that are available to more highly trained people; they have specialists who sometimes work along with the coach in the same facility to keep the athletes functioning; they select the most talented athletes they can find and make the best possible training available to them; they educate and nurture the most talented coaches they can find; and they continually conduct research on how to better train the athlete.

Unfortunately, we are only marginal at providing these services. It is my hope that this section will suggest to you what a gymnastics program should offer a young athlete in order to be considered worthy of bringing up the most talented children. Defining what we want to do, where we want to go, and how we expect to get there is a first step we seldom take. We are much too quick to get down to the specific preparation of athletes without looking at the panoramic picture of all their needs. We always want to move forward, and usually we do move forward; but we never stop to figure out which way we are facing and where we want to go. Eventually, the ability of an organization to exist in spite of itself runs out. We must continue to enlarge and enhance the program portions of gymnastics or face defeat. The choice is ours.

In the following chapters I have tried to cover all the bases you'll have to run so that you can use this section as a blueprint or a template for developing your gymnastics program. I can swear that I followed these guidelines in developing my own program, and they helped spell success for the athletes and the program. It made life a lot easier for me to know where we were going before we went there.

5

Schedule
and Training Load

The control of the schedule and training load is often one of the most critical factors involved in any athletic training program. There are only a limited number of hours during the day when the athlete will be productive (prior to fatigue), and efficient use of this time is vital if you want to develop your athletes to their fullest potential. It is very important that you have an overall picture of all aspects of the training program and do not get so bogged down with problems in one area that you neglect the other areas.

In this section, I will talk about some of the relationships of the use of time and schedule and the means of determining time utilization. Unfortunately, our knowledge of sport science is not developed to a point at which many definitive answers can be given. Besides, the body cannot read a calendar or watch. Time measurement is an invention of man; the body of the athlete obeys principles of chemistry and physiology that are not so conveniently placed in terms of the clock or calendar. But we can help the athlete with some general rules of time management and with some understanding of the relationship of schedule, stress, and training to the ability of the athlete to perform well.

CONTROLLING SCHEDULE AND TRAINING LOAD

When we talk about schedule and training load, we are actually talking about how much stress we place on the body within a specific time period. Stress can be identified as anything that makes the gymnast react or causes the gymnast to take action, either mental or physical action. Many authors have dealt with the phenomenon of human reaction to stress, both physical and mental. Unfortunately, there are still few hard and fast rules, largely because each individual responds to stress somewhat differently. Eastern European nations are said to have the control of training-stress managed by a computer and blood lactate. This idea has been disputed by some of our best exercise physiologists, but it is very interesting that these nations consider stress management of training important enough to do something about it from an experimental and scientific standpoint. For example, these eastern European nations reportedly use the lactate level in resting blood as an indicator of fatigue (lactate is a product of energy metabolism in the working muscle). The level of lactate in resting blood can be an indicator of fatigue, but to determine this level a qualified person must extract the blood, and laboratory facilities must be available for analyzing the blood. I hope that eventually we can all use sophisticated tests like these that will help us control the amount of work we subject the athlete to during training to promote success and avoid injury and failure.

TRAINING LOGS AND DIARIES

Such tests are not likely to be used in the near future because of the objections from athletes and parents — and of course, because of the expense and lack of laboratory facilities. Therefore, what you need most as a coach are methods of controlling training that are inexpensive, noninvasive, and simple to administer. We can use the eastern European model in a way that can help us better administer our training process. We must keep accurate records of training and some physiological parameters. We must use something to tell us how the athlete is responding to training loads and this will require a diary of training kept by the athlete or by the coach regarding as many facets of the training as can be recorded without encumbering the training process with data collection. The data must be easily retrievable and must be in usable form.

Methods

A chart for a training diary is included in Appendix A as an example of an easy way to record information. Dots drawn for each parameter can be connected later to show the various patterns that accumulate over time. I strongly recommend that this information be handled by computer. Since many people still shy away from the computer, I have included a computer program for storage of data by the gymnasts (in Appendix B). A sample printout of the data is included to give you an idea of the real power of the computer in handling this type of data painlessly and graphically. Using the modern microcomputer is not as expensive nor as complicated as you might think.

The intelligent use of data collected daily on these types of charts allows you to keep track of everything the gymnasts are doing (training, work, rest, etc.). You can then keep one eye on the data and the other on progress to make sure that the gymnasts are not pushing too hard or too little, and bringing them to high-level condition at the right times. Of course, the charts assume that the athletes will be honest in their records and that you will take the time to analyze them. (All too often the charts are kept but are not analyzed closely by the coach to keep constant track of the progress of training.) This is another reason why the computer is so useful. The gymnasts can enter their own data, and then you can have this data analyzed in seconds by the computer anytime you need information on any athlete who might not be adapting well to training.

Content

All the data that is kept may be very interesting, but what do you look for? How do you use the data to make decisions? Here are some general rules you might find useful in making judgments about the training state of the athletes in the program.

- If the heart rate rises steadily, this may be an indication of overwork. (Of course, the heart rate should be taken under similar circumstances each time.)
- If body weight should suddenly fall and continue to fall, this may be a sign of overwork.
- If heart rate rises steadily and body weight continues to fall at the same time, this is a more reliable sign of fatigue, overwork, or illness.
- If the weight of the athlete continually goes up, the athlete will obviously be more susceptible to injury.

Refer to the charts and printouts in Appendices A and B to see the patterns that can be discovered by observing the data after computer processing. Illnesses and injuries recorded on the page can give you an idea of the severity and the duration of these problems to ascertain if one time of year is more dangerous than another. Figure 5-1, showing the results of a study I did on competitive injuries over a 17-month period, is based on insurance company records. This clearly shows that January is the most dangerous time of the year for competitive injuries. If you study your data, you'll be able, before long, to see marked patterns among your athletes.

The diary will help you and your athletes learn about how they respond to work over a specific time period. And as you begin to see the interplay of time and stress on the athletes, you and the athletes can learn how to regulate the amount of time and amount of stress necessary to gain, main-

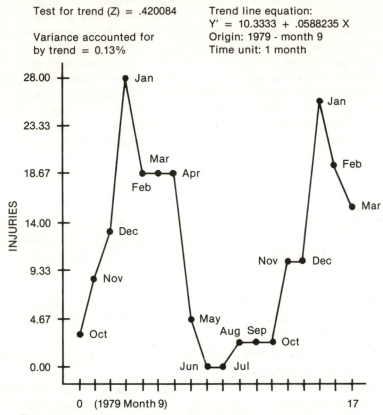

TIME SERIES ANALYSIS I

Test for trend (Z) = .420084   Trend line equation:
                                     Y' = 10.3333 + .0588235 X
Variance accounted for   Origin: 1979 - month 9
by trend = 0.13%   Time unit: 1 month

Figure 5-1   Injuries reported by months. Line and points represent total number of injuries reported to Bayly, Martin, and Fay for that particular month. The date is taken as the date of the injury and not the date of the report. (Data from Bayly, Martin, and Fay, in Sands, 1981).

tain, and rest from high-level conditioning. The diary does not promise a quick solution to training problems. It is simply another very useful tool that will give you more information and assist you in decision-making.

DETERMINING A TRAINING SCHEDULE

In the following pages, I will talk about some general rules and ideas for determining the training and competitive schedule for gymnasts. I like to call the training schedule and competitive schedule a "curriculum," since there are well-established rules for setting up and maintaining curricula that can be of immediate and easy use to the gymnastics coach. Let's look at the overall picture first before we get to specific requirements.

In a typical gymnastics year, athletes may be competing throughout the 12 months, particularly if they are very good. I don't recommend this, but assuming such a schedule forces us to develop rules for scheduling rather than simply providing a specific calendar for each gymnastics season.

The training program for gymnasts consists of three stages. Stress literature calls these by many different names, but attributes similar durations to each of the stages. The triad of stages is useful since each stage can be further divided into three smaller sections. The stages are:

1. Preparation for upcoming competition;
2. Competition, or the period during which the athlete is ready to participate in top form;
3. Recovery or rest from the first two stages. (This third stage is the one we most often leave out.)

In some Russian coaching literature, these stages are also described as the acquisition of athletic form, the stabilization of athletic form, and the temporary loss of athletic form. Hans Selye calls these stages the alarm stage, the resistance stage, and the exhaustion stage (Larson, 1971).

The entire training schedule should consist of large-scale and small-scale examples of this three-stage model. The training season should consist of preparation, competition, and recovery. Each competitive event also should consist of a direct preparation time for that event, the actual competition, and a recovery period. Again, it is this recovery period that we most often neglect in our overzealous striving for winning. I find it particularly interesting that while volumes have been written on the *quality of work*, there is an extraordinary lack of information concerning the *quality of rest*.

Stage 1: The Preparatory Period

The preparatory period, which can last anywhere from weeks to months, is the time when the athletes are working on their skills, combinations, and routines. This stage can be broken down further into three substages or sections:

1. *Learning and working on conditioning.* The skills are usually new or incompletely learned skills that will be included in the routines used in the later stages by the athlete. The conditioning consists of general and specific strength, flexibility, and muscular endurance training.
2. *Refining and gathering these skills into combinations.* A period of four to six weeks is often necessary for the gymnast to complete the

transition from skills to combinations. The combinations rarely consist of full routines, but they will later be included in the gymnast's routines.

3. *Chaining these combinations together to form routines for competition.* The duration of this stage is rather stable, usually involving four to six weeks.

This third section immediately precedes the competition stage. A gymnast coming from a period of training in which no routines at all were done, to this stage of doing precompetition routines, should be given six weeks to fully prepare the routines for competition. If the gymnast has been doing some routine work during the second substage of the preparatory period, then four weeks may be enough time to get routines under control prior to the competition period. By the end of the third section the gymnast should acquire "athletic form" and the ability to perform in competition at or near the best of her ability.

Stage 2: The Competitive Period

The end of the third substage of preparation marks the end of preparation and the beginning of competitive stature or readiness. The competitive period, which marks stage two for the gymnast, has been given various time limits. Russian literature available through the U.S. Elite Coaches Association and other literature from work on stress usually lists four to six weeks as the time required for the athlete to perform at peak levels before dipping into the final exhaustion stage. It is important that training be timed so that this second stage coincides with the time of the most important competitions. Little information is available on the nature of this period. For example, could we drag out this period by carefully resting athletes between competitions? If athletes are intentionally undertrained through the early phases of the preparation, can they prolong their competitive peak period to last through more competitions? These answers remain to be discovered.

Stage 3: The Recovery Period

The recovery period (the period where exhaustion sets in and the gymnast must rest due to fatigue) immediately follows the competition period. This stage usually consists of a kind of recuperation called "active rest." This means that the gymnast may still work out and take part in activity but that the activity should be less serious, perhaps involving different sports or a very different approach to gymnastics. Usually four weeks is given as the typical time necessary before another preparatory period can be begun. Table 5-1 shows the relationship of the three stages to each other.

TABLE 5-1   Training Cycle for One Competitive Season

Preparatory Period			Competitive Period (4-6 Weeks)	Recovery Period (4? Weeks)
Section 1 (Unlimited Time)	Section 2 (4-6 Weeks)	Section 3 (4-6 Weeks)		
Skills & general conditioning	Combinations for future routines	Pre-competitive period for routine training	Competitive period with most important meets Athlete in peak form	Recovery time for period of active rest
Acquisition of athletic form			Stabilization of athletic form	Temporary loss of athletic form

→   ←

Target date for readiness

This graph depicts the total training schedule for one training season or cycle. The divisions and concepts are explained in more depth later in this chapter. The most important competition should be placed roughly two-thirds of the way into the competitive period so that some time has been set aside for preparing by actually competing in some less important meets prior to the most important meet.

A THREE-LAYERED LOOK AT A TRAINING SCHEDULE

In presenting these guidelines for setting up a training schedule I have purposely omitted the physiological considerations that have gone into its development. I suggest that you read texts listed in Appendix E to gain insight into the actual physiology of the gymnast accommodating to stress. What I want to do here is to provide an example of a structural framework that you can build your own training schedule around.

The competitive period is usually assigned by looking at the competition and qualification calendar. The time for readiness or peak performance is pretty easy to determine by simply looking at the date of a national championship or trials. Selecting the peak period might depend on the gymnast's ability (a gymnast with less ability might need to peak at a time of qualification for an important meet because she may not qualify for the championships or trials). Therefore, you may wish to have the gymnast peak at the competition, allowing her to enter the most important meet and hope that she can hold on through the later competition. At this point we should begin to get more specific about how the time will be utilized by the athlete. This closer look at the time available should begin with a few format assumptions and an overall knowledge of the complete training cycle or season.

SOME ASSUMPTIONS: THE OUTERMOST LAYER

The format I recommend for training assumes that an athlete must perform compulsory and optional routines in competition. If the gymnast is simply performing optional routines, then you will have to modify this format somewhat. The second assumption is that the gymnast will train 16 hours per week or more — this boils down to a training schedule averaging over three hours per day five days per week. A gymnast who trains less than this should not be competing in optionals and compulsories. (A shorter training time would be typical of a recreational rather than a competitive gymnast. Recreational gymnastics is a very important and useful part of gymnastics but not the target of this text.)

The time devoted to gymnastics per week can be broken down into levels of aspiration or desired accomplishment. The following suggestions are based completely on my own experience in dealing with athletes of these levels for several years.

- A gymnast who is a member or an aspiring member of the senior national team (age 15 years or older) should be training from 25 to 35 hours per week. ("Aspiring" means that the gymnast is actually in contention for such a position, not simply that she desires it.)
- A gymnast who is a member or an aspiring member of the junior national team (age 12 to 14 years) should be training 24 to 30 hours per week.
- A gymnast who aspires to be a top Class I or advanced level gymnast should be training 20 to 30 hours per week.
- A Class II gymnast should train from 16 to 25 hours per week.
- A Class III gymnast should train from 16 to 20 hours per week.

These are rather broad time distributions to ensure that the full spectrum of individual programs and talent levels of athletes can be accommodated.

A further refinement of the time devoted each week is necessary because of the young age at which gymnasts begin training. Very little is known about the effects of training on these young people, or about their physical and mental well-being. No one can be presumptuous enough to believe that simple assignment of time parameters will be a panacea for healthy training for young people. Nothing can replace good judgment. Modifications may have to be made with regard to school schedules, demands on the young person, and other nontraining influences.

MIDDLE LAYER

Let's try to set up a hypothetical training schedule as an example of how to juggle time and activities. Starting with what we know about stress management and logical preparation of a gymnast, we can begin by looking at what is involved in one training season.

Our athlete is beginning serious training for a series of important competitions to be held between May 15 and June 15. She is beginning to train for these competitions after returning from Christmas break, so we'll say that January 1 is our starting date. This gives us the period between January 1 and May 15 as the preparatory period, the period between May 15 to June 15 as the competitive period, and the period between June 15 and roughly July 15 as recovery period.

Preparatory Period

The preparatory period is that time when most of the important work takes place. It is divided into a skill preparation section, combination preparation section, and routine preparation section. This is easily the most important period relative to the amount of time spent and the learning and work completed. The accomplishments of the rest of the season or training cycle are built on the skills developed in this period. Once we understand the other periods and how they fit together, we will return at length to the preparatory period, since it is the most important time for thorough and thoughtful planning.

Competitive Period

The competitive period is broken into as many sections as there are competitions or meets. Let's say that during the competitive period there are two competitions our gymnast must be ready for, and they are spaced about two weeks apart. During this stage the planning is fairly simple. But the individual differences among gymnasts may make significant changes in the application of time due to outside factors. Essentially, the preparation for competition during this stage consists of the immediate preparation, the competition, and a short recovery period.

The immediate preparation consists of

1. preparation of the routines to gain consistency;
2. some sort of quasi-pressurized rehearsal of the competitive circumstances;
3. a short recovery period; and
4. an acceleration of training into the actual competition.

Let's consider what would happen during the week prior to the competition. If the competition is on a Friday and Saturday, the gymnast will perform compulsories on Friday and optionals on Saturday. Our normal day off from training in this example is Wednesday. The previous Friday we should do many compulsory routines to gain experience and consistency. Saturday we would perform many optional routines. Sunday would be used for lighter routines for polishing some sections. Monday would also be used for light routines to polish some sections. Tuesday would be used to perform some routines—compulsory or optional or both—in a quasi-competitive atmosphere (i.e., judging all routines at normal or full training load in number, limited warm-up time, with the goal of accumulating lots of practice in the decisive moment). Wednesday is a day off. On Thursday the athlete works on two-thirds of the normal number of routines. On Friday the gymnast begins compulsory competition. On Saturday the competition for optionals takes place. On Sunday the athlete takes a day off or trains very lightly. Monday is a rather light day, and Tuesday hard work begins again for the next competition. This plan helps to keep the gymnast working at near optimal levels all the time without overtaxing her on any particular day or series of days.

Although this plan seems simple, seldom do we encounter a simple preparation for competition, since many other factors soon come into play. A major factor is whether the competition entails compulsories and optionals or just optionals. Other intervening factors are injury, how well the gymnast is actually doing at the time of preparation, illness, other competitions that may have come up unexpectedly, and so on. However, if you start out the preparation with this plan, even though you might have to modify the training for some reason, you at least know where you have been, where you are supposed to be, and roughly how far away you might be from the basic plan at any given moment. Planning like this gives direction to the training process and preparation rather than scheduling activities randomly. You can assess the preparation and the problems that have come up and determine whether to work on all the skills the gymnast has planned or to water down the routines and make other changes.

This plan can be followed for both competitions during our hypothetical competitive period. The period between competitions, or that period that is just after the recovery period and just before preparation for a new competition, is usually the most dangerous time. Routines are already learned, the gymnast is already in good shape, and consistency has probably been achieved. The maintenance of this momentum through the periods between competitions is very difficult, and this is the time when overtraining is most likely to occur. Therefore, you and the gymnast should monitor training carefully and act at any sign of loss of form, fatigue, or slumping performance. If problems surface then, schedule a little rest and return to a Section 1 preparatory period for a short time. This means that the gymnast should return to training skills while waiting to get ready for the next major competition.

Recovery Period

The recovery period is that time when competition is over and the athlete is training down to levels that do not require the extreme conditioning necessary to perform routines. This does not mean that they have to leave the gym; they simply need to take active rest by training lightly in a non-pressurized way and looking to the future. Trying a different activity is often helpful at this time—for example, bouncing trampoline, or introducing a guest dance teacher with a specialty that will be useful to the gymnasts but is different from what they've seen in the past. Hard conditioning, routines, and fixing old problems are not suitable for this time period.

A SPECIFIC LOOK: THE INNERMOST LAYER

The preceding information was designed to give you an overall picture of how the general plan works before we concentrate on specifics. Now, let's begin looking at how to use specific days and minutes to make the final training schedule consistent with our plan.

The preparatory period consists of the three subsections or stages listed previously. By counting backwards from May 15, when we want our athlete in peak form, we allow four to six weeks for the third section for preparing routines and for drilling (we will say five weeks). Then from this date we count backwards, again four to six weeks, for the second section of the preparatory period, when the gymnast is preparing combinations (again, we allot five weeks). This leaves the remaining time, going backwards to January 1st, for the first section of the preparatory period, when the gymnast will train skills. Table 5-2 shows how this breaks down.

Our gymnast trains on the following schedule shown in Table 5-3 because of facility limitations and school attendance. This gives our athlete Wednesday off for rest.

TABLE 5-2   Time Distribution for Preparatory Period

Section	Days	Weeks	Activity
1	66	9.4	Skills
2	35	5.0	Combinations
3	35	5.0	Routines

TABLE 5-3   Weekly Training Schedule

Compulsory Days	Hours	Optional Days	Hours
Sunday	5	Monday	6
Tuesday	6	Thursday	6
Friday	4	Saturday	6

TABLE 5-4   Training Schedule

Time Frame	Compulsories	Optionals	Total
Hours per week	15	18	33
Days in preparatory period	68	68	136
Hours in preparatory period	291.4	349.7	641.1
Hours in Section 1	141.4	169.7	311.1
Hours in Section 2	75	90	165
Hours in Section 3	75	90	165

Calculations then give the distribution of time for training our gymnast as shown in Table 5-4. A look at such a time schedule can sometimes be a very rude awakener: there's only a very small amount of time for you and the gymnast to work with in preparing for competitions. A chart like this can also be helpful when you are looking at whether or not there will be enough time to learn a new skill and put it into the routine with an acceptable level of consistency. The above information can make such appraisals much more realistic.

DIVIDING THE AVAILABLE TIME INTO ACTIVITIES

Once we know how much time we have to work with, we simply divide that time among the various activities the athlete must perform to be 100%

TABLE 5-5   **Weightings by Percentage of Effort**

| Compulsory Days | | Optional Days | |
Activity	Percentage	Activity	Percentage
Warm-up	5	Warm-up	5
Dance	5	Dance	5
Vault	20	Vault	0
Uneven bars	20	Uneven bars	20
Balance beam	30	Balance beam	30
Floor exercise	15	Floor exercise	20
Tumbling	5	Tumbling	15
Conditioning	0	Conditioning	5
Total	100	Total	100

trained and prepared for competition. You must look carefully at your program to decide what you need to emphasize, and then start planning to see that this occurs. The hypothetical training situation referred to here includes certain activities whose percentages of effort and time are shown in Table 5-5. I have chosen to consider compulsory and optional portions completely separately. This facilitates calculations and administration when the gymnasts' training is considered in strictly compulsory and optional days.

This time distribution in percentages represents an estimate of the emphasis our gymnast should give to each of these activities to reach her goal. The distribution is purely an example, not a recommendation. Each program and athlete may require a different set of percentages and perhaps some different activities. This method of assigning priority is very important for determining the direction of training. Often the athlete will prefer to perform the skills and events that she is good at. This means that her weaknesses are being neglected. You probably often operate the same way: if you are strong in one particular area, then you tend to spend more time there and neglect to build up your weak areas. As we apply these percentages to the actual amount of time available then we will see how you can place checks and balances on the training to assure that everything that is supposed to be happening is indeed happening.

By performing further calculations on the information we have, we will come to the distribution of time for each day of training shown in Tables 5-6 and 5-7. This time distribution resulted from taking the percentage of effort listed for each activity and calculating the actual minutes of activity each percentage represents.

With these numbers, you can look at the available time and determine quickly how much time the gymnast has per day for each activity. Then you might notice that there are only 15 minutes of time for tumbling on Sun-

TABLE 5-6   Time Distribution for Compulsory Days

Activity	Sunday	Tuesday	Friday
Warm-up	15	18	12
Dance	15	18	12
Vault	60	72	48
Uneven bars	60	72	48
Balance beam	90	108	72
Floor exercise	45	54	36
Tumbling	15	18	12
Conditioning	0	0	0

Numbers represent the number of minutes per activity.

TABLE 5-7   Time Distribution for Optional Days

Activity	Monday	Thursday	Saturday
Warm-up	18	18	18
Dance	18	18	18
Vault	0	0	0
Uneven bars	72	72	72
Balance beam	108	108	108
Floor exercise	72	72	72
Tumbling	54	54	54
Conditioning	18	18	18

Numbers represent the number of minutes per activity.

day—not enough time to get anything accomplished. Therefore, you take all your tumbling times for compulsory days and lump them together on one day so that there is enough time for some learning to take place. You know that this will require some juggling, but you know that when the end of the week rolls around, the actual time spent on each activity should correspond to the total amount of time indicated per week (by adding up all the times of each day). This will, in turn, correspond to the percentage of time and effort indicated by your master plan for getting the gymnast to her goal.

You will soon find that your system may not fit the actual time requirements given in this breakdown (because of availability of equipment, school schedules, and so on). If this is the case, then you know from the beginning that you'll be coming up short on something and that other compensations must be made to adhere to the master plan. In short, this plan gives you an opportunity to check the direction of training and to control the use of time in reaching a goal; it also provides some checks and balances for keeping the system in order.

This approach to setting up the training curriculum should be used with each of the three preparatory sections. The demands on the athlete must be constantly checked and rechecked. There is no such thing as a master plan without maintenance. The maintenance of the plan consists of constantly evaluating to see if the plan is really working and making modifications if observations dictate that something has gone off course.

USE THIS METHOD FOR ALL SECTIONS AND STAGES

When you use this type of curriculum design for the competitive and the recovery periods, the activities and the percentage weights assigned to each activity will change as the priorities change. In fact, you can break down the process even further by adding up all the time available for an event or activity and seeing if you can actually teach a skill in that amount of time. For example, if the gymnast would like to learn a very difficult vault, we should add up the available time for vaulting in the preparatory period. Calculations show that about 58 hours of training are allotted for vaulting during the entire preparatory period. Then if we take out time for gaining consistency on the vault and doing it in mock meet situations we are left with about 45 hours of training time left for actual learning. Realistically, we can then see if this particular athlete is far enough along to learn the vault safely in this amount of time. It is also helpful in assigning these times and playing with numbers to remember that the athlete may become ill or injured during training, which might throw some real wrenches into the schedule. By keeping careful records in our computer we should know the particular athlete's rate of absence and injury so that we can add a factor to our calculations that would statistically allow for the absences of the athlete due to illness, injury, and so on. This way we won't bite off more than we can chew in asking the gymnast to come up with an unlikely performance. By using records and a few calculations, we can be very much in control of time instead of victims of time.

CONCLUSION

In conclusion, we are beginning to see time as a useful measure of our resources. We can use time and training to gain significant control over the process of preparing our athletes and to help them in the process of training. Your thinking becomes multidimensional as you come to grips with the factors affecting the final outcome of the athlete's readiness to perform competent gymnastics. The athlete can be more comfortable knowing that a concrete and well-conceived plan for progress is being used to direct her work.

6

Facility
and Equipment

FACILITY

I've seen a tremendous number of different facilities and floor plans over the years, and it seems to me that just about anything will work if used wisely. However, there are a few general rules (more like guidelines than absolute law) that can help you in setting up the floor plan of the training gym. The safety of the athlete is our most important consideration, and safety can be greatly enhanced by careful and thoughtful planning. The general guidelines I'm going to give you concern traffic patterns, placement of equipment, use of thick matting, protective padding, building structure requirements, and movement of equipment.

    The traffic of the gym consists of the movements of the athletes around the event, and to and from different events; it also includes the relationship of each event's traffic patterns to other events' traffic patterns. We should attempt to make the gymnasts return to the line for their next turn by bypassing other working athletes by as much distance as possible. This will help keep the athletes from striking each other, getting kicked, or being fallen upon. Each event should have some imaginary boundaries that the gymnast must stay within while working. The athlete should be required to ask permission to leave this area and enter some other traffic pattern. The traffic around a single event can be controlled by careful placement of the chalk boxes, and by establishing fixed, defined patterns for returning to the end of the vault or tumbling runway, or for moving from one beam to another.

BUILDING REQUIREMENTS

No building structures should encumber the traffic or training areas of the athletes (posts in the way, slanted roofs that are too low, stairs that lead directly to traffic areas, etc.). Ceiling heights are important: they must meet the requirements of specific gymnastics skills. For example, the ceiling for uneven bars must be 16-18 feet to allow the taller gymnasts to do handstands on the upper rail without striking their feet.

The facility for gymnastics training is often a warehouse, since such a building is a clear span structure with plenty of open area. It is not easy to find a facility that is inexpensive, efficient, and safe. It generally takes many hours of planning to work out the floor plan for any facility to provide for the future growth requirements of the facility, the addition of more or better equipment, storage, traffic patterns, distance from building structures, and placement of matting and chalk boxes. The advent of foam pits has made planning ahead even more vital, since the pit can be placed in the ground or built above ground. Any pit will take a considerable amount of space, and the effect it has on traffic patterns and the structure of workouts is very great. You must plan for these factors and others that may be a problem in your particular environment (such as heat, cold, humidity, necessity of ventilation, and so on). Unfortunately, the types of facilities available vary so widely that it is beyond the scope of this text to define the guidelines for keeping the facility safe. Check with the ASTM (American Society for Testing and Materials) and check your local building codes for other pertinent information about the requirements of facilities and the relationship of facilities to the people who work in them.

You can promote safety by the correct placement of equipment. Obviously, the equipment should not be placed so close that the gymnast is likely to strike a piece of equipment while falling from another piece. But it should be close enough for you to be able to stand in one position and be able to supervise all the activity you are responsible for. This idea is very important. A potentially dangerous situation can often be avoided if you can see all the attempts leading up to the point of potential injury. If it's obvious to you that the attempts are getting worse, the athlete is beginning to fatigue, the mats have shifted, or the traffic pattern has changed, you can probably avoid the injury. That kind of sixth sense that teachers develop when they know that an accident is waiting to happen is very good if the coach is completely aware of what is happening in his/her area.

THICK MATTING

The use of thick matting is vitally important to the safety of all the athletes at all times. Unfortunately, the ability to predict all falls is not humanly possible. Therefore, those falls that are sudden and unforeseen should be guarded against by policy. The use of heavy "crash mats," 8 inches or more in thickness, should be mandatory under equipment or as landing surfaces nearly all the time, and certainly during learning stages. A small crash mat under the balance beam may not be large enough to cover the area a few feet from the beam where the gymnast will ultimately land if she falls from a far out-of-balance position. In this case two crash mats may be necessary, or a larger mat; or the beam might be lowered to keep her fall trajectory within the confines of the soft mat. Each coach should look at a skill carefully to try and be clairvoyant enough to predict where the gymnast would end up if she were to let go there, or where the athlete would be most likely to fall if she does this one very well and over rotates the skill. This clairvoyance may indicate that the coach will have to pad almost everything, since the gymnast can fall in a variety of places at any given time.

PROTECTIVE PADDING

Protective padding should cover all the areas where a falling gymnast might land. Therefore, the wall, areas of the floor, and the sides of other equipment may have to be padded—particularly the corner areas of the floor exercise mat, the landing areas of all events, the area under the horse, and the areas around the bases of the equipment. The matting should have as few creases and overlaps as possible. The joints, overlaps, and creases are likely places for the athlete to catch a foot, turn an ankle, or get caught in.

Protective padding can also cover the gymnast. Various types of pads that are made for gymnastics and other sports can be used to keep the gymnast safer and more comfortable. Any time the gymnast is likely to fall on a particular body part she might be safer with a pad on this area. For instance, there are skills on bars that often lead to striking the rail with certain body parts; while performing knee spins in floor exercise, the athlete sometimes knocks her knees together, so padding would help here. The knee pads of basketball players and wrestlers can be used in a variety of ways to keep the gymnast from bruising her heels on the bars. Heel cups and pads used by runners can help prevent heel bruises on balance beam and vaulting. The injury research I have done with my own gymnasts has shown over and over that most of the injuries result from falling and striking something. Therefore, the introduction of more protective padding can go a long way toward improving the training conditions of the athlete.

EQUIPMENT MOVEMENT

The movement and adjustment of equipment should be kept to a minimum for a variety of reasons.

1. Equipment will last longer if it does not have to be moved around.
2. Various injuries occur from dropping equipment on feet and hands while it is being moved (unfortunately, all gymnastics equipment is heavy).
3. Injuries occur from adjusting the equipment: fingers are pinched, rails fall on heads, and balance beams run over toes.
4. The adjustment of equipment can also be avoided somewhat by putting similar size athletes in the same groups for bar settings and beam and horse heights.

The more fixed the facility, the more likely that these types of problems will be avoided.

LEGAL CONSIDERATIONS REGARDING EQUIPMENT

The apparatus, matting, and pieces of equipment used in modern gymnastics have undergone some dramatic changes throughout the past decade. In fact, I believe that most of our improvements in difficulty and new skills have resulted more from equipment changes than from better coaching techniques. Our American equipment companies should be commended for their foresight and dedication to gymnastics as a sport. They should receive much of the credit for the gymnastics improvements seen in the United States and across the world, since they have led the world in producing innovative and safe equipment.

The new equipment we are enjoying today that did not exist 10 years ago includes spring floors, padded and covered balance beams, springier vaulting boards, springier and nonbreakable fiberglass rails for the uneven bars, thicker and safer matting, foam pits, and carpeted floor exercise mats. These innovations have done much to promote the safety, comfort, and longevity of our athletes.

I would like to give some guidelines that can help you make coaching decisions that involve the use or adaptations of gymnastic equipment. The ASTM (American Society for Testing and Materials) has a gymnastics committee that has been in existence since around 1972. This committee has been charged with coming up with standards for gymnastics equipment. They have established and revised specifications for trampolining that have been used for many years. The committee is presently working on specifications for matting that will be used to determine resiliency, size, thickness, and other factors as standards for tumbling and other mats. Equipment companies and coaches should adhere to these guidelines to keep the athletes safe.

Current specifications are available from (a) the International Gymnastics Federation, regarding equipment used in international competitions;

(b) the United States Gymnastics Federation, regarding equipment used in domestic competitions; and (c) the NCAA or AIAW, for their own particular adaptations of the current International Gymnastics Federation specifications. The gymnastics governing bodies in the United States have changed and adapted some of the International Federation's specifications in some areas, but all the changes have been to exceed the specifications required by the International Federation. These rules and guidelines are important, since you cannot talk about equipment and its use without considering the legal implications of any actions you take that are not within the guidelines and framework of the gymnastics sport governing bodies. Unfortunately, there are not many specifications that go beyond the simple competitive equipment requirements. It is your responsibility, not the equipment company's, to ascertain what equipment is needed for learning and performing any particular skill. You must see that all the necessary equipment is present, properly placed, well maintained, and properly used.

The grind comes when you may want to adapt a piece of equipment or design a completely new piece that makes it easier for the gymnast to learn certain skills. You must be aware that if you do this, and if an accident occurs, you may have to prove to the court that the adaptation was better than the normal equipment specifications would have been. In addition, you will have to definitively prove that the adaptation of the equipment did not contribute to the injury. What you might consider innovation the court may consider negligence.

Some examples of the adaptation of equipment are tilting trampolines, home-made balance beams, home-made spring floors, home-made bars, and single rail set-ups. Modifications include putting tennis balls in the springs of the vaulting board, constructing many different styles of pits, and using mini-trampolines for tumbling or vaulting take-offs. If you use adaptations or modifications like these, and someone gets hurt, you'll have great difficulty proving that these were actually improvements upon already accepted standards and specifications. Therefore, you should carefully document, test, and analyze each of your modifications or changes so that these changes are assuredly safe.

You should always make sure that you purchase equipment from a reputable company that can defend itself in case a piece of equipment does fail. Some of the equipment presently available is provided by a single person or some small business that could not possibly accept a legal challenge; in this case, the injured party would have no choice but to strenuously pursue the gymnastics program for recovery of damages. This puts you in a very risky position.

The real key to the avoidance of these legal nightmares is to keep the gymnasts from getting hurt at all. The small injuries that are seemingly inherent in all sporting activities are not the ones that the coach need fear. The spectacular injuries that cause disability are the ones that cause the legal problems. You can place yourself in the best position by not letting your gymnasts get hurt at all. This is done by careful training, good judgment, careful selection of equipment, genuine concern for the well being of the athletes, and constant vigilance.

The maintenance of the equipment is as important as, or more important than, its purchase and design. Gymnastics equipment is really very durable, but in time it will wear to the point of not providing the safety that it did when it was new. You should inspect the equipment daily for defects of materials or parts, and you should record any such defects. The records should be filed and dated. You must see that each defect is fixed or replaced before the gymnasts are allowed to use the equipment.

This all sounds easy enough, and we all do it in some form or another. However, problems arise because of the fact that the equipment wears out very slowly, often imperceptibly. The crash mats one day are suddenly too bottomed out to protect the falling gymnast. The tumbling mats are so thin in the middle that they have lost their resiliency. The beam covers have been used for so long that the turns (and other wear and tear) are grinding little holes in the tops. Keeping careful records of these equipment failings can show you roughly how long it takes for a piece of equipment to wear out. Then, as the end of one of these time periods come up, you can mark the calendar to remind you to order new parts or see if the equipment really does require replacement or repair this time. This procedure will allow you to be one step ahead of the game when buying equipment: you can look for bargains before the equipment gets unsafe and you have to replace it quickly.

SAFETY FACTORS

Let's begin looking at some individual pieces of equipment and a few specific cautions and guidelines related to their safe use. The factors mentioned below are not the only ones that contribute to increasing safety, but are listed to help make the coach more aware of influential factors surrounding safety and potential injury.

FOAM PITS

The use of foam pits has been prevalent in the United States for only a few years. American coaches who visited some of the training gyms in Europe saw large rectangular holes in the floor filled to overflowing with small pieces of soft foam. The type of foam that is found in seat cushions is used: it is soft, nonmoulded, and does not have the bubbly looking skin that is a result of its manufacture. The pits are used for landings and falls of all types. The gymnast can land in some very uncomfortable looking positions and not be hurt because the pits are so deep and soft that the impact is spread over a very large distance. A Russian coach supposedly said that he believed they lost a whole generation of gymnasts to injury before they started using foam pits. I think that might be an exaggeration, but I can testify to the fact that the pits help tremendously in avoiding injury, promoting learning, and making gymnastics safer.

The pit allows the gymnast to do many repetitions of a skill without having to suffer the pain and risk of mistakes. The gymnast is in an unusual situation as an athlete since she must not only perform some very complex skills but must also repeat them many times to improve her consistency; this may be dangerous, because each time she makes a mistake it may hurt her ankles, knees, or some other body part. A typical tennis player practicing a serve may serve 300-500 times in a practice session. The mistakes are seen when the ball hits the net or goes out of bounds. The gymnast may be performing a double somersault, much more complex than hitting the ball. She will only get a couple of dozen attempts in a practice session. If she makes a mistake, she may not walk away from it. The pit allows her to perform many repetitions without getting hurt. Repetition is the key to learning and to safety. The safe repetitions of a skill will develop learning and consistency so that the chance of getting hurt becomes smaller and smaller.

Pit construction is relatively simple in concept. The pit consists of a large hole filled with foam, carefully padded to prevent the gymnast from striking anything hard. Some pits use loose, torn up, or shredded foam; some have large crash mats encased in nylon mesh as the soft landing area. Pits are constructed above the floor by building platforms and using lumber, or they are built into the ground by digging a hole in the floor. I would recommend the following minimum dimensions for a pit with loose foam for women's gymnastics. The pit for women should be a minimum of 6 feet deep, 12 feet wide, and 15 feet long. (A pit for men's gymnastics will require a significantly deeper and larger area due to the fact that the men are heavier, fall farther, and fly farther before they land.) The pit should have very thick padding in the bottom so that it is impossible for the gymnast to penetrate through the foam and hit the bottom hard surface without being stopped by the padding at the bottom of the pit. The walls of the pit should be padded around the edge and downward along the side of the pit. This is done because now and then some gymnast goes crooked and penetrates the foam near the edge. Although she may not hit the top of the supporting structure, she may penetrate the foam near the edge and the remaining inertia of her fall could carry her into the wall of the pit. Again, these are recommended as general guidelines, so that you are aware of possible problems that can occur with the pit and therefore will use good judgment in its construction and use.

The foam that goes in the pit should be soft, of rather small size, and not the variety that will powder with age. The foam pieces should be soft, for obvious reasons. The size is also important. The foam pieces should not be so large that they tip or do not compress enough to allow the gymnast the complete penetration of the foam that gives the pit its absorptive qualities. After all, all the pit really does is allow the gymnast to absorb or slow her impact over a large distance. It is the abrupt stop that causes injury when the gymnast strikes or lands on the floor or equipment. The pit allows the gymnast to slow her descent gradually in the soft material. As a general rule, try not to have the pieces larger than one cubic foot.

The foam that goes into the pit is made from a process that uses a form of cyanide to fluff up the plastic. The iso-cyanide compound results from a chemical reaction that combines cyanide with another substance. When the compound is complete all the cyanide compound is combined with another substance to form an inert material. Unfortunately, there may sometimes be more cyanide present in the reaction than can combine to form the inert substance that makes the foam fluffy. When this happens the free cyanide radical can combine with other things that come in contact with it (such as people). This combination may produce some rough skin irritations and a few other symptoms. You should be especially aware of any skin problems that show up in the athletes using new foam or a new pit for the first few times. And if the pit ever catches fire, head for the hills; the cyanide gas that results from the combustion can kill you in minutes. Do not try to save anything, just get the kids out.

The pit should be fluffed up often. The constant use of the pit by gymnasts falling into it makes the foam compress to tighter and tighter proportions, and it gets harder and harder. The pit finally becomes a deep crash mat. The ability of the pit to absorb the fall over a great distance is reduced and therefore the purpose of the pit is reduced. This makes for a higher risk of injury, particularly since the athlete may fully expect to have her fall cushioned and is abruptly surprised. Fluffing the pit consists of simply unpacking the foam that has been packed tightly through continued use. This should be done as often as the circumstances indicate, and more often where the athletes tend to land most — generally just a few feet from the edge nearest the take off.

The foam should be kept clean and dry, and the pit should be cleaned from time to time by throwing out all of the foam and cleaning the accumulated materials out of the bottom. This is necessary to keep the foam particles that rub off out of the eyes of the gymnasts as they fall into the pit. As the foam ages it will need to be replaced from time to time. Regular attention paid to fluffing and cleaning the pit will go a long way to keeping the gymnasts safe and comfortable.

A pit is not a panacea. It simply makes falls more comfortable. The pit will not allow the gymnast to stand up her double back somersault if the round-off and flip-flop are not efficient. The pit will not teach the gymnast how to perform the skill better. Teaching is your responsibility. There is a phenomenon that occurs upon introducing a pit that seems to promote learning through reduction of fear, but this does not in itself teach gymnasts the skill nor ensure that they will perform without fear away from the pit.

The careful instruction of the gymnast must still continue. The pit simply allows the coach to stand away from the gymnast and avoid the spotting that was so essential before pits came into use. Spotting forced the coach to be a catcher rather than a teacher. Spotters could not possibly see the results of the gymnast's technique if they were always standing near the gymnast and were responsible for catching and manipulating the gymnast through the air. Now we can safely stand some distance from the gymnast and watch the technique carefully to ascertain performance errors and devise drills, give pertinent information, and describe clearly how the skill should be performed and exactly what went wrong.

In summary, the pit is probably the single most necessary piece of equipment in a modern gymnastics training facility. The pit allows the gymnast to perform thousands of repetitions in comfort and safety. The use of the pit will not make great athletes but it will aid the learning and drilling process. The coach can make much more informed and consistent judgments about the readiness of the athlete to perform the skill in "competitive circumstances" by watching the thousands of repetitions that the same athlete will perform into the pit. Placing a soft mat on the top of the foam also gives information as the gymnast is gently trained to land on harder and harder surfaces. The test of a finished product in the pit may be to land on a crash mat with a 4-inch landing mat on top of it and slightly above the floor level. This would indicate that the gymnast has a large margin for error and that training of the skill onto competitive types of landing surfaces can begin. In short, the pit allows us to be more sequential and thorough in our teaching than ever before, and we can be much more sure about our decisions to "go for it."

CRASH MATS

Crash mats were an early answer to safer landing areas before the advent of pits, and in my opinion are, next to the pit, the best method of protecting the gymnast. I consider crash mats to be those soft foam slabs (at least 8 inches thick and a minimum of 5 feet by 10 feet) covered with a nylon or mesh material. They are still vital in all training situations, and they are particularly useful in the learning and drilling stages that come after the pit stages. The gymnast performs her skills with crash mats as her landing area for a considerable time before landing on the actual 4-inch landing mat or the floor exercise mat itself. I believe that a crash mat should be placed under every piece of equipment during training at all times when it is feasible and practical. This will help prevent the injuries from the unforeseen falls.

The portability of the crash mat is one of its greatest assets. The mat can be used to pad a landing area almost anywhere. It can be tilted, made into hills, placed against the wall, draped over the bar or beam, and folded to facilitate safety and learning opportunity. The crash mat is so vital that I believe every event must have one or access to one during each training period.

The crash mat should be cared for carefully. The crash mat suffers from use mostly in dead center where most of the landings occur and where most of the wear occurs. You should check the crash mats for this wear frequently. If you can jump and land in the center of the mat and feel your feet penetrate through the foam and touch the floor, the crash mat needs to be replaced. Sometimes stacking crash mats on top of one another can prolong their life and be a helpful learning aid (see Sands, 1981).

TUMBLING MATS

Tumbling mats are constructed in a variety of different ways. The old ones might be made of canvas with horse hair as the cushioning substance. New ones use a foam product called ethafoam as the absorptive material. It is important for you to understand that the tumbling mat is used primarily for its absorptive qualities to protect hands, feet, wrists, and knees rather than for its resilience. In other words, the mat is used primarily to keep the athlete comfortable rather than to provide greater springiness for added height of tumbling or aerial maneuvers. (It's helpful to remember that, historically, floor exercise was performed on hardwood gym floors long before mats were used.) Tumbling has used matting for some time, but if you have ever tumbled on a horse hair mat you will gain instant appreciation for the ethafoam we now use.

You must inspect the tumbling mats periodically along with the other equipment in the gym. The principal sign of wear on the typical folded tumbling mats is softness in the center. When they are folded and stacked on top of each other, the center portion dips considerably lower than the ends. If you can slide your foot along the width of the mat when it is placed on the floor and feel a different consistency of the ethafoam in the center than on the ends, this is a sign that the mat must be replaced. Other obvious signs are defective stitching of the joints, inability of the velcro fasteners to hold the mats together at the ends, and torn covers.

The use of tumbling mats for tumbling and as matting under the apparatus is very widespread. You should attempt to maintain the mats in good condition by observing the signs of wear and by providing additional matting to prevent the gymnast from striking other objects related to the apparatus. You must not make the mistake of considering the tumbling mat to be enough matting to catch gymnasts when they fall. The crash mat, landing mats, and pits are designed for this purpose. When the gymnast performs a skill on the tumbling mats then she should be perfectly able to do so. ~~Her~~ The margin for error should be enormous and there should be no question about ~~her~~ the ability to perform the skill safely.

FOUR-INCH LANDING MATS

The 4-inch mats are those used for competition in dismounting and landing the vault. These mats are roughly 4 inches thick and are constructed of a variety of materials. In tumbling, you should use the 4-inch mats as another developmental step prior to the tumbling mats alone and after the crash mats. In other events, these mats are used for dismounting, and they do provide a significant added measure of safety and comfort. The gymnast who is performing a dismount, or landing a vault, should always have these mats as a minimum landing surface. Additional matting should be used as necessary, depending on the experience of the gymnast and the difficulty of the skill.

Maintenance of the 4-inch landing mats is the same as for the crash mats. More care must be taken in moving and modifying the uses of 4-inch landing mats since their construction is markedly different from that of the crash mat.

THE VAULT

The vaulting equipment consists of the vaulting horse, a landing mat or area of the pit, the take-off board, and a suitable run-up distance of 75-80 feet. The equipment for vaulting is really rather simple. Its maintenance is also simple. The horse will generally not require much maintenance at all. If the horse is being raised and lowered to accommodate different sized athletes, then the piston should be oiled periodically so that it moves easily and will not contribute to pinched fingers and long struggles to move the horse body up and down. The base of the horse should be padded so that the aborted attempts at going over the horse do not result in striking the hard metal base. The old style horses that are used for pommel horse and have holes for the pommels should have the holes covered or plugged. This will prevent the young athlete from getting her fingers caught in them during the support phase.

The landing area for vaulting should be carefully padded, with the amount of padding reflecting the abilities of the gymnast and the difficulty of the vault. The less ability and experience, the softer and larger the matting. If the landing area is near a wall or some other object, then this object should be very carefully padded so that a gymnast who lands out of control and runs several steps before falling will not be injured upon striking the object.

The vaulting board has long been a source of considerable controversy. The added springiness of modern boards has been greatly responsible for the increasingly difficult skills high-level gymnasts are able to perform. The maintenance of the vaulting board is usually more simple than that of the other pieces because as the board wears out it becomes obvious to the coach upon viewing the vaults. Since the board is responsible for helping the athletes get over the horse, much of the effectiveness of the vault is determined by the board. As the vault loses quality the coach will usually check the board, or the athletes will complain that the board feels "dead." These are signs that the board needs to be replaced or repaired. New types of vaults now being developed consist of doing a round-off that lands on the board followed by a flip-flop or Arabian dive to the horse. The advent of these vaults makes the safe construction and maintenance of the board even more paramount. The gymnast is forced to hit the board very accurately during the take-off phase of any vault. The addition of a skill like the round-off while running at full speed (to take off on a small "sweet spot" of the board) makes the event considerably more difficult. The use of these vaults may require some apparatus changes to promote their safe execution. The edges of the board may have to be padded and a structure that enlarges the top surface of the horse may need to be added to promote safety.

The runway for vaulting should be long, padded, and unencumbered. Since the gymnast is standing some distance from the horse and board when she begins her run, it is not easily apparent that she is performing; so people often cross the runway of the vaulting approach without regard for the vaulter about to begin her approach. This should be prevented by roping off the vault runway in practice and competition to prevent easy access to this area. The runway should be padded to prevent the shin and foot injuries that occur with frequent pounding during running and take-offs. The padding should be soft enough to prevent these problems but firm enough to provide good traction. The runway should also be a different color than the vaulting board so that those gymnasts who have poor eyesight can easily find the board during the full-speed latter portions of their runs. The nap of the carpet of the vaulting board should not go in the direction of the run, in order to help prevent the gymnast from slipping at board contact.

THE UNEVEN BARS

The uneven bars receive a great amount of attention during training. The uneven bars are probably the place where the gymnasts spend the second-largest portion of their training time. This large amount of time is likely to result in a larger proportion of injuries in this area, so it is important to take some extra precautions to ensure safety.

The competitive athlete is likely to get injured on the uneven bars through two avenues — falling from the bars and striking the floor, or falling onto the bars and striking the rail, uprights, or spreader. In a previous section we underlined the importance of using crash mats under each piece of equipment and putting the bars over a pit to decrease the likelihood of falling to the floor and being injured.

The uneven bars have considerably more moving parts than the other pieces of equipment, so constant checking and maintenance of the adjustment mechanisms is vital. The easy adjustment of the equipment not only facilitates speedier workouts but helps avoid the finger pinching and rail dropping accidents that are likely to occur when the gymnast has to struggle with the equipment. Checking the rails for splits or defects is also important. The new fiberglass rails with wood laminated on the outside of the fiberglass tube require more careful maintenance and checking than did the older style solid piece of wood. Oiling the moving parts of the equipment will help keep the athlete working without problems. (It is a little unnerving to the athletes when the squeaky bars are oiled and suddenly become silent. The sounds of different squeaks and strains of the equipment are often used by the athlete to get cues for position and action in learning and performing a skill.)

The semi-violent actions performed on the bars by casting and stomach whip on the low bar cause the bars to be quite mobile. The bases of the bars should be secured to the floor to prevent them from moving. In competition the types of bars that have mobile bases should have the floor around the bases taped to show where they were during warm-ups. The setting the gymnast uses to ensure that the low bar will strike her exactly on the thighs where she can handle the impact during a stomach whip can be drastically altered if the bases of the bars are moved.

I have labeled some skills as rail-dependent skills. These are the types of skills that rely greatly on the resiliency of the rail action for their performance. Such skills as the stomach whip to handstand on the low bar, Janz front somersault, wrapping skills, and at times even the larger swinging skills like reverse hechts can be greatly affected by a change in rail action. This is a dilemma you have to consider in composing the bar routines of your gymnast. If she is going to use a rail-dependent skill, she may have problems in transferring this skill to another set of bars. If the rail action of the bars changes from one type of bars to another, then the gymnast will actually have to relearn the skill during the warm-ups of competition. Of course, warm-ups in competition are not the place to be relearning skills. Therefore, if the gymnast uses rail-dependent skills she should have the opportunity to practice these skills frequently on other types of bars and she should be drilled very thoroughly on these skills prior to competition. I have often seen problems occur when the athlete must go from the type of bars cabled into the floor to the portable or "water"-weighted types of bars. Most portable bars are more springy or mobile when set than the versions cabled into the floor.

The type of chalk and the temperature of the gym can have some effects on the safety of the gymnast. The use of powder or block chalk in itself is not the issue, but changing from one type to another may require some adjustment. The gymnast may need to rehearse a few more skills (to adjust the movements of her grip around the bar) when the type of chalk is changed. The temperature of the gymnasium, combined with humidity, can also affect the safety of the athlete. High temperature and high humidity conditions cause gymnasts to perspire, and this usually makes their hands slippery and their thighs sticky. In a hot, humid environment you should exercise caution by placing extra matting under the bars for the occasional slip, by placing additional matting farther from the center of the bars to catch the falls with flight, and by careful spotting or progressions for the thigh support and departure skills. Thighs will have to be chalked during hot humid weather to prevent sticking. Stickiness of the thighs is dangerous during hechting skills when departure from the rails is by the thighs. The retarded sliding caused by temperature and humidity keeps the gymnast closer to the rail during these actions and may cause the gymnast to come too close to the rail for the nature of the skill she is performing.

As the breadth of the swings, the flights, and releases increase for uneven bars, the coach should pad all of the parts of the bars that are not used for gripping and may be struck by the crooked-swinging gymnast. The heels are prime candidates for hitting the rail on releases. Some somersaulting and releasing skills may expose the gymnast to landing on her back on one of the rails. The rail should either be padded or removed in these cases, the gymnast should pad herself, and/or a competent spotter should be there. Although I do believe that spotting should be kept as minimal as possible, this is the one exception I believe is very important. We can usually pad the floor or do the skill over the pit to keep the falls to the floor from causing injury. However, falling and striking the equipment cannot be stopped with pits, and therefore the equipment must be softly padded or the gymnast must be spotted. As the uneven bars become more like the horizontal bar, we must be increasingly aware of the risk and likelihood of flight before landing. Again, you have to be a little clairvoyant in seeing that the gymnast will have the protection where she needs it and when she needs it.

THE BALANCE BEAM

The balance beam is a simple piece of equipment. It has few moving parts and requires little maintenance. You can see the cover of the beam when you watch the gymnast, so defects in the equipment are usually obvious. Yet, balance beam accounts for most of the injuries among the highly trained competitive athlete. This is not due to its complexity but rather to its simplicity. The balance beam injury is typically caused by falling and striking the beam with some body part. These types of injuries are not likely to respond well to increasing the matting on the floor, since the gymnast usually strikes the beam before she gets to the floor. The use of higher mats (so that the gymnast falls only a short distance and therefore recovers quickly) to prevent striking the beam is a help, but does not assist the athlete in gaining the perspective of altitude that will help control her balance as she performs on the beam at competition height. The balance beam is the great equalizer of the women's all-around. The competitive athlete should spend more time on balance beam than on any other event. The real key to protecting the athlete on balance beam is adequate training. The athlete should be drilled and drilled until the proper technique for skills is so habitual that injury is only a remote possibility.

The balance beam should have a crash mat under it during training as often as possible to catch the unforeseen falls. There are mats available that the gymnast can attach to the beam to pad the top and sides of the beam. These mats are very helpful in taking the sting out of landings, promoting early confidence, and protecting the gymnast if she strikes the beam. These mats should be examined carefully for wear since the foam material attached to the beam wears faster than the tumbling mats do. Any place where a foot can be caught in the padding must be eliminated. I have seen some poorly designed beam mats that have allowed the gymnast's foot to get stuck in the place where the mat folds to go around the corners of the beam surface. However, beam mats are a great boon to the early learning of skills that require heavy impact or many repetitions using the same body area.

The beams should not be placed so close together that the gymnast cannot run a step or two without striking another beam. The falls from balance beam usually do not fly very far, and the gymnast usually does not run far after falling from the beam, but a little extra room will allow two gymnasts to fall simultaneously without hitting each other. The bases of the beams should not be in the path of the falling gymnast. The beams should be as parallel as possible and provide room for falling 360 degrees around the apparatus.

THE SPRING FLOOR

The spring floors that have come into wide use recently are a great addition to gymnastics. The spring floor has provided considerably more comfort to the gymnast and a more "forgiving" surface during landings. Maintenance of spring floors is essential to maintain consistent resiliency. The floor areas likely to become overused are the corners and the diagonals. These areas should be checked frequently for defects; any "dead spots" should be lifted and springs replaced. The foam-type spring floors are more susceptible to these problems and should be checked more often and more carefully.

The spring floor is very expensive, and most gymnastics coaches are likely to seek inexpensive alternatives to purchasing the spring floor. Home-made versions may be perfectly adequate, but you should remember that if any accident occurs and the floor is blamed, you must be able to provide evidence that the floor meets all specifications and did not contribute to the injury by design or materials.

FIRST AID AND TREATMENT AREA

A training area should be provided for the care and rehabilitation of injury. This does not mean that you have to set up a small doctor's office; you simply must have an area where taping, checking of injuries, and rehabilitation of injury occurs. This area can include the whirlpool, tape, taping table, water, a cabinet for scissors, and other supplies. Weight training equipment might be included, to help gymnasts regain strength as they return to full activity. Ice should always be available and easily accessible. A great idea I saw once was to have an instant cold pack (you have to break the inner bag to make the inner contents cold) hung from a clip board placed near every event. This was to ensure that anyone could run over and get the ice pack immediately upon noting an injury that needs ice. Then more ice was available in the freezer of the gym's refrigerator. Of course, a lot of criticism accompanies these instant cold packs because they don't retain cold as well as real ice does, but in the interest of speed and convenience they can be a very useful first line of defense. This type of first aid and therapy equipment is very important in keeping athletes healthy and returning them to activity as quickly as possible if they should receive an injury.

MISCELLANEOUS EQUIPMENT

Videotaping and filming athletes is very important for analyzing technique and providing feedback for learning. You should acquire a high-speed film camera and a videotape machine. They are expensive, but I have used both and I find them both quite necessary. The videotape gives instantaneous feedback to the coach and athlete, but at roughly 30 frames per second this is not as clear or as useful as film that can be shot at higher frame rates. The high-speed film is better for clarity and longevity. You want to get the kind of videotape that allows you to do frame-by-frame advancement so that the skill can be thoroughly examined for flaws in technique. To make use of computer analysis, you just about have to have film rather than videotape, and I consider the computer an almost indispensable adjunct to training and skill analysis.

The modern microcomputer has given me the ability to do more for the gymnast than ever before. The computer can record daily physiological data on each gymnast, display the data in graphic format to discern the condition of the athlete in a variety of parameters, perform biomechanical analysis of film in a very accurate and graphic format, perform literature searches of hundreds of data bases on nearly any information known to man, and keep literally millions of records, statistical analyses of any factors affecting training, communications with other coaches, word processing, and mailing lists. I use two microcomputers to perform all these functions and many other functions as well. The computer provides fast and very accurate information regarding many facets of training. Since you are unlikely to have a huge staff, the computer provides a faster means of doing many of the jobs that simply go undone otherwise or require exhaustive amounts of time and preparation. This frees you to do what you do best — coach.

CONCLUSION

This chapter on facility and equipment was designed to provide added awareness of safety, help in the judgment of wise use of equipment, and some idea of minimal types of equipment that should be used for training high-level athletes. Of course, there will be exceptions and additions owing to the needs and abilities of the various coaches. You are encouraged to explore all the possible avenues of equipment to help ensure the safe and productive training of the athlete.

7

The Support Staff

SPECIALISTS

No single coach can be every answer to every athlete. You will encounter unusual problems that you have never seen before. I have found that many typical problems of young athletes are well documented and can be dealt with in a rather cookbook fashion. However, these are not the problems that will prevent the talented, high-level athlete from getting to her goals. The types of problems these athletes experience may become career limiters, and they are usually quite exotic by typical gymnastics standards. For me, these types of problems included a child who had a calcium deficiency (because she could not handle normal formula as a baby, which resulted in knee problems due to soft bone), a child who ran into a glass patio door and fractured her nose, which kept her from training at maximum for several weeks, a girl who fell off a horse during a horsemanship lesson and received a concussion that kept her out of training for several weeks, a girl who was being harassed by her teachers for representing the United States in international competition and missing school (these teachers would not allow the girl to make up her work, since they did not believe that these absences were legitimate reasons for them to have to give extra privileges to her when she returned), a girl who experienced real depression and inability to cope with stress as she attempted to deal with the weight gain and sudden mood swings associated with the onset of her menstrual periods, and a child who was extremely disturbed about the impending divorce of her parents. These symptoms and problems might give you an idea of the nightmarish types of problems that you'll have to deal with that have absolutely nothing to do with whether or not you can teach a flip-flop, spot a somersault, or choreograph a beam routine. In fact, these problems will be more devastating than most any gymnastics problems. Much of the success of the program will be determined by the coach's ability to assist with all these "personal" problems of the athlete.

Although it's obvious that you'll have to call on outside specialists to help solve such problems, it's not always easy to figure out how and where these people can help. I have been very lucky in this, and I believe that specialists have made an enormous contribution to our success as a competitive program. Injuries must be seen by qualified people within 24 hours. Emotional problems must be dealt with in days. Dietary and weight problems must be solved by competent people and not left to the latest diet fad. Research must be done to ascertain the effects of training and of the particular program in question on the health and longevity of the athletes involved. Those injuries that are not incapacitating must be treated and rehabilitated, and limitations defined on a daily basis to prevent further injury. All these factors should be provided for in the comprehensive program for training high-level athletes.

The problem you face is finding such people close by and determining their interest in assisting in the gymnastics program. The types of specialists break down roughly into three categories: health and medicine, science, and psychology. The following list is rather like a large shopping list of specialists that every program should have. Ideally, these specialists should be available to give you quick advice by telephone and be able to see any athlete within 24 hours for defining and beginning solution to a problem.

The health and medicine category should be headed by an orthopedist or podiatrist. The injury statistics I have kept over the years have shown dramatically that most of the injuries suffered by female gymnasts are from the knee down—the province of the orthopedist and the podiatrist. These two specialists can provide a large portion of the help needed by any training athlete. Next on the list would be a general medicine practitioner for help in various illnesses and speedy treatment of the more general problems such as colds, flu, etc. In addition to these doctors, I'd want a competent athletic trainer and/or physical therapist. This person will aid in the treatment and rehabilitation of injuries that the athlete might suffer. Since we are dealing with female athletes we should also have a gynecologist on our list. Although seldom used, the gynecologist may be of assistance in helping the athlete through changes occurring in the adolescent period. Finally, a nutritionist or dietician will help in the dietary and weight problems that most of the athletes will encounter at one time or another. These health and medical professionals can provide immediate help in solving any health-related problems the gymnast might encounter.

Experts in the science category are concerned with the fields of exercise physiology and biomechanics. These experts will be used somewhat less than the health-medicine experts, since their area involves more research than clinical solving of problems. They can assist in the analysis of skill techniques and the facilitation of sound training regimes for the athlete. Their role is largely preventive in nature, and although they might get less "business" than the health experts, they will help prevent injury and will give advice about minor problems the athletes experience during training, a situation much preferable to sending athletes to another specialist once the problem has become serious enough to interfere with training.

The psychology category is one that has become more and more important in recent times because of reports that eastern Europe is using sport psychologists to make "super-athletes." I do not see the psychologist in this role as much as I do in the role of facilitating the teaching process. The sport psychologist can be of immense help to your program; he or she can teach the athlete to deal with many of the stress-related facets of sports, assist in learning problems, help the athlete through rough times, help with stress management, teach techniques in relaxation, and generally provide outside and unbiased emotional support. Since the athlete is such a complex person and you are often so close to the situation that the obvious blends into the background, a competent sport psychologist can provide just the unbiased evaluation that you both need to keep the situation in realistic perspective. Be sure to check on the credentials of any psychologist who is going to be assisting.

Fortunately, I have found that most people who have specialties in these fields are more than eager to help. They are usually very interested in children and enjoy assisting in their development. Most will perform their role on a "fees for services" basis and although their services are not free, their ability to deal with your problem quickly more than compensates for the cost. The gymnast would usually have to pay for any treatment, aid, or counselling anyway, and the fact that it is done quickly is extremely important to the needs of the athlete. Often you can have the specialist who is nearby stop at the gym to check on the progress of the athlete on the way to and from the office. This kind of support is very helpful to everyone in the program. You know that a problem can be solved by just a phone call; the athlete knows that there are a lot of people who are genuinely interested in seeing that she does well; and the specialist can be named a "team physician" or "team specialist," which will look impressive on a resume and will provide him or her with greater access to the community.

In my opinion, these specialists are what make or break the program. Although most gymnastics problems are relatively easy to solve, the problems these people assist in are much more difficult. I have found that getting a child to do a trick is a very simple matter compared to getting the child through adolescence, through a divorce, over an injury, or into a training regime that will guarantee success. These specialists are the resource people for the ambitious coach to solve the problems occurring during training and thereby increase productivity and the likelihood of success.

Appendix C includes addresses and helpful associations that might help you find competent specialists. It is very important that the people involved must have a background in sports medicine or sports science in order to be effective. Countless times I have seen a well-meaning emergency room physician tell the athlete to put heat on a sprained ankle. This continually surprises me. At the same time I write a quick thank you to all of our specialists. It may take you a while to find these people, but they will put the program into the 20th century.

8

The Selection Process

The selection of athletes to train is a tricky, yet vital part of any comprehensive program in gymnastics. You must have a means of determining the ability (or potential ability) of the athletes who are entering training so that you can direct them to a system of training that best suits their needs and abilities. A high-level, very demanding training situation is not the place for gymnasts with only marginal ability, since they will probably be totally frustrated in attempting to keep up with much more talented children. On the other hand, I have often seen the dreams of a fine young athlete lost, simply because she was training in a program that offered no challenges. So it is very important for you to devote a great deal of time and thought to the selection process.

You will be involved in three types of evaluation — evaluation that will attempt to determine:

1. whether the child has potential in gymnastics;
2. whether the gymnast has potential to become a great gymnast; and
3. whether the gymnast should be promoted within the program.

The first type of evaluation is, in my opinion, a critical facet of the program. The intelligent judgment of the coach, coupled with results of some useful tests and supplemental information, can greatly enhance the training of the athlete.

There are really three types of programs in gymnastics. The first is a program designed for the high-level training of very talented athletes to national and international prominence. The second is a program that dabbles in competition but does not have the requisite system and ambition to train athletes to high levels. This second type of program may eventually develop into the first type; or it may remain at an intermediary level (the gifted young athlete will not be able to reach very high level goals in this type of program). The third type of program is strictly recreational in outlook and ambitions. The gymnast in this type of program neither seeks nor desires high-level training and the commitment it entails. Obviously, evaluation for these three types of programs is different. The first type of program is the target of this text; we will look at the evaluation of young gymnasts to determine if they should be selected for high-level, rigorous training.

Testing athletes to determine potential is a big, big gamble. In the following paragraphs I will attempt to give you some concrete concepts and tests that should be helpful. But the truth is that there is no foolproof way to determine potential. The instincts of an experienced, knowledgeable coach are probably still just as reliable as most tests.

Finding tests and doing some simple statistics to determine their reliability and validity is relatively simple for making a determination of gymnast versus nongymnast. Finding tests to determine if the gymnast will be better than another gymnast is quite another story. It would be nice if we could simply give a battery of tests to determine potential (if we simply wanted to categorize people). Fortunately, this is not the case, so you must rely heavily on instincts and good judgment.

You will be interested in the size of the child, weight, likelihood of gaining weight during adolescence, strength, power, flexibility, courage, determination, intelligence, and skill. The child may come to the program because her parents are tired of having her doing cartwheels all over the house (or they may believe that they have a real star on their hands). Children who are in a recreational program may need evaluation to see if they might want to commit themselves to a more rigorous training regime if an expert believes that they have high potential. This type of evaluation is the biggest gamble of all; who can really be sure what the abilities of a child will be in 5-10 years? The coach must use good judgment, a few simple tests, and keen observation to make a wise determination. Although we all probably recognize that this is a risky affair it is not uncommon for a typical coach to have to make such a determination hundreds of times a year. Therefore, it would serve both athlete and coach if this determination were based on some useful criteria. It is most important that the attitude of the coach and the results of the evaluation are used not to discourage the child, but simply to channel her in the appropriate direction. The evaluation is never final; the child should be evaluated often to ensure that no mistakes have been made and that the child always has the opportunity for upward mobility. We do not want to close doors. We would rather open doors that lead to the paths of fun, accomplishment, and success.

SIZE

In general, we would like to have a small child, light-framed and light in weight. The size and weight of the child are immediately apparent to the coach. Although size and weight are not usually handicaps to the young child, they may later cause problems if the child is going to be tall or heavy upon reaching adolescence. Adolescence is the period when the child will be capable of reaching her goals and will be eligible for national teams and national championships. It is therefore important that the early decisions to pursue gymnastics—training many hours each day and developing year after year to reach these goals—should not end when the child physically outgrows the sport. It is an interesting commentary on our sport when only a few exceptions to the small-body, light-weight rule can actually make it to the pinnacles of gymnastics accomplishment.

Gymnasts must be on the lean side of lean, and the ratios of height and strength to weight are very important. As a general rule of thumb I have developed a table of heights and weights, shown as Table 8-1, that I've found very reliable in determining team membership and acceptable weight. I got these figures by checking my entire team of 30 girls, aged 8-17, who at the time of this research were all of admirable body type, with weight under control. Then I performed a correlation between height and weight of these athletes. We all know that the gymnast will gain weight as she grows, so this table was developed to help fill in the heights and weights that did not exist on my team. What I found was a correlation of .982 by computer analysis of height and weight. This is quite high for human characteristics. Then the computer gave me the following linear regression equation or the "formula" for predicting "Y" or the weight of the athlete if I provide the "X" or the height. It is a simple matter for the computer to calculate each "Y" for any given "X." The resulting equation is listed below.

Weight in kilograms (Y) = Height in inches (X) $\times$ 1.55119 − 51.7046

What this means is that the relationship of height and weight during the growth of our young athletes is nearly linear. The weight that is being added is probably lean weight because it is so closely correlated with growth in height. I expected a slightly more curvilinear relationship. (I had thought that as the athletes' height increased their weight would probably increase at a greater rate.) The use of such a relationship can help us predict the expected weight of an athlete of a given height. This allows us to make some useful comparisons and helps us decide who should diet and who should not. Actually, I have found that this chart has been more useful in determining who is underweight than who is overweight. None of these athletes had been on any type of restricted diet prior to this analysis of heights and weights.

TABLE 8-1   **Heights and Weights Table**

Height (Inches)	Weight (Kilograms)	Weight (Pounds)
45	18.1	39.8
45.5	18.9	41.2
46	19.7	43.2
47	21.2	46.6
47.5	22.0	48.3
48	22.8	50.1
48.5	23.5	51.8
49	24.3	53.5
49.5	25.1	55.2
50	25.9	56.9
50.5	26.6	58.6
51	27.4	60.3
51.5	28.2	62.0
52	29.0	63.7
52.5	29.7	65.4
53	30.5	67.1
53.5	31.3	68.8
54	32.1	70.6
54.5	32.8	75.7
55	33.6	73.9
55.5	34.4	75.7
56	35.2	77.4
56.5	35.9	79.1
57	36.7	80.8
57.5	37.5	82.5
58	38.3	84.2
58.5	39.0	85.9
59	39.8	87.6
59.5	40.6	89.3
60	41.4	91.0
60.5	42.1	92.7
61	42.9	94.4
61.5	43.7	96.1
62	44.5	97.8
62.5	45.2	99.5
63	46.0	101.2
63.5	46.8	103.0
64	47.6	104.7
64.5	48.3	106.4
65	49.1	108.0

Table 8-1 shows the results of the preceding equation as the calculations are performed on heights from 45 to 65 inches. Weights are given both in kilograms and in pounds. This table is consistent with the weights of the gymnasts as they have grown since this initial measurement (plus or minus 2 pounds). Although I do not pretend to think that this is a definitive study that would stand up to academic scrutiny, I do believe that the correlation is alarmingly high and it can form a useful *portion* of the evaluation of the young gymnast to see if her weight is within these guidelines. If there is a gross difference, then perhaps the athlete (a) must have other very special redeeming characteristics to be accepted, (b) may need to be channeled to a less rigorous program, or (c) may need a period of time to get her weight within these guidelines in order to be accepted. Since, as I said before, these guidelines are not gospel, you may need to expand or contract the plus or minus 2 pounds suggested. The lower the intensity of the program perhaps the broader the guidelines for acceptability.

Once the athlete has been measured and weighed, then you need to know a little family history. How tall are the parents and grandparents? Is the family overweight? Do the brothers and sisters follow the same pattern as the parents? (This kind of information can tell you a great deal about the likely growth pattern of the young child.) The eating habits of the household can also be discerned by looking at the stature of the mother, father, and siblings. Although I have seen some notable exceptions to this concept, there have been relatively few of them in my experience. If acceptance or rejection for the program is going to be based almost entirely on height-weight criteria, then extreme care is needed. And some period of observation under training may be required for any exceptions admitted to see if the growth pattern will occur. I have seen 6-foot parents raise a gymnastics daughter who is barely 5 feet, a mother and father who were extraordinarily heavy with a daughter who was light-framed until well into college. The use of weight and size criteria simply allows the coach to make a more informed and intelligent decision—but none of these tests or criteria should be your only basis for acceptance or rejection.

STRENGTH AND POWER

The next phase of evaluation is that of strength. We naturally would like to attract those children who are strong and powerful into higher level training. Although there are academic differences in the definitions of strength and power, we usually find one when we find the other. The strength of the athlete is vitally important, since the difficulty of many of the modern skills has risen to a point that without strength the susceptibility to injury and failure rises to unmanageable proportions. I have seen a few marked exceptions to the strength and power criteria—so again, this should not be the sole reason for acceptance or rejection of an athlete. Although we will make our athlete stronger and more powerful through training, it is my experience that to *develop* the degree of strength and power that will be needed by the high-level gymnast is rare if she has very little strength and power to begin with. It is extremely important that if the athlete is not strong by gymnastics standards she must be extraordinarily skilled.

TESTS FOR STRENGTH, POWER, AND FLEXIBILITY

The following tests should be considered together for determination of a gymnast's strength and power. I have adapted these tests to make them easy and fast to administer and rather foolproof. The gymnast has a hard time failing and the coach can have any of the staff administer them with a little information. The strength and flexibility tests are divided into two main categories: inexperienced and experienced gymnasts. This gives us a means of evaluating gymnasts seeking entry into a program to begin training, and those athletes who have already been training and seek promotion or analysis of strengths, weaknesses, and progress.

These test items are taken from the following sources:

1. translations from Russian literature provided to me by the translator for the Elite Coaches Association;
2. Canadian Gymnastics Federation testing materials;
3. our own U.S. Junior Elite National testing program;
4. the United States Association of Independent Gymnastics Clubs testing program;
5. physical education texts; and
6. tests I designed and adapted, building on all of the above sources.

Most of the test items from these sources are actually adaptations of Russian literature. I have adapted these items for my own use and for this text on the basis of their ease of application and relevance, and on my own estimation of their validity in measuring the qualities necessary for the elite level athlete in various stages of training.

Strength and Power Tests

Each of the inexperienced athlete tests is given in a one-try format. Only one attempt is allowed except when big errors occur, like slipping on the start of the run, falling down, and so forth. Each child is allowed as many practice attempts as she desires, but only one testing attempt. The test items attempt to give a good strength profile of the athlete.

Section 1: Inexperienced Athletes

Item 1: Vertical Jump (Inexperienced Athletes). The gymnast stands near a blank wall with one side (usually her dominant side) nearest the wall. She stretches the arm closest to the wall vertically and touches the highest point that she can reach (see Figure 8-1a). This point is marked and she lowers her arm back to her side. The gymnast then swings her arms in a for-

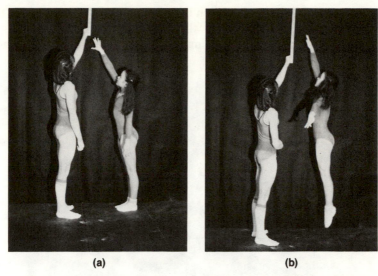

(a)   **(b)**

Figure 8-1   Vertical jump test. (a) The reach; (b) Jump and reach.

ward upward fashion to jump as high as she can and reach as far above her first point on the wall as possible. At the height of her jump she touches the wall again with the fingers of the arm closest to the wall and this spot is marked (see Figure 8-1b). The coach then measures the vertical distance between the marks and this becomes her vertical jump height. The gymnast can chalk her fingertips in order to leave some chalk on the wall at the peak of her jump. (This removes any subjectivity in determining the peak of the jump.)

The height and age of the gymnast will have some effect on the results of this test item; the floor surface can also affect the results, especially if the only open wall area is over the spring floor. Because of these problems, it is difficult to develop criteria for determining how high the athletes should actually jump. Table 8-2 gives approximations of heights gymnasts might at-

**TABLE 8-2   Vertical Jump Chart
(Inexperienced Athletes)**

Height of Jump (Inches)	Points
18 or more	10
17	9
16	8
15	7
14	6
13	4
12	3
11 or less	1

tain in the vertical jump. Adaptation may be necessary for particular programs. On this test as well as all the others you can select from the table the number of points necessary for passing or failing depending upon the goals of your program.

Figure 8-2 Leg lifts (without foam).

Item 2: Leg Lifts (Inexperienced Athletes). The leg lift test is performed on a wall bar, stall bars, or some piece of equipment that allows the athlete to have her back flat against the wall, with her grip on a bar only a few inches from the wall. (This prevents the gymnast from using her shoulders to assist in lifting her legs to the bar.) The gymnast begins by hanging by her hands on the wall bar, her body fully extended. She then lifts her legs straight forward and upward to touch with her feet or ankles the bar she is gripping and then returns to the hanging position (see Figure 8-2). When the gymnast begins the first leg lift, the coach starts the stopwatch, and gives the athlete 10 seconds in which to perform as many leg lifts as possible. If the gymnast bends her knees, separates her legs, or fails to touch the bar, that particular leg lift does not count. When 10 seconds are over the coach tells the gymnast to stop and records the number of times she touched her feet or ankles to the bar. The score is determined from Table 8-3.

TABLE 8-3   Leg Lift Chart
(Inexperienced Athletes)

Number of Leg Lifts	Score
6	10
5	8
4	6
3	4
2	2
1	1

Figure 8-3   Sprint start position for 20-meter dash.

Item 3: 20-meter Dash (Inexperienced Athletes). The 20-meter dash is an attempt to measure the explosive running speed of the athlete. The starting line should be some immovable object such as the wall, a heavy mat, etc. The gymnast begins with her rear foot at the starting line which is the beginning of the 20 meters. This gives the gymnast something to push off from for her start (see Figure 8-3). Then the coach uses a stopwatch to measure the time from the start to the finish line. The coach announces "ready, set, go," starts the watch on "go" and stops it when the gymnast crosses the finish line. The time of the run is recorded and points are given based on Table 8-4.

TABLE 8-4   20-meter Dash Chart (Inexperienced Athletes)

Time (Seconds)	Points
3.2	10
3.3	9
3.4	8
3.5	7
3.6	5
3.7	3
3.8	1

Item 4: Pull-ups (Inexperienced Athletes). This test is performed on the high bar of the unevens (see Figure 8-4). The gymnast begins in a regular or overgrip hang and is given 10 seconds to do as many pull-ups or chin-ups as she can. The gymnast should not be allowed to swing, so the coach may have to place a spotter next to the gymnast to keep her from swinging. The coach starts the watch upon the first movement of the gymnast. The coach announces "stop" after 10 seconds and the number of chins are recorded.

Figure 8-4   Chin position of pull-up test.

The gymnast must pull her chin completely above the bar each time and she must return to a full hang or that particular attempt does not count. The number of chins is translated into a score by Table 8-5.

**TABLE 8-5   Pull-ups Chart
(Inexperienced Athletes)**

Pull-ups	Points
6	10
5	9
4	8
3	6
2	4
1	2

Item 5: Push-ups (Inexperienced Athletes). These push-ups are very traditional (see Figure 8-5). The gymnast has 10 seconds in which to perform them. The gymnast's chest must touch the floor each time or that particular push-up does not count. The gymnast should raise to full extension on each push-up and should keep her back straight; any deviation from these rules and that particular push-up does not count. The coach uses a stopwatch and starts the watch as the gymnast begins her first movement. The coach should watch carefully that the chest touches the floor and may wish to have someone else keep time or place their hand on the floor so that the ribs must touch the hands on each descent. Table 8-6 shows the number of push-ups and commensurate scores.

(a)

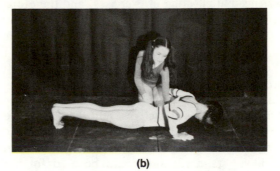

(b)

Figure 8-5 Push-up test. (a) Up position; (b) Down position. Note hand of assistant for count.

TABLE 8-6   **Push-ups Chart**
(Inexperienced Athletes)

Push-ups	Points
10	10
9	8
8	6
7	4

Summary: Strength and Power Tests for Inexperienced Athletes. These tests form the evaluation of strength and power of an inexperienced athlete coming to seek high-level gymnastics training for the first time. They will help provide you with some additional criteria to assist your instincts in determining the placement of the child in the program or recommending her for another program that better suits her needs. The tests require no previous gymnastics ability and should be used for the younger gymnast 8-11 years old.

Section 2: Experienced Athletes

This section covers strength and power evaluation for athletes who are already experienced in gymnastics and who are being assessed for possible promotion or physical condition. The tests can also be used for determining whether to accept or reject a gymnast who has received some training.

The athlete who has been in training for some time and may have already competed provides a slightly different problem for evaluation. In testing such an athlete for strength and power, we can make a few assumptions. For example, this athlete should be considerably stronger than the athlete who is coming to train for the very first time. The athlete may be a bit more experienced at cheating in exercises, and therefore the test items should be more strict in their evaluation. The actual demonstration of skills and the ability that the gymnast shows in some skills that have strength requirements can show as much or more about the gymnast than can these simple tests. You should combine the testing results with all the other information gathered to determine the needs of the athlete.

The following items are administered in a three-attempt format. The gymnast is allowed three tries at each test and the best of the three is taken as the final score. The items are listed with scoring formats to help the coach apply the testing to athletes of different skill levels. The scores in column 1 are somewhat lower standards and could be used for athletes who are testing to gain membership on a team. The scores in column 2 are for very accomplished athletes who are being assessed for their physical condition or setting standards for promotion.

Item 1: Glide Kips (Experienced Athletes). The glide kips are performed on the low bar set at regulation height. All the glides must be done with legs together (not straddled). The gymnast must perform the glide, return swing, kip, a small cast, to another glide kip all without pause or poor form. The gymnast who stops during any portion of the glide kips is allowed to continue from that point but the glide kip that produced the stop is not counted. If the gymnast touches her feet to the floor, that particular glide kip does not count. If the gymnast casts from her stomach and not her thighs or hips, then that particular glide kip does not count. The coach must watch carefully for these errors and announce the count as the test proceeds. Therefore, if the coach is counting 1, 2, 3, 4, etc. as the gymnast proceeds, when an error occurs the coach simply does not announce the next number but repeats the previous number. This will tell the gymnast that she did not perform one of the kips correctly and must do an extra glide kip to receive her appropriate score (see Table 8-7).

Item 2: Vertical Jump (Experienced Athletes). The vertical jump test is administered as it was in the previous section. Table 8-8 shows how to score this test for experienced athletes.

TABLE 8-7   Glide Kips Chart (Experienced Athletes)

Number	Column 1	Column 2
12		10
11		9
10	10	8
9	9	7
8	8	5
7	7	3
6	6	1
5	5	
4	4	
3	2	
2	1	

TABLE 8-8   Vertical Jump Chart (Experienced Athletes)

Height (Inches)	Column 1	Column 2
22		10
21		9
20	10	8
19	9	7
18	8	6
17	7	5
16	6	3
15	5	1
14	4	
13	3	
12	2	

Item 3: Leg Lifts (Experienced Athletes). The leg lifts are administered similarly to the test item listed previously for inexperienced athletes. The gymnast must perform the test using a wall bar so that she cannot use her shoulders to pull her legs up. The test is administered with a stopwatch so that the gymnast must lift her legs quickly against time. The exception is that the gymnast must keep a small piece of paper, foam, etc. between her ankles or feet throughout the exercise (see Figure 8-6). If the piece of foam or paper falls out, then the test ends with that number of repetitions. This will prevent the gymnast from separating her legs during any portion of the test. The athlete is given 12 seconds in which to complete her repetitions. If she fails to touch the bar or does not come to a complete hang between lifts then that particular lift does not count. At the end of 12 seconds the coach

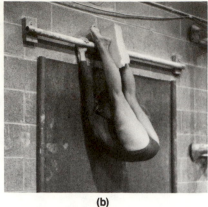

(a)   (b)

Figure 8-6 Leg lifts (using foam piece). (a) Intermediate position; (b) End position.

announces "stop" and the number of times the gymnast has touched her feet or ankles to the bar is recorded as the number of attempts and the score is awarded (see Table 8-9).

TABLE 8-9   Leg Lifts Chart (Experienced Athletes)

Number (12 Seconds)	Column 1	Column 2
10		10
9		9
8	10	7
7	8	5
6	6	3
5	4	1
4	2	

Item 4: 20-meter Dash (Experienced Athletes). The 20-meter dash is administered exactly as in the preceding section. Table 8-10 shows scoring.

TABLE 8-10   20-meter Dash Chart (Experienced Athletes)

Time (Seconds)	Column 1	Column 2
3.0		10
3.1	10	8
3.2	8	6
3.3	6	3
3.4	4	1
3.5	2	

Item 5: Back Hip Pullovers (Experienced Athletes). The back hip pull-over is performed on the high bar of the unevens. The low bar is set exactly half-way out (in other words, half-way between maximum and minimum width). This is to prevent the gymnast from swinging during the downswing portion of the pullover and making the test too easy. The gymnast begins in a stretched hang on the high bar with a regular or overgrip hand position. The gymnast has 10 seconds in which to do her pullovers. The coach begins timing as the gymnast begins her first movement. The gymnast performs a pullover to support and immediately and quickly lowers to a stretched hang to begin another pullover. The gymnast must keep her legs straight during the entire process and is allowed to bend her arms. The gymnast repeats the pullovers until she has done the maximum for score or the coach announces "stop" after the 10 seconds have expired (see Table 8-11). The pullover is considered completed when the gymnast is resting on her thighs on the high bar.

TABLE 8-11   Back Hip Pullovers Chart (Experienced Athletes)

Number (10 Seconds)	Column 1	Column 2
6		10
5		8
4	10	6
3	8	5
2	6	4
1	2	3
		2
		1

Item 6: Handstand Push-ups (Experienced Athletes). The handstand push-ups are performed against the wall or some other object that is firm enough to substitute for a wall. The gymnast kicks to a handstand resting her feet against the wall with her hands not more than 12 inches from the wall. The gymnast is given 10 seconds in which to complete her push-ups. Her head must lower and touch the floor on each repetition or that particular repetition does not count. The gymnast is not allowed to "climb" up and down the wall with her feet. If she falls from the handstand position, that particular attempt is completed and the number of repetitions to that point are counted as the total. The coach may have to use his or her own judgment concerning the depth of the down portion of the handstand push-up. If the coach can see that few can get down to the floor and complete even one push-up, then a small piece of foam that allows them to miss the floor by a few inches may be worth using. The coach starts the watch at the first downward movement of the gymnast from the handstand and announces "stop" at the end of the 10 seconds. The total number of acceptable

TABLE 8-12   Handstand Push-up Chart (Experienced Athletes)

Number (10 Seconds)	Column 1	Column 2
8		10
7		9
6	10	7
5	8	5
4	6	3
3	4	1
2	2	

push-ups is counted for the score (see Table 8-12). The handstand is considered complete when the gymnast raises to fully extended elbows.

The area between the hands of the gymnast should be very soft so that the gymnast does not "bang" her head on the floor in an overzealous attempt to "bounce" off her head into the next push-up.

Summary: Strength and Power Tests

These tests for strength and power should be used as part of the total evaluation process. You can modify, add, or remove items to suit your particular program and any equipment considerations that have a bearing on how the test can be administered.

You should pay as much attention to the behavior of the child taking the test as you do to the raw scores derived from the items. Although the scores are important I believe that I have learned as much about the athlete from watching her approach to the tests as I have from the actual outcome. Is the gymnast aggressive or passive? Does she practice before the test or not? Does she make three determined attempts at the tests she cannot complete? If the tests are unfamiliar, does she ask questions? A variety of information can be gathered from the testing process other than the simple raw data. You should remember that instinct and experience are still useful tools, and use of the tests to bolster your good judgment will be the best application of the results.

Tests for Flexibility

The flexibility of the gymnast must be measured to get a more complete picture of the physical abilities of the gymnast as part of the selection process. As in the previous sections on strength the testing of flexibility will be done in two major sections, the first for inexperienced gymnasts and the second section for experienced gymnasts. Flexibility is a much overlooked area in gymnastics training and deserves more attention. When you watch the best gymnasts from nations around the world you realize very clearly that we do not spend enough time on flexibility. The following tests are included to give you a consistent way of measuring this quality in your athletes. Fortunately, flexibility can be developed fairly easily by gymnasts with conscientious work.

The gymnast who comes to test for training in a high-level program for the first time should have her flexibility checked and recorded so that later improvements or lack of progress can be determined and action taken. Although there is some indication that flexibility is related to genetic factors, it is still one of the most changeable of physical qualities. A certain minimum amount of flexibility is necessary to realize success in gymnastics. The young gymnast, aged 8-11, should come to the gym with a degree of natural flexibility. The youngest infants usually show remarkable natural flexibility that quickly goes away because of disuse and growing. The active child is generally more flexible than the inactive or sedentary child, and therefore likely candidates for gymnastics are usually a little more flexible than unlikely candidates.

The following assessment of flexibility for the young and inexperienced athlete is of the pass/fail variety rather than a point system. The initial assessment of flexibility can be made by quickly checking a variety of positions to simply see how far the gymnast can go through a range of motion. The test items given here are often familiar positions to gymnastics, and you just want to see if the young gymnast can perform them. In the second section for experienced athletes the testing is done on a point system for finer assessment of ability.

Section 1: The Inexperienced Athlete

The young gymnast is usually ambitious and anxious to please and impress the coach during a testing period. In her zeal the young gymnast testing flexibility will attempt to go to positions she may never have tried before. This causes some risk of pulling muscles. Therefore, the gymnasts should be carefully warmed up prior to the testing session, and you should make it clear (particularly to young gymnasts) that you are not so interested in actual accomplishments as in the *potential* for accomplishment. The gymnast should go only to where she is comfortable in the position since you certainly don't need a reckless gymnast who continually hurts herself.

Item 1: Splits (Inexperienced Athletes). The split is a simple and common position that all young gymnasts will need to master. This test item consists of seeing if the gymnast can get her hip flat to the floor on both her right and left side (see Figure 8-7). In all cases the strong, or favorite side, of the gymnast should be flat. The weak or nonfavorite side of the gymnast should be flat or within a few inches of the floor. The gymnast should be able to keep her hips reasonably square in the position. This means that a ruler placed on her hip bones is not running parallel to the split but close to perpendicular to the split. In my years of coaching I have never seen anyone

Figure 8-7 Forward split position.

actually get perpendicular, but the closer the better. The back leg of the gymnast should be turned so that the top of the knee cap is down or resting on the floor. The back leg should not be turned out for the sake of this test. The front leg should be turned out so that the little toe side of the foot is closest to the floor.

Item 2: Side Split (Inexperienced Athletes). The side split is also called a lateral split, Chinese split, Japanese split, etc. The gymnast should perform this split on a tape line on the floor so that the coach can see if her legs are directly sideward (see Figure 8-8). The gymnast places both heels on the line and slides her feet sideward along the line until she can touch her crotch to the line or come within a few inches. The gymnast can support her weight on her hands while she is lowering. The knee caps of the gymnast should remain upward, pointing to the ceiling. The legs should not roll forward so that the big toe side of the foot is touching the floor. The gymnast

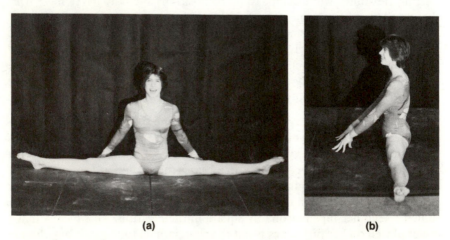

(a) **(b)**

Figure 8-8 Side split. (a) Front view; (b) Side view.

should be able to get flat on the floor or come within a few inches in order to pass with the leg positions described above.

Item 3: Piking (Inexperienced Athletes). The ability of the gymnast to pike tightly is very useful for some skills on all events, but particularly on uneven bars. The gymnast should sit on the floor with legs straight, together, and toes pointed. The gymnast then reaches with straight arms as far past her toes as possible (see Figure 8-9). The gymnast should be able to get her fingertips past her ankles. (In other words, the gymnast should be able to touch the top of her foot as a minimum.) The gymnast should not pull with her hands on her ankles or feet but should use her hip flexors and flexibility to reach her feet rather than the strength of her arms and shoulders to pull her down. Passing this test requires that the gymnast be able to reach past her ankle so that she will be flexible enough to perform the stoop through actions required on a variety of skills. At times the gymnast who can touch her head to her knees by pulling with her arms cannot reach past her ankles with her hands. Touching the head to the knees is some evidence of flexibility in this position but is not a recommended position. Often, the gymnast with a flexible back can touch her head to her knees without being able to reach past her ankles with her hands.

Figure 8-9   Pike position sitting on the floor.

Item 4: Backbend (Inexperienced Athletes). This test requires a little strength and skill to perform. However, the strength and skill for the type of gymnast we are likely to be looking for should be rudimentary and not of concern. The type of backbend being sought here is not of the contortionistic variety where the athlete tries to move her hands as close to her feet as possible. The backbend for this test item has the gymnast in a comfortable backbend position with bent knees. Then the gymnast straightens her knees while keeping her feet in one place (see Figure 8-10). The result is that the gymnast will move her shoulders over or just past her hands. The position the coach is looking for consists of a backbend with straight legs, head in line with arms, and shoulders above the hands or slightly past the hands,

Figure 8-10 Backbend.

toward the armpit side of the arms. This indicates that the gymnast is able to stretch her shoulders more than her lower back and is a vital part of safe and productive gymnastics. Every coach has seen the floppy and loose back of a gymnast who cannot control her lower back while doing gymnastics skills. A gymnast with a loose back can still pass this test, but you need to know if she can stretch in her shoulders. The process of educating the athlete to stretch in her shoulders rather than in her lower back is a long but important one. The gymnast who simply cannot stretch in her shoulders and must stretch in the lower back is at a distinct disadvantage in learning, health, and safety.

Summary: Flexibility Tests for Inexperienced Athletes. The preceding test items form the first line of evaluation of the gymnast as she enters training for the first time. You should be aware that simple flexibility is not enough to make a good gymnast. The athlete must also have the strength to move to the limits of the range of motion available and be able to use this flexibility. You should observe the gymnast performing a few skills that require the use of flexibility and see how she performs them. If she uses her flexibility with a commensurate amount of strength, if she muscles her attempts even though she has the flexibility, or if she collapses due to inability to control her flexibility, this would be an indication of lack of skill and ability to control her flexibility.

Section 2: The Experienced Athlete

The following test items take considerably more time to administer than the preceding flexibility tests. They require three attempts with the best score to count. The coach will need a yardstick, a wooden stool or substitute, a small dowel, and the balance beam or ballet bar.

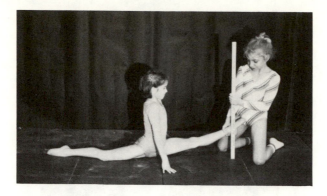

Figure 8-11   Forward split test (with yardstick).

Item 1: Splits (Experienced Athletes). The split will be performed on the left and right sides. I am assuming that the gymnast can get flat on both sides if she has had experience before. The gymnast adopts a split position and the coach kneels near the forward foot. A yardstick is placed perpendicular to the floor next to the forward heel of the gymnast (see Figure 8-11). The coach then lifts the forward foot from the floor, slowly and gently, while watching the height of the heel relative to the yardstick. When the gymnast's hip lifts off the floor the coach stops lifting, and the number of inches to the bottom of the gymnast's heel is read. The number of inches is translated into a score by the table below. Then the same procedure is repeated for the other leg. The gymnast receives two scores for this item (see Table 8-13).

**TABLE 8-13   Splits Chart
(Experienced Athletes)**

Placement (Inches)	Score
Over 12	10
9-12	9
6-9	7
3-6	5
0-3	3
Hip touching, split flat	1

Item 2: Side Split (Experienced Athletes). The side split test is administered exactly the same as the side split in the preceding section. Table 8-14 gives the point breakdown for awarding points to the gymnast.

**TABLE 8-14   Side Split Chart
(Experienced Athletes)**

Placement	Score
Flat	10
Crotch within 2 inches	7
Crotch within 6 inches	4

Figure 8-12   Piking test on box (with ruler for measurement).

Item 3: Piking (Experienced Athletes). The piking test is administered with a stool and a 12-inch ruler or yardstick. The gymnast stands on the stool with her toes at the edge. By keeping her legs straight she reaches her hands as far past her toes as she can (see Figure 8-12). The distance from the top edge of the stool to the tips of her fingers is measured and the distance is translated into a score with Table 8-15.

**TABLE 8-15   Piking Chart
(Experienced Athletes)**

Inches	Score
9 or more	10
8	8
7	6
6	5
5	4
4	3
3	1

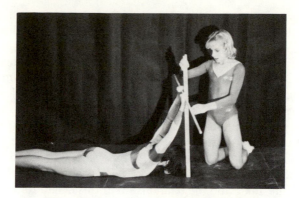

Figure 8-13   Shoulder flexibility test.

Item 4: Shoulder Flexibility (Experienced Athletes). The flexibility of the shoulders of the experienced athlete is a more important measure of upper body flexibility than the simple backbend, in my opinion. Anyone who has been involved with gymnastics for any length of time will improve their lower back flexibility; however, the flexibility of the shoulders is hard to improve without direct training. This flexibility is measured as active so that it will have relationship to dance positions as well as simply having the range of movement available. The gymnast begins by lying on the floor on her stomach with her arms outstretched overhead. The gymnast holds a small dowel in her hands in a regular grip with the thumbs of both hands touching each other. A yardstick is placed perpendicular to the floor near the dowel where the gymnast's thumbs are placed. The gymnast then raises her arms with straight elbows as high above the floor as she can (see Figure 8-13). The gymnast must keep her chin on the floor. When the gymnast reaches the limit of her movement, the number of inches is measured from the floor by viewing the yardstick. Table 8-16 shows the scoring table.

TABLE 8-16   Shoulder Flexibility (Experienced Athletes)

Height (Inches)	Score
Over 20	10
15-20	8
12-15	6
6-12	4
Less than 6	1

Item 5: Leg Raises (Experienced Athletes). The leg raises are done on each leg, both forward and sideward. The gymnast will end up with four

separate scores from this item. The scoring system for these skills is the same for both forward and sideward and both directions are listed together here.

Forward: The gymnast begins with her back to the balance beam. She may hold onto the beam without leaning against it. The gymnast should keep an upright and aligned posture at all times. The support leg should not bend and the torso should not hunch forward. The hip of the raised leg should be kept square and level with the support hip. The gymnast raises one leg forward with a straight knee and extended ankle. The coach stands to the side of the leg with a yardstick and moves it upward in line with the ankle bone of the gymnast. The coach keeps the yardstick level and watches the height of the ankle and the relationship of this height to the body of the gymnast. When the gymnast reaches the height of the leg lift then the coach looks down the yardstick to see what level the ankle bone attained (see Figure 8-14a). The level is interpreted as being as high as some part of the head or torso. This height is translated into a score with Table 8-17. The gymnast then performs the same lift but with the other leg.

Sideward: The gymnast stands with her side next to the beam or ballet bar. She may grip the bar or beam but may not lean against it. The gymnast then raises her leg sideward. The coach stands in front of the gymnast and moves the yardstick upward as the leg moves upward, always keeping it in line with the ankle bone of the gymnast. As the height of the lift is reached the coach notes the position of the ankle bone and its relationship to the torso and head of the gymnast by looking down the level yardstick (see Figure 8.14b). The relationship is noted and the score awarded on the basis

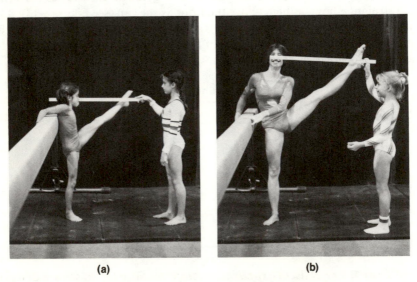

(a)   (b)

Figure 8-14 Leg lift test. (a) Forward; (b) Sideward.

**TABLE 8-17   Forward and Sideward
Leg Raises Chart (Experienced Athletes)**

Height of Ankle Bone	Score
Overhead	10
Eye level	9
Chin level	8
Shoulder level	7
Chest level	5
Hip level	3
Below the hip	1

of Table 8-17. The gymnast cannot bend her support leg, have her hips out of alignment, or hunch her body over. When the gymnast completes one side she lowers the leg, turns to the other side and performs the same action with the other leg.

Compiling the Scores of Flexibility Tests for Experienced Athletes. The testing scores for experienced athletes can be compiled in a variety of ways; passing or failing is left to the discretion of the administrator. One coach may wish to set the criteria very high so that passing requires a very high average score; another coach for a lower level program may set passing scores at much lower levels. This problem is left up to you so that the tests are applicable to many programs with different philosophies and goals.

BEYOND OUR SIMPLE TESTS

At the conclusion of testing flexibility we leave the realm of simple testing. The simple tests for basic physical abilities can help you gain a better idea of what the gymnast's potential is. The use of testing, however, is fraught with holes and problems. It is vitally important that you recognize these limits and use good judgment in applying tests to the athletes. This does not mean that testing is worthless; it is still the best instrument we have, even with all its imperfections. But as you progress through the years of coaching much of the formality of testing will be eliminated, since you will soon be able to simply take a look at the child as she performs some skills to note that in order to perform the skill in such a fashion she must be flexible or inflexible, strong or weak. This can be further substantiated with the use of tests.

There are many other types of tests, some very simple. Take a look at texts on exercise physiology, biomechanics, and biochemistry for tests that might be used to determine other important factors about gymnasts. We could insist on testing body fat and lean body mass with skin calipers or underwater weighing; we could insist that a force plate is necessary to analyze the power of the gymnast through a few selected skills; we might want a computer to analyze the layout somersault in tumbling or the run of the athlete to determine if there is potential for more development in the child. I have been involved with such work and I have found it to be very interesting, very informative, very expensive, and largely impractical. The use of high technology will be of significant help for all sports, but even this technology carries problems with it. Since we do not generally have easy access to such devices, their use is limited to times when the testing will not interfere with training. We are forced to use such testing only rarely. When our facilities are routinely equipped with this kind of instrumentation so that we can run a test at will, then the instrumentation will be of use and testing will put gymnastics into the 20th century.

I believe that simple tests and good judgment can go a long way to improve our direction of training. The use of high technology often becomes a problem of diminishing returns. Although high technology may give a more definitive answer to a question, it does not solve the problem of getting the athlete to her goals, and the expense and time involved often make it outside the reach of a typical gymnastics program. As if this isn't enough, there are a lot of arguments among the experts as to which method of testing will provide the best results. For example, in biomechanics, do you use digital filtering for the smoothing of the curve of data points? In physiology and use of the cybex there is some evidence that if the machine is not calibrated properly the results will be erroneous. Is the fatigue of the young gymnast more a result of nutrition and glycogen depletion due to cutting weight, or of high levels of training loads, or both? It is important that the coach understand the limitations of testing and the very fact that we know so very little about the preadolescent (especially the preadolescent female) athlete. So you should use all the tests that you can find that are applicable and practical—but wait and see what the results might show you. It is too easy to extrapolate beyond the data and try to prove an assertion that seems to hold some truth based on experience but may be nearly impossible to prove scientifically.

TESTING SKILLS

This section looks at skills, courage, and determination. These concepts are considered together when appropriate because they are rather interrelated as our thinking takes on more dimensions. Your eye is a good tool for gaining great amounts of useful data to be processed by your own instincts and past experience.

Assessing the skill of the athlete requires some basic understanding of gymnastics and the process of training. I will attempt to give you a look at the skills I believe are important and are good indicators of the ability and potential abilities of the athlete. These skills are usually simple, and you can determine the gymnast's competence in them by merely observing carefully. While you are observing these skills, you also want to be looking for indications of courage, determination, and nervousness, and observe how the gymnast handles such problems as a missed attempt.

The general format for administering the evaluation of skills that I use is to have the gymnast perform some simple skills for each event. Then I ask her to perform any skill that she is particularly proud of, then to tell me the names of the skills she has worked on in the past. If the athlete is brand new to gymnastics, during this portion of the evaluation I try to teach her a few of these skills in a very basic and patient approach to see how she responds. If she can do some skills already then I simply ask to see the skills listed below.

We always start with floor exercise and tumbling. I ask to see her stretch for a while first to see how diligently she approaches this portion of her training. Then I begin looking at her handstand. I would like to see a nice ramrod-straight handstand under control. So I ask her to do a handstand to a forward roll. Then I observe all the various factors that I believe are important for the correct execution of the handstand. In particular, I look for head position, good form, straight elbows, and both hands touching the floor at the same time. Anything that is crooked about the handstand is noted.

The next skill I check is a cartwheel. I ask the gymnast to perform a cartwheel both on her strong side and on her weak side. I usually can tell a lot about the thoroughness of her training if she looks aghast at doing a weak-side cartwheel. As she performs the cartwheels I note if they are straight, and look for the head position and straight elbows.

After checking the cartwheel, I ask to see a forward and a backward walkover. These skills are somewhat self-explanatory, so what I am interested in is the alignment of the shoulders and whether the gymnast actually uses her shoulders to attain the bridge or uses her lower back. The gymnast who places one hand on the floor in front of the other, has one shoulder crooked or collapsed, or takes one hand off the mat before the other, usually faces rejection unless she has other redeeming qualities. In my opinion, the squareness of the walkovers is vitally important for all skills that follow from them. Keeping the gymnast square on balance beam is very difficult if she has inherent problems in the symmetry of the walkover to begin with. Symmetry of the body is a very important factor in gymnastics and must be maintained at nearly all costs.

When I have looked at the stationary tumbling skills, I ask the gymnast to show me her round-off and handsprings or flip-flops, depending on the skills that she can do. Observing these for symmetry, power, and competent execution gives me a good picture of the ability of the athlete. Finally, I check on some simple dance skills, a full turn, chaîné turns to see if the gymnast can spot, a leap to check flexibility and quickness, and a body wave to see if her movement concept is fluid.

If the athlete has had no experience with these types of skills then I have her do a jump full turn and stick the landing on the floor with her feet together, a straddle jump, and finally a jump down from the balance beam onto a 4-inch mat with a 12-inch circle drawn a few feet from the end of the beam. The gymnast must land within the circle and stick the landing. The ability of the gymnast to hit the target and remain motionless is noted and then we move on to the next event.

The second event I go to is uneven bars. On uneven bars I usually need to see only one combination from the gymnast who has experience. I ask the gymnast who has had no experience to show only two skills. The experienced gymnast performs a glide kip to front hip circle and then casts as high as she can. The height of the cast, strength and power of the kip are noted along with the efficiency of changing her grip in the front hip circle. The inexperienced gymnast is asked to do a pullover and a cast. Even though I may have to teach her these skills on the spot they will give me a good indication of the gymnast's strength, ability to learn fast, and courage. The intermediate type of gymnast who may be pre-kip in her learning is asked to do a cast and a back hip circle. The cast and back hip circle are observed for all of the above characteristics.

The gymnast then moves to a low or floor balance beam where she is asked to run along the beam quickly but not to run off the end. Her dynamic balance is observed along with her speed. The gymnast is then asked to perform an English handstand as high as her skill will allow. The inexperienced gymnast may not kick up all the way, while the experienced gymnast is expected to kick to the handstand, hold it, and return to the beam without falling. The experienced gymnast is required to do a double toe turn, a leap, a jump, and a cartwheel. The inexperienced gymnast is asked to do a jump, a hop, kick to a side handstand for a moment, and step down to the floor. Both types of gymnasts are asked to stand on the balance beam on one foot with the other foot resting against the knee of the support leg. The hands of the gymnast are on the hips. The gymnast then closes her eyes and the coach uses a stopwatch to measure the length of time the gymnast can stand on one foot, eyes closed, and maintain her balance. All these items should be observed carefully for indications of fear, insecurity, and so on. They will help give you an idea of the child's concept of the skills, as well as where she has been, what she considers difficult or easy, and how quickly she is likely to progress.

I do not test the child on vaulting since I do not find these skills to be difficult to learn; anyone who is competent in the other events can be taught vaulting. I use measures of strength, such as the run speed and vertical jump, to determine potential in vaulting, rather than request a jump over the horse.

I like to get an idea of the determination of the gymnast to complete a task, and I'm also interested in how cooperative she might be. To do this I ask the gymnast to perform some kind of grueling strength test, such as leg lifts against the wall. I give the gymnast the following instructions: "I want you to perform the leg lifts as long as you can, do not come down until I tell you to." Therefore, the gymnast must continue to try and perform leg lifts even after she cannot reach the bar anymore. She must wait until I tell her to stop. I simply continue to ask the gymnast to keep going, I encourage her to try one more because "I know she can do it." The child can choose to keep going, stop, whine about the difficulty, complain that she cannot do anymore, or just hang there. The choice of which behavior is appropriate for top-level athletes is obvious. Observing the child through this test item helps me understand the determination and coachability of the child.

CONCLUSION

The selection process and the myriad issues it entails forms a significant part of every gymnastics program. You can use the selection process to gather the finest athletes available or avoid it and simply confuse the issue of talent procurement. It is important that you have exact and meaningful criteria for the acceptance or rejection of athletes. The athletes form the raw material for the training process. The use of inferior material will usually result in an inferior product. This sounds somewhat mercenary but it actually serves both the athlete and the coach. The proper placement of an athlete in a program appropriate to her needs and abilities is vitally important. It helps no one to place an athlete in a program over her head where she cannot hope to compete or keep up. On the other hand, it helps no one to put a talented athlete in a program that does not challenge and nurture that athlete. I believe that our selection process can go a long way toward arriving at a good match between child and training program.

9

Talented
and Enthusiastic
Coaches

The hardest part of setting up and running a productive gymnastics program for high-level athletes is staffing. There are few people who can coach this kind of athlete, and finding them and keeping them happy, productive, and creative is difficult. We are looking for a sort of thoroughbred coach and teacher to handle our thoroughbred athletes.

The stability of the coach is very important. The stresses and strains of gymnastics are many and far-reaching. The coach should be a pillar of stability and consistency around the gymnast. This does not eliminate a certain colorfulness that accompanies all creative people, but when the chips fall, the coach must be present and decisive.

The term *motivation* always comes up when we talk about coaches and athletes. The term is a little hard to define. The coach always wants a motivated athlete. The athlete always wants a coach who can motivate her. In the end we are never quite sure who is responsible for the motivation. I believe that motivation begins at the top and goes down, and that a motivated and enthusiastic coach can bring about the same qualities in the athlete. The athlete, in a sense, is the receiver of motivation from the coach. This helps teach the athlete how to motivate herself. The coach must pick up the ball of motivation and hand it to the athlete for her to run with it. The coach should not expect the athlete to provide 100% of the motivation from within, nor should the athlete expect 100% motivation from the coach. In the final analysis, the enthusiasm demonstrated by both coach and athlete is a complex process in which each bolsters the other's excitement.

TEACH THE CHILD . . . NOT THE SKILL

The gymnastics phenomenon is suffering from a genuine lack of good teachers of the sport. I believe the cause of this problem lies in the way we educate our potential gymnastics coaches and teachers. The typical process of becoming a gymnastics coach is to compete in college, graduate from college with an interest in gymnastics, open a gymnastics school or enter the public school system upon leaving college, and begin teaching young people to do gymnastics. The situation of the new coach is markedly different from that he or she experienced as a high-level gymnast who was continually training routines. Although the teaching aspect of gymnastics was present, it was always subordinated to the competitive routine and the quest for consistency and high scores. The new coach will face young children who will not be ready for routines for several years and who need an educational program that will take them quickly and safely to a competitive stature. Our colleges and other teacher-training institutions do not prepare teachers for this problem. A sort of compromise approach in our national age group program is to teach routines but make the routines very simple so that the inexperienced athlete may be able to learn the skills. This often prevents the young athlete from reaching the higher levels of achievement, since no compulsory can contain all the skills and abilities needed for high-level gymnastics. It is simply easier for the teacher to read the skills from a compulsory book rather than learn to teach thorough and safe gymnastics on all events, through a variety of levels, and with progressive steps.

The older or more experienced coach of gymnastics and the program that uses new coaches must prepare to give training in the teaching of gymnastics to all levels of new coaches. The assumption that the gymnast who was a good competitor will automatically be a good teacher is a very dangerous one. The good competitor often cannot understand the reluctance or the difficulty the less accomplished or talented child will face in learning skills. Teaching gymnastics — or almost anything — to children must proceed from a child-centered approach. This means that the coach educates the child, not the skill. The typical technical approach to gymnastics and the correction of various deficiencies in the skill often forces the child aside in the interest of correct technique and perfect execution.

The new coach has come from a situation where everyone is motivated, everyone assumes that the gymnast wants to learn the skill being presented, and everyone knows that some skills are inherently uncomfortable, that the discomfort will pass, and that technical perfection is a paramount consideration. The coach is, in a sense, someone whose interest in gymnastics has remained strong while others suffer a natural attrition of their interest in gymnastics. The coach will have to face many children who do not share his or her own determination and who ultimately will not survive this attrition.

The technical facets of gymnastics are important, but they must be presented with the limitations of the child in mind. The most modern or popular technique is not necessarily appropriate for young children. It will prove helpful for all new coaches and programs to step back from the training part of gymnastics to enter the teaching part with conscientious concern for teaching each child as much gymnastics as safely possible.

THE PROGRAM CAN HELP

Gymnastics programs can enhance and nurture the talent and enthusiasm of the coaches by providing a variety of experiences and perks to enlarge their body of knowledge and encourage their creativity. The programs should subscribe to a variety of magazines and journals related to coaching and teaching; these should be available for the coaches to borrow, read, and discuss. Personal subscriptions to a few desired journals may even be provided for coaches in an effort to help increase their abilities and creativity. The addresses for a few of these journals and magazines are included in Appendix D.

The program can hold clinics or seminars, bringing outside experts to the facility for informative sessions in which staff members are allowed to participate and gain information. The program can also pay the way for these coaches to attend outside seminars and clinics held in other areas. These activities will also help the coach see new ideas and question others about their programs and teaching methods. The annual United States Gymnastics Federation Coaches Congress is a good forum for this type of interchange, along with the United States Association of Independent Gymnastics Clubs, the U.S. Elite Coaches Association for Women's Gymnastics, and a variety of other programs offered throughout the year. There are also programs offered in separate but related fields, such as dance, sports medicine, biomechanics, and preschool education. The comprehensive program in gymnastics should provide for these growth experiences for the coaches and staff to help convince the coaches that they are an integral and important part of the gymnastics program.

IDIOSYNCRACIES AND CREATIVITY

The idiosyncratic personalities of creative people are often the source of their creativity and of friction that occurs in a program. The friction often comes from a pride of authorship and disdain for interference in the work that the coach may have done with a gymnast. The lack of communication among the coaches — which prevents efficient use of their time and energy — is also a consistent complaint. A new coach may be aiming for the head coach position, yet may see no opportunity of ever moving upward. A coach may not understand his or her role in the training process and therefore will not feel like a valuable part of the program. These problems are not unlike those experienced in other professional situations but are somewhat peculiar in that remedies have not been proposed with any consistency. For instance, at the 1980 Olympic Trials for women's gymnastics there were only three coaches present who had coached an Olympian in 1976. This means that at least four productive and knowledgeable coaches out of seven were not coaching or at least not coaching at the international level four years later. This should lead us to believe that the attrition rate of coaches in gymnastics is pretty high. IT IS.

Each program should take steps not only to enhance the productiveness of the coaches but also to ensure the longevity of the coaches. We should consider that each time a new coach replaces an old one we have lost some experience that could help the new coach learn much more quickly and more thoroughly, perhaps avoiding the same mistakes. However, we simply continue to start over every few years.

The following suggestions might be useful in enhancing the longevity of coaches: The programs should spell out the jurisdiction of each coach's work so that the portions that can belong to the individual coach (and are a particular source of pride to that coach) are not tampered with, and those areas open to everyone are acknowledged as such so that everyone knows that they are free to contribute. The coach should be given some of the more glamourous duties, such as speaking at conferences, taking gymnasts to meets, assisting in decision making, and contributing to any special activities undertaken by the program. The head coach or administrator who denies these opportunities to other coaches will soon have a small mutiny underway. The coaches must feel that they are filling a valuable role, and since most are creative, they must have the latitude to perform their functions with a minimum of interference. This kind of atmosphere helps keep everyone in the program productive and happy. The coaches should all remember that if they are not part of the solution they are part of the problem. Each should attempt to contribute to a team effort in solving problems of training, yet take pride in his or her own individual accomplishments.

THE CHICKEN OR THE EGG

The coaches are the real backbone of any program. I have seen a variety of programs work with poor facilities, poor talent, poor location, little or no technical knowledge, yet produce great gymnasts year after year. Although the other factors in the program are important, coaches are the ones who will make the greatest and most decisive difference. Doug Gilbert, in his book, *The Miracle Machine* (1980), talks about the fact that East Germany had to decide how to build a sporting machine out of a postwar, beaten country. They had to ask some vital chicken-or-egg questions: which comes first—the coach, the facility, the athlete, the doctors? The answer they chose, much to our embarrassment, was coaches. They knew that the coaches would design and build the facilities, they would find the talent, and they would set the tone for the ambitious sport machine that they have. They chose wisely. We should learn from their example.

10

Research

Research is the evaluative portion of the gymnastics program. Research can help you determine where the program or any aspect of it stands and where it is going. The research portion of gymnastics is usually the most overlooked, poorly performed part of the program. I don't want to give the impression that the type of research you have to do is carried on in some ivory tower wearing a cap and gown. Research is simply the process of gathering data (making observations, finding consistency in the observations to show some case for cause and effect, and then manipulating the cause to change the effect).

We want to use research data to help us train our athletes to higher levels of accomplishment, train them more safely, and train them more economically or efficiently. In other words, we are looking for a better way. Since the program has so many widely varied facets we must have a means of departmentalizing our approach or we will be forced to take shots in the dark at whatever we might think is a likely cause of our problems. We all know that gymnastics coaches cannot afford much sophisticated technology for gathering data or making observations. I believe that coaches can use their own observations to take control of the evaluative portion of the program without having to invest in much equipment in the initial stages. The coaches will soon find that their questions are much more sophisticated than simple eyeball observations will allow, and they may then be forced to look toward technology for help in gathering more accurate information. But we don't have to start there.

THE PERFORMANCE CHART

Researching the present position of the program without machinery can be done with a simple business technique that uses a chart, scores, and a little arithmetic. The chart is designed to analyze performance and can begin to tell us a great deal about how our program is doing. The performance chart can be adapted to almost any situation and purpose that you have the imagination to use it for. The performance chart can be one of the most useful tools in your arsenal of instruments to bring to bear on any particular problem. The chart can be as broad or narrow as necessary to attack a particular problem.

A simplified version of a performance chart is given in Table 10-1. Note that the athletes' names are listed along the side and the important qualities being looked at along the top. The numbers are scores given to each athlete on the basis of her demonstration of the quality listed through her performance. The scores listed are based on a 1-10 rating scale (10 is high). The scores are based on the coach's observations of the gymnasts and on a comparison with other programs producing at a similar level in the area. The chart can help you find out which areas of your program need to be strengthened the most.

You add up the rows to see the ranks of each gymnast with respect to the chosen qualities and the columns to see where the team or group is relative to each quality. As an example, you can look at this chart and see that Nancy is probably the best gymnast and Julie needs the most work. You could look at the columns and see that flexibility ranks lowest and therefore might be a good place to concentrate on to improve the entire team. Strength and uneven bars look in good shape, so you might decide that you could take a little time away from these activities and put the time into flexibility and dance. This should help you improve the weakest areas.

This chart is very simple. It could contain many more columns and rows to be more thorough. The comparison of all these factors together is somewhat of a corruption of the use of comparative analysis but it will help you see where to begin looking for improvement. This chart is not designed to give big answers (as you can see, it does not tell you what the causes are, only that flexibility is probably where you should spend more time and energy).

If you can use actual scores on the performance chart rather than simply your own judgment to give a 1-10 score, then the chart will be more accurate, valid, and useful. The scores for strength and flexibility (shown in Chapter 8 on the selection process) could be easily translated into a 1-10 score using the point systems provided and placed into a performance chart. Then we can add the 0-10 scores obtained from the judges on each event; we already have some data for a chart. Next we can convert other types of scores or qualities into percentages and we can add more data to our chart.

TABLE 10-1   Performance Analysis Chart

| Name | Flexibility | Strength | Dance | Quality | | | | | Total | Rank |
				Vault	Uneven Parallel Bars	Balance Beam	Floor Exercise			
Suzy	7	6	8	5	6	7	7		40	2
Nancy	6	8	5	5	8	4	6		42	1
Christy	3	7	3	8	9	6	3		39	4
Donna	3	8	4	5	9	7	4		40	2
Julie	3	7	4	4	5	5	6		34	5
Totals	20	36	24	27	37	29	26			
Rank	7	2	6	4	1	3	5			

With a little imagination the performance chart can become a very useful early tool in the analysis of problems and the concentration of effort.

A SECOND LOOK

A further refinement of the performance chart might have you take a more thorough look at flexibility training. The idea is to see where the program is falling short in performance. A new chart is made that lists each day of the training week along the top, each event or activity along the side. You then put the number of minutes being used for training (not a score from 1-10) for each day and each activity. Then you add up the totals and find, for instance, that balance beam is where the most time is actually spent emphasizing flexibility through the drills. You decide that this is not enough (or not appropriate) and a new portion of training time is then devoted to gaining flexibility. Warm-up and conditioning are given a few more minutes and you implement the change in the training schedule. You begin looking for the best flexibility exercises available. The research goes on until the exercises are found and the next evaluation shows an improvement, no improvement, or regression.

You can evaluate the exercises by giving the athletes the flexibility tests listed in the chapter on the selection process. The scores are recorded and form a pretest. The gymnasts then take part in the new schedule and exercises for training flexibility for a period of time. You then make another chart and test the athletes again to see if the exercises and schedule actually produced results. If they did, then a new evaluation of the program must decide if this is enough improvement, or if more work is necessary. If there was no improvement you must look deeper to see where the source of the problem might lie (selection of different exercises, devoting more time, giving up, etc.). This continues until the problem is eliminated.

Understanding the performance chart takes only a few minutes. The chart is a little time-consuming to design, and collecting the data takes a bit of time, but it can condense a huge amount of data down into a few simple numbers so that separate judgments can be made to provide clear and decisive direction to solving a problem or enhancing progress. Again, the chart is not the solution to a problem, it simply helps the coach ask the right questions. Defining the question is a step we generally forget in solving our problems. Once the question is suitably defined, the answers usually fall right into place.

INFORMATION AND DATA GATHERING

It's up to you to gather the information or observations that will most help your program. Gathering information must be a well-defined process, since we could gather information forever without any means of knowing what is pertinent or not. The following paragraphs will give an idea of the information that needs to be gathered to gain control of the training program. This information needs to be obtained, stored, analyzed, maintained, and compared. The means of doing this is left to you. Handwritten diaries are common; the computer can be useful; a secretary would work. I strongly recommend the use of the computer since the processing of this information can be very time-consuming and you never have enough time. Also, gathering information and then never using it is a crime we're all guilty of. We try to find an answer to a problem, and begin collecting data. Then we lose interest, the problem changes, or another crisis comes up that requires more time. The computer seems the only viable answer. A program for storing information is included in Appendix A for you to try out once the computer is purchased.

INJURIES

You must keep track of all injuries. The injury data should contain the date and time, the body part, the event, the skill it occurred on, the treatment taken, any limitations that occurred, and each subsequent day that the athlete suffered from the injury. This data will tell us which events and skills are most likely to cause injury, what time of year is dangerous, how incapacitating an injury might be, how long it took to recover, how long the gymnast trained with the injury, and what body areas are most predisposed to injury. I have been keeping injury statistics for years on my own athletes. The latest report on my own athletes was done for a 9-month period (October 1, 1981, to July 1, 1982). An injury for my purposes is anything that causes pain and is the result of trauma. The classic definition of injury, that of loss of training time, is not applicable in this case since very few injuries ever cause loss of training time. From my data in this area I found that balance beam was responsible for the most injuries (34.15%), and overuse was second (29.27%). Strains were the most common injury (26.83%); contusions were second (21.95%). The foot suffered the most injuries (26.83%); the shin and knee tied for second with 12.20% each. The mean number of days that the athlete recorded an injury for the 9-month period was 33.27 days. This means that a total of 18 athletes in the group recorded an injury before training on an average of 33.27 days during the 9 months of training. The most dangerous month was October, with 11 new injuries recorded, and second was January, with 9. The percentage chance of being injured for my team during a training session was 2.03%. This data was collected on 18 female athletes, ages 9-17, for a 9-month period.

This data may not seem too important until you consider what we did to change our program as a result of these statistics. The data indicated that the types of injuries suffered were from falling and striking something or from overuse and the continual pounding of the lower extremity. We made policies to combat this. We insisted that beam pads were used longer for the balance beam skills, two thicknesses of mats were used for tumbling, and everything that could be padded to avoid striking it, was. Since that time we have had a significant drop in these types of injuries by my observation. New data analysis will be done in the future. Without this information we would be helpless in determining cause and effect and then take steps to keep our athletes safer.

SLEEP AND ILLNESS

You should be constantly aware of the health of the athlete: the length of sleep, illnesses, and so on must be documented and analyzed for trends. My study of these factors of the same 9-month period showed that my team averaged 8.98 hours of sleep per day. An interesting statistic showed that the trend for sleep time declined through the 9 months. That is, the team members slept steadily less and less from fall to spring. This may have been the result of school pressures, less insistence by parents on observing bedtimes, or a variety of other factors. These sleep records also show consistently when exam time comes. This may indicate that more time off is necessary during the spring months than during the winter. March showed the highest incidence of illnesses. The gymnasts averaged 9.75 days with an illness in March. Second was December with an average of 7.38 days of recorded illnesses. Headaches led the pack in symptoms and Monday was the day with more illnesses recorded than any other. I found no relationship between sleep time and injury or illness at all. You can begin to see immediately that keeping such records will aid you in determining new approaches to training that will lend more safety to the system and assist the athlete in coping with all the stresses presented.

WEIGHT

Weight records are also important. The athletes should gain weight throughout their growing years. In Chapter 8 a table is included to show recommended weights by height. The weight records also provide other interesting information. In every case of an athlete quitting gymnastics because of a change of interest I have seen an increase in weight. The athlete becomes less diligent about keeping her weight under control prior to throwing in the towel. The gymnast who suddenly loses weight and has an increased heart rate along with an illness or injury is a prime candidate for overtraining, so this pattern is quickly checked and appropriate actions taken. Girls approaching 15-17 years of age show a sudden weight gain commensurate with the increased metabolic demands of puberty. This time period is usually the most traumatic for these young athletes as this is the time when most will quit or experience extreme frustration or depression about themselves, gymnastics, family, and so on. The sudden weight gain usually amounts to 4 to 7 pounds. There is also an increase in height. The interesting thing is that after several months these same athletes will lose some of this weight and bring their weight more under control. I do not have enough data to fully substantiate this for academic scrutiny but my clinical observation of this pattern goes for every gymnast I have trained through these mid-teen years. This indicates that during this sudden weight gain and change of metabolism we should not get too carried away with harassment about weight. The weight change of the child of this age and younger in some cases is beyond our control. Most importantly, it seems that with a little patience the child's weight will come under control. The duration of time for this weight gain seems to be from 6 to 12 months. This little piece of information has made an immense difference in the way we handle gymnasts in this age group. This sudden weight gain accompanies the other characteristics of puberty (acne, breast development, etc.). This weight gain is no longer seen as a threat to a career but as a transitory period for the gymnast to simply live through. It also provides enough evidence that the young girl is growing up and that a different, more cerebral approach may now be necessary for keeping her interest and making her a part of her training. We try to apply a little friendly counseling rather than harassment.

RESTING HEART RATE

The resting heart rate of the gymnast should be tracked, and it should be taken by some consistent means. An electronic heart rate monitor is best suited for this job, since these young athletes make many mistakes in taking their own pulse rate. The resting heart rate shows very little over a few days but over a few weeks we can begin to see some patterns. The patterns can be compared to weight and give some early indications of overtraining. Gymnasts who have experienced significant illness have shown clear patterns in their resting heart rate. For example, a gymnast who suffered from pneumonia showed a clear increase in heart rate prior to the onset of symptoms. Upon returning we monitored her heart rate daily and found it took four weeks to lower significantly and two more weeks for it to return to pre-illness levels. This was vital information for us, since now we lower training loads for six weeks after a significant illness. The gymnast mentioned above got pneumonia and came back to training after two weeks of bed rest, and she had four weeks to prepare for the Coca Cola Invitational in London as a member of the U.S. National Team. We watched her data daily and adopted a training regime that had her train very hard on one day and not even break a sweat on the next day. This allowed her more than the usual time to recover. Her heart rate went steadily down, she went to London after this training pattern for her first international contest, took sixth all around, and won the bronze medal on bars. Without this information an overzealous coach like myself would panic, with only four weeks to prepare. I would have worked her too hard trying to get her ready fast and she would have broken down. The daily record keeping helped give me reason to temper my own anxiety. Record keeping proved to be beneficial beyond simply encouraging my insatiable curiosity.

Heart rate can also indicate signs of stress. One gymnast showed a heart rate increase that was steady over several months and very alarming. I sent her to a doctor for tests because I thought that she had mononucleosis. The gymnast then saw a sport psychologist who enlightened us as to her particular problem. Actually, she was simply afraid of the balance beam and as her skill grew she was being asked to do harder and more scary things.

DIET AND NUTRITION

The dietary intake of the gymnast should also be recorded. I have been continually astonished that we have a group of athletes who are overfed and undernourished. In looking at the dietary information, the amount of sugar being eaten and the lack of vegetables and fruits is simply amazing. It is obvious that the gymnasts will eat only what is convenient. This is an important consideration for all programs which cannot control the training table. One look at the diets of your gymnasts and I guarantee that you will want to have a dietician come to talk to them about proper nutrition.

TRAINING LOAD

Finally, there must be a measure of the amount of work being done by the gymnasts. This is easy in sports that perform or work through a selected distance or time. In gymnastics it is very difficult to quantify the amount of work being performed. The only measure available, without being invasive, is counting elements. The number of elements on each event should be counted daily and recorded. The number of elements divided by the number of minutes of training can be used to give some idea of the intensity of training for that particular day. The raw data can indicate whether an event is receiving more emphasis than another and whether anything is being neglected. The number of routines should also be recorded. This data can then be correlated to the success or failure of learning and competition. You can see the patterns that show up concerning learning and gaining confidence after many repetitions. My study has shown that the gymnast will perform 300-600 elements per day. Also, the recent competitive season showed a very interesting relationship between rank at USA Championships and number of elements performed. It is very nearly perfect for the total number of elements performed versus the rank attained. I found only one exception to the relationship, and this was partly accounted for by other factors. Some simple statistical procedures can begin to condense all these numbers into some meaningful trends and patterns that will help you in controlling training more thoroughly.

CONCLUSION

The use of research and record keeping can help you control the training of the athlete to a point that the process is very understandable. This makes training more efficient and safe and gives the gymnast a much better idea about the direction she is going and the speed with which she is moving. The gymnast can be assured that we can bring her to a peak or near peak level for any important competition as long as we know in advance when it will be. This helps her train with the comfort of knowing that she will be ready for the competition. Knowing this removes some of the doubt that necessarily accompanies any activity dealing with unknowns. The outcome of the competition is not certain, but the athlete knows that she will be well-prepared and understands that all she has to do is prepare her own mental state to realize her best performances. Athletes generally want to do their very best. If they win then everything is wonderful. If they do their best but lose, most can exist with that also. The control of training attempts to ensure that the athlete will be able to do her best, regardless of who wins. We cannot ask much more from a training process.

III

PREPARATION

Preparation is the aspect of training in which the actual work gets done. The gymnast begins with a philosophy (Part I); she works within a program (Part II); but most of what she does is preparation (Part III). This portion of gymnastics is the one that seems to receive the most effort and clinic and seminar time. In the preparation portion the gymnast acquires a vast array of knowledge, involving technique, conditioning, mental training, and other concepts vital to gymnastics. The coach must have a program that offers tools for preparation before the concepts in preparation have meaning. Part III deals with these factors in a categorical approach that can give you additional structure to your methods of teaching and coaching gymnastics.

The concepts acquired during preparation can be placed into five general categories: physical, psychological, technical, tactical, and theoretical. The *physical* category is the realm of conditioning, physiology, flexibility, rest, and so on. The *psychological* portion involves mental preparation for learning, for competition, and for interpersonal relationships. The *technical* category is where most of us spend the largest amount of time — the technique of gymnastics and the correction of skill errors. The *tactical* portion concerns routine composition, knowledge of politics, and prediction of trends. The *theoretical* category includes those concepts related to the philosophy of training and sport. The gymnast must learn where she fits into the panoramic picture of training and competition, winning and losing, working and resting.

By carefully considering your program in terms of how well these categories are covered during preparation, you can help ensure that all your bases are covered. The wise coach should be aware that athletes are not simply creatures who perform gymnastics. These young people need to prepare all facets of themselves for and through gymnastics. The systematization of this portion of training is very important for all coaches. The categories or concepts of preparation will help you determine your own strengths and weaknesses not only in the program, but also in yourself. This can be a useful vehicle for you to use to begin understanding, then improving, in areas where knowledge or experience is lacking. The vast amount of new information available in modern sport and the diversity of personal opinions make it difficult for the coach to sift through the information to develop a concentrated, effective, ethical, and determined plan of attack for realizing the most from the athlete and gymnastics. Appendix E lists some books that will help you gain greater understanding of the many factors related to gymnastics training.

11

Physical Preparation

The five areas of concern for gymnastics conditioning are strength and power, flexibility, endurance, cardiorespiratory endurance, and rest. Each of these categories can be further divided into two major sections: general and specific conditioning. By general conditioning we mean the conditioning that gets the athlete ready for activity, but is not a specific skill or routine. These are the types of exercises and activities any gymnast might engage in to get in better shape for her sport. General conditioning has sometimes been referred to as "baseline" conditioning, which means that a certain amount of strength and power, flexibility, cardiorespiratory endurance, and muscular endurance is necessary in order to begin gymnastics activity. This baseline level has aerobic and anaerobic components. An aerobic base is often referred to in the literature, and although we do not use many of the aerobic components in the actual performance of gymnastics routines, aerobic energy processes are important for the gymnast, considering that the athlete trains from 4 to 8 hours per day. By conditioning for development of an aerobic base, the athlete should recover faster from routines, be able to last through long workouts with less general fatigue, and be able to call upon some aerobic energy processes before relying totally on anaerobic sources.

Specific conditioning relates more exactly to the particular sport and skills being employed. Specific conditioning may be a series of exercises designed to improve the casting ability of the gymnast on bars. These types of exercises are unlikely to be performed by other athletes, since the types of movement used in gymnastics are generally not used in other sports. Specific conditioning includes the very exacting exercises that are aimed at one or two skills: splits to improve the split leap, a bridge to improve the aerial walkover, or back-to-back floor routines to improve the athlete's endurance for that particular routine. Specific conditioning has some aerobic components but is mostly anaerobic, since specific conditioning exercises usually take less than 90 seconds.

PREPARATION AND SCHEDULE OF TRAINING LOADS

Let's begin with a rather broad view of where conditioning fits in the total training of the athlete, looking at conditioning by the stages of training described earlier.

Stage 1: Preparation

Section 1: Learning

In the first section of the preparatory period, the gymnast is doing skills, primarily: a great deal of learning is taking place, fatigue is not much of a factor, and meets are still far in the future. The gymnast should undertake more general conditioning than specific conditioning during this period to enhance her total level of fitness. Aerobic fitness should be of great concern at this point to provide a foundation upon which the gymnast can build the other energy systems more efficiently. Some of the benefits of this aerobic base include better circulation, loss of fatty tissue, and enhanced recovery from anaerobic processes.

The gymnast should devote 75% or more of the conditioning time to general exercises, including running, windsprints, calisthenics, and resistance training. Specific exercises that will enhance later development of specific skills occupy the rest of the time. Specific exercises include kips in a row, handstand push-ups, leg lifts, and so on.

Section 2: Combinations

At the second stage of the preparatory period the athlete is doing combinations. Now in better condition than before, she is narrowing down the number of different skills that she performs per day. She performs a smaller number of different skills and more skills in sequence. These combinations are more stressful for her than are individual skills, and longer rest periods are necessary between turns to perform. The gymnast should increase the amount of specific conditioning (to about 50 to 75% of the total conditioning time) during this stage to acquire more quickly the skills and combinations she is training. (Because conditioning includes both strength and flexibility, an inordinate amount of time should not be spent on strength.) During section 2 of the preparatory period you are more likely to know which skills are going to work and which ones will not. It is easier at this time to design specific exercises for specific skills or qualities and the gymnast is more likely to do them willingly because she can see how these exercises can benefit her performance.

Section 3: Routines

The precompetitive period is the time when the gymnast is performing a large number of routines to gain consistency. The gymnast now has a higher level of physical preparedness, confidence, and endurance. This is the period which is most stressful on the gymnast's physical capacities. The performance of routines provides a good deal of general conditioning, building upon the foundations laid in earlier stages. Specific conditioning should not be so necessary by this stage, since by now any skills being performed in the routine should be completely learned and 100% safe. Strength and power, flexibility, cardiorespiratory endurance, and muscular endurance are maintained as much as possible at this stage by virtue of the type of work and number or routines being done. Improvement of muscular endurance throughout the routines is an important goal during this stage. For example, the gymnast may not do many handstand push-ups and pull-ups during this stage; she now conditions by doing rows of back handsprings, series of round off flip-flop layouts, or many repetitions of kip cast, kip catch sequences. These are designed to increase the strength, flexibility, and endurance of the athlete for specific skills in routines.

Stage 2: Competition

The competitive stage is the period when the gymnast is actively engaged in performing routines for competitive evaluation. This stage has little conditioning of any type. The gymnast uses conditioning during this time period to maintain what was acquired during the previous stage. Since the routines being performed involve some hazards (due to the risky nature of falling in gymnastics) we try to prevent the athlete from becoming fatigued with too many outside activities. For example, running is almost entirely omitted because it can contribute to shin splints. The emphasis in this stage is more completely on the anaerobic energy systems specific to the routines being performed. We want to build up muscular endurance by enhancing the various blood buffers and anaerobic energy system enzymes.

Conditioning exercises are performed less frequently and as needed, depending upon the circumstance. If everything has gone smoothly to the point of competition (no significant illnesses, vacations, injuries, time off, etc.), then the athlete should be conditioned once or twice a week for strength, and every day for flexibility. Since flexibility training has proven to be beneficial for recovery from muscle soreness, and since at this time we really want to avoid injuries at all costs, the additional flexibility gains will help prevent some of the silly injuries that occur because of boredom and failure to maintain concentration.

Other factors that intervene may require the athlete to perform more conditioning exercises. If the athlete has been ill or injured, she will lose some of her previous fitness, and she will need some rehabilitative conditioning to get her back to where she was previously. You should be aware that any athlete who has been out of training for more than a day or two will require special exercises to get her back into a fit condition—and you should not simply rely on normal training to do this. In fact, the training period immediately after the gymnast has returned from a break of some kind is one of the most dangerous training times. The athlete is anxious and expects to perform at the peak levels she had prior to the lay-off; she cannot, and this sets her up for injuries of all kinds. In short, the competitive period has less conditioning and the conditioning must be more carefully monitored.

Stage 3: Recovery

The recovery period should include conditioning of nongrueling nature and should be very casual in format. The conditioning should include a large amount of flexibility work and activities that may be of a conditioning nature but are fun for the athlete to do. These are usually games, different or new skills, playing at another sport for a time, and actual rest. Remember that rest is also a part of conditioning. The athlete can be active during the recovery period, but it is a big mistake to attempt to cover too much ground during this time. At this point, the atmosphere for conditioning should be more one of cleansing the aches and pains and rejuvenating the physical capacity than one of the same drudgery the athlete has faced throughout previous stages. This is a good time to use aerobic activities that are fun, like soccer and running games.

SOME GENERAL COMMENTS ON CONDITIONING

Before focusing on the particulars of conditioning, I want to make a few general comments about conditioning that I feel are important. I know I will make a few enemies with the following statement but here goes: In my opinion, it is better to get the strength, flexibility, and endurance for gymnastics by actually doing gymnastics rather than lifting weights, pulling on isokinetic machines, eating bee pollen, and so forth. My opinion has come from studying the specificity of training.

Specificity comes from a time-honored concept of training. The body will adapt to what is demanded of it, no more and no less, provided it has adequate time and the stress is progressive. This means that the body of the young gymnast will acquire what we train it to acquire, and nothing else. We must make the training progressive, and provide for rest and recuperation. We must design all of our exercising with specific goals in mind. For example, in designing specific conditioning for a skill, the exercise must *perfectly* imitate the actual skill or quality we are trying to improve. It is very difficult to overload our gymnasts' strength systems in direct relationship to how they will perform a skill.

Now, I don't object to conditioning or strength training. But I do think that we must understand what we are likely to gain from these things. The strength-building equipment companies would like us to think that by moving the buttons, whistles, and paraphernalia of their particular equipment we automatically get better athletes. This is not completely true. We may get a stronger athlete, as measured by a variety of instrumentation, but the athlete's strength must be a perfect imitation of the strength needed in the skill to realize helpful benefits in skill execution.

I do understand that certain stabilizer muscles and groups must be strengthened for the best performances of skills. Conditioning greatly enhances this strength and thus aids the development of skills. To make a long story short, in my opinion, the best way to get stronger for gymnastics skills is to do the gymnastics skills. We must allow for the time necessary to perform many repetitions of skills so that the gymnast strengthens the exact muscle groups she needs and increases the speed of contraction that is necessary, utilizing the same amount of power and the same range of motion that she will need for performance.

The strength, power, and flexibility tests in Chapter 8 on the selection process would seem to deny this rule, but we are forced to use them for other reasons. If we want to test the potential for skill development by analyzing the components of strength, power, and flexibility (using skills themselves) the talent or motor skill ability of the athlete would be an interfering variable in our results. In order to make the testing valid and reliable from one person to the next we must remove the skill variable and ensure that we are testing only the qualities we want to.

To repeat, conditioning for gymnastics must use exercises that perfectly imitate the skills or qualities trying to be improved: the athlete must work with an overload (she must increase the weight or force used, or accomplish the skill in less time than before), and the training must be progressive from the simple to the difficult. When we discover these exercises and methods we will begin to remove the charlatanism and conjecture that seems to surround the entire field of strength training. Believe me, I have tried them all. I have experienced everything from isokinetics, weight training, electromyostimulation, negative weight training, isometrics, and on and on.

The gadgetry around now for strength training and conditioning is amazing. Everything from huge, heavy, expensive multistation weight machines to small devices that pinch a rope for resistance while the athlete pulls on it are being used in the name of gaining strength. If you can afford this type of equipment for strength training and conditioning then by all means, buy it and use it. I frankly cannot. The athlete will get stronger by pulling and pushing against almost anything, regardless of its price tag. The following exercises and methods have been used with more than adequate results and in most cases cost nothing. The premise of using gymnastics itself to gain strength is not only logical and sound, it is cheaper. The extra paraphernalia that might be used in the following exercises are the result of my imagination or are borrowed from other sports. A little knowledge about strength, flexibility, and endurance coupled with some imagination can bring impressive results without costing a fortune, taking loads of time, and becoming an end in itself. We want to condition athletes to make them better gymnasts, not simply to condition them.

Now I want to say a word about administrative problems that arise in conditioning and physical preparation that are related to the use of time and equipment. The gymnast should spend the majority of her time learning and perfecting skills. This should tell you that a relatively small amount of time must necessarily be devoted to conditioning. Therefore, the conditioning exercises must be effective, easy to administer, and quick. The gymnast should not be forced to finish a 5- or 6-hour training session only to face another hour or so of conditioning exercises. Practicality dictates that the length of conditioning time should be no more than 30 minutes. Preferably, conditioning should take 20 to 30 minutes at most. This is not a large amount of time and can therefore be planned and implemented in most training schedules. (It is somewhat self-evident that if conditioning cuts into skill learning, it will be difficult to get everything done and we may have misplaced our priorities.) The exercises must work, and the gymnasts must be able to perform them without complex positions that must be explained.

The quicker and more efficiently the exercises can be done, the more benefit the gymnast can reap, and the more time the gymnast might have to devote to school or other activities. Selecting exercises that meet these criteria is paramount, especially in programs with limited training time. The use of free weights is almost impossible to schedule, since just changing the weights will take too much time. The use of other fancy equipment — although perhaps sound from the standpoint of effectiveness — often will not stand this test because it takes too much time for each person to get her turn, to change the equipment to accommodate different heights, to change the resistance to accommodate different strengths among the gymnasts, and so on. For example, to get a dozen or so gymnasts through a strength workout with only a few machines or weight stations is prohibitively time-consuming.

PHYSICAL PREPARATION FOR STRENGTH AND POWER

The following methods are just a few that I believe are useful for the young female gymnast. They are not magic and are not designed to be foolproof.

They do follow as many of the principles of strength and flexibility training as possible and they are designed to get at the heart of the young gymnast's needs, which consist of only a few movements and strengths. I have included a few exercises that will help the athlete acquire some relatively simple movement and strength concepts.

Let's begin with strength and look at a few simple applications of conditioning principles along with the needs of the gymnast. I heard about some of the strength and conditioning work that Diane Hollum did prior to the 1980 Winter Games as Eric Heiden's coach. She used inner tubes filled with lead shot as the weights he had to carry around for his speed skating. This got my imagination going. I thought about how I might use inner tubes filled with sand or other material for training my gymnasts. I believe it is one of the smartest things I ever did.

After acquiring some inner tubes of various sizes from bicycles all the way to truck tires I began cutting them open and tying the ends together. Then some of the gymnasts' parents took some sand from their children's sand boxes for me to put in the tubes. What I found was that I had weights that could be literally tied to any part of the athlete. By using various sizes and weights the gymnast could perform skills with them. This was a very fascinating development. The thicker bicycle tire inner tubes would hold 3 to 6 pounds of sand. By tying a tube around the waist of any of my gymnasts I could add from 5 to 10% of their weight to them. The inner tubes could fall off and hit them, the equipment, or the floor without hurting anything or anyone. Best of all, they did not cost a cent. I can imitate nearly any strength training exercise you can mention using these tubes.

The most important thing is that the athletes can do gymnastics skills with them on. The gymnast can do casts, kips, handstands, jumps, runs for vault, pull-ups, leg lifts, and hopping while wearing extra weight. This allowed me to condition for kips while actually doing kips, to get stronger for casting by actually doing casting. Inner tubes can also be used for other purposes. For example, they can be tied around the ankle for knee extensions for kids with knee injuries. Two inner tubes can be used around the waist for greater resistance. They can be hung around the shoulders of the gymnast during pull-ups. The gymnast can hang the tubes around the waist and do depth training or jumping up to and down from objects for leg conditioning. They can be made almost any weight you like, attached to any body part you wish, and every child can carry one in her gym bag. Any exercise we do can be done with them. Each gymnast can have her own in a variety of sizes and weights for pennies at most. And, they can be used like surgical tubing if you don't put sand in them.

My goal with the inner tubes was to give the gymnast some overload, safely, while performing gymnastics skills. The overload will help improve strength, the gymnastics skills will help in the learning and specificity of training, and the gymnast can do it quickly. Initially, it does not sound like a few pounds of sand in an inner tube would supply the overload necessary for most gymnastics skills. But surprisingly, when the gymnast has to perform the skill with a little extra weight, she fatigues very quickly in the muscle groups being used for the skill. Inner tubes may not win a prize for being pretty or obtain much grant money from companies trying to prove how great they are. But they work like a charm, and the uses you can put them to are limited only by your imagination. Figures 11-1 through 11-18 show inner tubes in use to give you a general idea of how you might use them in your program.

The inner tubes are used for the specific skills in gymnastics during training and sometimes for general types of conditioning designed to improve jumping and leaping skills. I have just a few cautions:

1. Don't leave the ends long enough to swat the gymnast.
2. Don't tie them to body parts that will compress the back or swing from the inertia of the weight.
3. Don't run over them with a mat truck because it's a mess!

Figure 11-1   Different sizes of inner tubes.

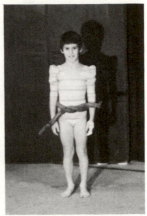

Figure 11-2   Inner tube tied around the waist.

Figure 11-3   Straddle leg lifts.

Figure 11-4   Lever pulls.

Figure 11-5   Circular leg lifts.

Figure 11-6   Straight leg lifts.

Figure 11-7   Casting on uneven bars.

Figure 11-8   Kipping.

Figure 11-9   Kipping.

Figure 11-10   Pull-ups.

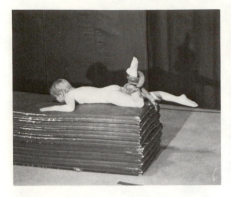

Figure 11-11   Hamstring strengthening.

Figure 11-12   Sit-ups or curl-ups.

Figure 11-13   Sideward leg lifts.

Figure 11-14   Knee extensions.

Figure 11-15   Knee extensions.

Figure 11-16   Hopping to and from a mat stack.

Figure 11-17   Jumping to and from mat   **Figure 11-18**   Press to handstand.
stack.

PHYSICAL PREPARATION FOR FLEXIBILITY AND STRENGTH

A second series of exercises that I particularly endorse is called partner stretching. This exercise is designed to improve the gymnast's ability to move her legs through a wide range of motion and to give her the strength to hold her legs in positions that are at the extreme ranges of motion. The gymnast's ability to hold her legs up will assist her in dance skills and on every event.

The gymnast needs a partner of roughly her own size for this exercise. The working gymnast will need the balance beam or a ballet bar on which to place her hands for holding her balance. All the exercises will be done on both sides and on both legs. I have described the exercise for one side and one leg only; you can simply apply the same format to the other side or leg.

The working gymnast begins by standing with her back to the balance beam and resting both hands on the beam to her side. The gymnast should not lean excessively against the beam, but gently use it for maintaining her balance. The working gymnast then lifts one leg forward to about a horizontal position while the assisting gymnast takes this leg and holds it horizontal by grasping it at the ankle (Figure 11-19a). The working gymnast then presses downward against the hand of the assisting gymnast for 6 seconds. The working gymnast should attempt to press as hard as she can and the assisting gymnast should not allow the leg to lower. The assisting gymnast may have to work pretty hard to keep the leg in one place. After the 6-second press by the working gymnast the leg is raised to a position roughly half-way from horizontal to the limit of the flexibility of the gymnast (Figure 11-19b). In other words, the working gymnast must lift her leg

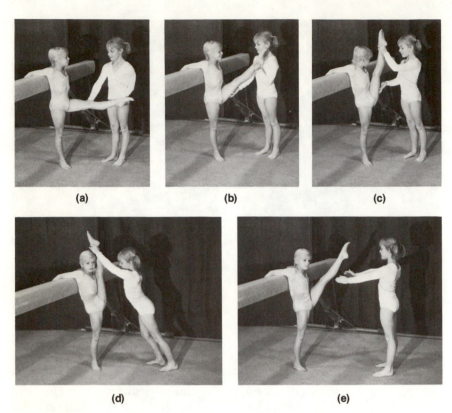

Figure 11-19 Partner stretching (forward position). (a) First press position hold; (b) Second press position hold; (c) Third press position hold; (d) Final stretch position, maximum range; (e) Gymnast can hold her leg this high.

(with some assistance from the assisting gymnast if necessary) to a position about half-way to the limit of her range of movement.

At this point the gymnast then presses down with her leg against the grasp of the assisting gymnast. The working gymnast does this for 6 seconds and then relaxes and tries to lift the leg to the limit of her flexibility, again with assistance from the assisting gymnast if necessary. The gymnast now has her leg near the limit of her range of motion and presses down against the assisting gymnast for 6 seconds (Figure 11-19c). At the conclusion of this 6 seconds the assisting gymnast pushes the leg higher, very gently, until the working gymnast announces "stop" at the completion of her full range (Figure 11-19d). This position is held for 6 seconds. Then the assisting gymnast gradually lowers the leg of the working gymnast while the working gymnast tries to hold it up. The assisting gymnast continues to lower the leg until the working gymnast can lift the leg from the assisting gymnast's hand. When the working gymnast can hold the leg on her own then this position is held for 6 seconds (Figure 11-19e). At the conclusion of the 6-second free position hold, the gymnast lowers her leg slowly to the floor and begins the same process on the other leg.

This process is repeated on the working gymnast's other leg exactly as the first leg. The assisting gymnast will find that it is hard work to hold the leg and push it higher. The working gymnast will find it difficult to hold her leg on her own very high without some thorough training. Both gymnasts must be very careful about the application of force during the portions of extreme range of motion. The assisting gymnast should always push gently and the working gymnast should always talk to the assisting gymnast so that everyone is aware of how far they can go.

The same procedure is followed on both legs in a sideward position with the working gymnast facing parallel to the length of the beam (see Figure 11-20). The leg is lifted sideward through the same relative positions as listed above and the assisting gymnast provides the same help in raising

(a)   (b)   (c)

(d)   (e)

Figure 11-20 Partner stretching (sideward position). (a) First press position hold; (b) Second press position hold (c) Third press position hold; (d) Final stretch position, maximum range; (e) Gymnast can hold her leg this high.

and holding the leg. The working gymnast should be careful to keep her posture and alignment correct during all of these exercises to avoid acquiring bad posture habits. In later transfer to skills that will require these large ranges of motion the gymnast must have correct alignment to guarantee that the skill will not develop with crooked aspects.

The rearward positions of partner stretching are a little more tricky to do. The working gymnast places her ribs against the balance beam by facing the beam and avoiding bending forward. The working gymnast then raises one leg rearward being careful to keep the support leg directly under her hips. The assisting gymnast then places one shoulder under the thigh of the gymnast (Figure 11-21a). The arms of the assisting gymnast then grasp the seat or hips of the working gymnast to keep her hip from rising during the exercise. The working gymnast then presses downward against the shoulder of the assisting gymnast. The assisting gymnast may have to stand on her knees in order to reach the thigh with her shoulder in a comfortable manner (Figure 11-21b). The assisting gymnast does not allow the leg to lower during the pressing phase of 6 seconds. After 6 seconds the assisting gymnast raises the leg about half way to the limit of the gymnast's flexibility and holds it there for another 6 seconds (Figure 11-21c). Then finally the assisting gymnast lifts the leg of the working gymnast to the limit of her flexibility and holds it for the last 6-second press (Figure 11-21d). The assisting gymnast then pushes the leg to the limit of the flexibility of the working gymnast and holds this for 6 seconds. The assisting gymnast then lowers her shoulder slowly while the working gymnast tries to hold her leg in the air. Once the working gymnast can hold the leg unassisted, she must hold it there for 6 seconds before lowering it slowly to the floor (Figure 11-21e). Then she repeats the same process on the other leg.

The range of movement through the rearward positions is significantly less than the range of movement through both forward and sideward. Whereas in forward and sideward the assisting gymnast may have to move the leg through a few feet of range, the rearward positions will usually only move through a few inches. The working gymnast should be carefully checked to assure that the arabesque position is well-defined. The hands of the assisting gymnast are on the seat or hips of the working gymnast and they should press downward against the seat or hips to keep the hips aligned. The assisting gymnast should also help the working gymnast with any other particular posture problems by telling her what was correct or incorrect as the exercise is being administered.

The final position for partner stretching consists of doing a classic needle scale position. The working gymnast moves away from the balance beam and stands with both feet on the floor. She bends forward 90 degrees from the hips with both hands on the top of the beam and arms straight. The working gymnast then raises one leg backward where it is grasped exactly as before by the assisting gymnast who simply presses it upward to the

(a)   (b)   (c)

(d)   (e)

Figure 11-21   Partner stretching (arabesque position). (a) First press position hold; (b) Second press position hold; (c) Third press position hold; (d) Final stretch position, maximum range; (e) Gymnast can hold her leg this high.

limit of the flexibility of the working gymnast (see Figure 11-22). At the full range of motion of the working gymnast the assisting gymnast checks posture problems while the working gymnast holds the position for 6 seconds. After the hold is finished the working gymnast holds the leg as high as possible while raising her torso to an upright arabesque position. This is performed on both legs.

The partner stretching exercises are a compromise between strength and flexibility since they are designed to help both. These photographs show the different positions of the exercises.

Partner stretching helps satisfy our requirements for conditioning; it is a very efficient way of getting stronger in the extreme ranges of movement. It is relatively fast, since all isometric types of exercises are done for short periods. It gets to most ranges of movement because of the repetition of the exercises by gymnasts themselves with their own peculiar tendency to seldom do something two times in a row exactly the same way. It does an ex-

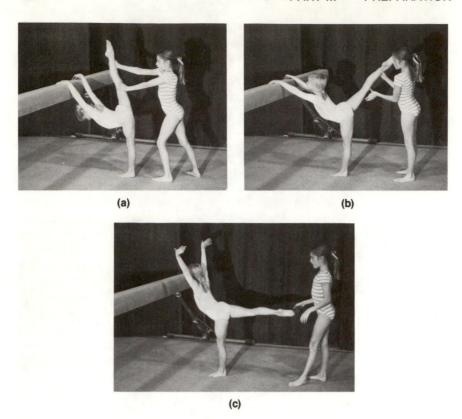

(a)   (b)

(c)

Figure 11-22   Partner stretching (needle scale position).

cellent job of getting to the extreme ends of a gymnast's range. It provides an overload for the gymnast since she must continually try to hold the leg higher and higher. It is easy to administer since the entire team can perform them at one time. And it is progressive, since the athlete holds her leg only as high as she can and only presses as hard as she can. The overload is under her control.

Partner stretching is one of the best exercises around, but it should be well-supervised to keep postures aligned, prevent horseplay, and discourage laziness.

PHYSICAL PREPARATION FOR FLEXIBILITY

The flexibility of the gymnast is enhanced to allow her to get into positions for skills that require a bit of contortionism for more efficient mechanics. Flexibility is best gained when the gymnast is warm, fatigued, quiet, and relaxed. The flexible gymnast will be better able to learn skills, avoid injuries, perform dance skills, and look more elegant while performing. Some Canadian research in flexibility showed that the gymnast should stretch for a full minute in each position. This was found to be the most economical expenditure of time for gaining and maintaining flexibility (Larson, 1971). The gymnasts who spent less time in the position gained less flexibility and the gymnasts who spent more time in the position gained more flexibility, but the gains were not worth the extra time it took to get them. Therefore, I would suggest instituting 1-minute stretching programs for the athlete to gain flexibility. The gymnast should perform forward splits, side splits, piking, and shoulder flexibility exercises for 1 minute. These exercises should also be done at the end of training rather than the beginning, with the warm-up suit on, and the gymnast quiet and relaxed. As a general rule the gymnast should go only to the point of mild pain in the stretching position. If the pain is really bad, then she is down too far or is applying too much tension. The gymnast should take some pressure off the position by raising up slightly, relieving the tension, or taking more weight on the hands, but she should be in the pain position for one full minute.

Flexibility work is often overlooked, but it is a simple and easily administered part of conditioning. Unfortunately, there is no good way of determining from day to day whether the gymnast is really trying hard — but ultimately results will be apparent. I've found that if you make flexibility as stylish as the double somersault or the Tsukahara vault, this will be strong motivation for the gymnast to work hard on her flexibility. Talking up the virtues and making a fuss over the flexibility of the people who have attained it also helps the younger athletes come to respect it and seek it.

PHYSICAL PREPARATION FOR CONSISTENCY

The combination and routine preparation of the gymnast is also part of the physical preparation. The sheer number of repetitions of routines and skills helps the gymnast gain the physical abilities to perform these skills and routines. In keeping with the idea of specificity it would be wise for the gymnast to repeat many times exactly what she will be required to repeat when she is competing. This is done in training by performing routines and combinations many times.

How many routines must be done before performance becomes consistent? This depends upon both the gymnast involved and the goals of the program. If the athlete is seeking high levels of competence and is looking toward national and international competitions, I make the following recommendations (subject to the limitations of the athlete and her individual program). The gymnast should be into the precompetitive stage, and should have performed the combinations previously with ease and confidence. She is preparing for a peak performance such as a national championship or international competition. The gymnast should be using a compulsory day followed by an optional day format and the competition will use compulsories and optionals for the final score.

Vaulting should consist of 20 to 50 vaults with the optional vaults performed first and the compulsory second (about 75% optional and 25% compulsory). Uneven bars should consist of 6 routines per day without a major error. This means that the gymnast must make 6 routines and simply do them, both compulsory and optional. On balance beam I recommend 15 optionals on optional days, and 15 to 30 compulsories on compulsory days. On floor exercise performance of 3 to 6 routines is usually sufficient for either compulsory or optional. Since floor exercise is the event which demands the most endurance, we might have the gymnast perform the routines back-to-back (without rest). This forces the gymnast to be overly prepared and capable of dealing easily with the fatigue present at the end of the routine. The gymnast should perform the second routine of the back-to-back without hard tumbling, for safety reasons. Doing consecutive passes of round-off flip-flop layouts back and forth across the floor exercise mat is another way of building endurance.

FATIGUE

The gymnast is subjected to many hard landings during routine training and is forced to take some chances. The fatigue of the floor exercise routine makes her more likely to make errors that result in uncomfortable falls. By using a mat in the pit the gymnast can avoid some of these problems during the initial stages. The gymnast performs her dance and tumbling pass into the pit with a mat on top, the music is then stopped, or the gymnast runs quickly to her place on the floor exercise mat depending upon the time and distance needed to continue her routine without interruption. This allows her to make a few mistakes during the early developmental stages without suffering injuries. Spotting during the tumbling pass most likely to cause injury is another tool. The physical preparation of muscular endurance for routines is as important as the preparation of strength and flexibility. The gymnast will find her ability to perform the routines with more ease, confidence, and competence if she is in good physical condition.

PHYSICAL PREPARATION FOR TRAVEL AND COMPETITION

An interesting area of physical preparation consists of the miscellaneous circumstances that surround travel to competition. The problems of jet lag and new surroundings subject the athlete to more stress than training and competing at home. The addition of the competitive stress and pressure from significant others can make the competitive experience a real test of endurance. You can help control this problem by regulating the precompetitive rest. You should look into the factors surrounding the competition (i.e., altitude, season of the year, temperature, weather, condition of the athlete, humidity, time zone, food, noise, etc.). These factors can be helpful or harmful for the athlete.

I believe that planning for travel and other related circumstances around competition has allowed a measure of success for us beyond the norm. Any of these travel-related factors can result in more fatigue for the gymnast, and if any are likely to be present the athletes must be more thoroughly conditioned. The experts say that altitude should have no effect on the performance of the athlete in gymnastics due to the shortness of the duration of the performance. Regarding the actual performance, I agree; however, the experts do not consider the extra headaches, sleep problems, and so forth that occur as a result of altitude. Prior to the 1981 World Championship Trials (held in Boulder, Colorado, which is not very high), we arrived a few days earlier than everyone else for the competition. The first day of training was fine, the second day was horrible, the third day was better, and the fourth day we entered compulsories. This pattern gave the athletes a good day of training prior to the competition. I believe this largely accounts for why the four girls all placed in the top 11. These girls got their "rough" day over with longer before the competition than everyone else. I believe this allowed them to forget about it before the competition time actually arrived. The way you plan for travel and other factors involved with competitions can help or harm your gymnast's ability to perform. The gymnast is usually so near the edge of peak training that any of these extraneous factors can spell problems by pushing her over the line into overtraining (see Appendix E for other texts that cover travel problems more thoroughly).

PHYSICAL PREPARATION AND COMPOSITIONAL FACTORS

The composition of routines is an area that can help or hinder the ability of the gymnast to perform the entire exercise with ease. Although the Europeans are now doing very difficult tumbling, on floor exercise the gymnasts usually set up all of their tumbling by standing in the corner several seconds to rest. They might wave their arms around but they are obviously resting. This will allow them to do a high-powered tumbling pass with greater ease than the gymnast who continually dances throughout the routine and does not rest before each tumbling pass. This tumbling approach to floor exercise, in my opinion, is counter to what floor exercise is all about: it nearly makes floor exercise two events taking place at one time. I believe that if we want to measure the dance ability of the gymnst separately from the tumbling ability, then we should have two separate events, tumbling and dance.

The events could be performed at different times, and the ultimate safety of the gymnast who wants to perform the high-level tumbling would be enhanced. Politically, we have seen that the exceptional dancer has trouble beating the exceptional tumbler. The floor exercise event should be a balance of these qualities, and the event should be evaluated as a whole, with dance and tumbling skills equally responsible for the score. My opinion indicates my philosophy of the event and explains why I do not let my gymnasts stand in the corner before tumbling passes. This forces them to be in exceptional condition if they want to do the harder tumbling skills. In making such a decision, you make a commitment to force your program to deal with a problem, and the preparation of the athlete must guarantee she will be able to do this type of exercise safely.

The uneven bars event should be choreographed carefully so that the gymnast will be able to perform the exercise with confidence and a minimum of fatigue. The connections should be kept to a minimum; for instance, kip catches should not be done near the end of the routine, if possible. The gymnast should try to do her most difficult skills as part of the 10 skills required without having to perform any extras to get the extra C part or the risk requirement. The careful choreography and development of the combinations during the second section of the preparatory stage will help with the problem of getting the weaker gymnast through her bar routine without undue fatigue and danger.

CONCLUSION

The physical preparation of the athlete in gymnastics is one of the most important factors in performance. Its relationship with other factors that will be described in Part III will become more apparent as we proceed. The issues that I've discussed are the ones I believe are most important for the coach to understand, but I've hardly scratched the surface; the issues do not end here. You should be constantly updated on new developments and research into the science of training and the effects of your particular program.

12

Psychological Preparation

The psychological preparation of a gymnast is one of the least scientific, least understood aspects of coaching. You can learn a lot from psychology that will help the athlete a great deal — even though psychology still leaves many questions unanswered. You can use psychology to obtain more control over the learning, interpersonal relations, preparation for competition, and personality of the gymnast and the coach. The whole point of psychological preparation is to allow the gymnast to make the best of her physical tools and preparation. It deals with three principal areas: motor skill preparation (learning skills); performance preparation (anxiety control); and interpersonal relations (social interactions).

SKILL LEARNING

All coaches are teachers. Since a gymnast's performance consists of skills, naturally you must be capable of teaching skills, and since the way the gymnast learns is much like the way any athlete learns, it seems obvious that by learning more about learning, you will become more effective at teaching skills.

Skill learning usually begins with attempting to impart to the athlete what it is we would like to have her be able to do as a finished skill. This usually means having an already accomplished athlete demonstrate the skill, showing the skill to the athlete via videotape or film, or describing the skill in very graphic terms so that the gymnast can develop a mental picture of what it is she is supposed to do.

After the initial conversations about what the skill looks and feels like, the initial attempts at learning usually take place. You observe the attempts offered by the athlete and make such comments as: higher, faster, slower, left, right, pike tighter, arch more, straighten this joint or that joint, and use reinforcement or words designed to push the athlete into performing more trials. This process continues through the learning of the skill: the athlete makes attempts that are closer and closer to the desired outcome, and you provide verbal encouragement and criticisms that are more and more finely tuned.

You can enhance this initial portion of skill learning by becoming a better communicator. The word pictures you use are very important. Using colorful words that the gymnast can understand is much more productive than trying to recite the various principles of angular inertia. Try to see and feel the skill from the gymnast's point of view. Look to see what the gymnast sees, listen to what the gymnast hears, note the scary parts, and watch for the subtle changes that help the gymnast feel more secure. Watch her grip on bars. If she looks lost during the skill, she probably is. Ask her what she feels, what she sees, what she hears, where she feels pressure or tension, and use this to design new and better learning drills and progressions to deal with this particular athlete. Often, the small bits of information you can glean from the observations of the athlete and from what she might report will show the way to proceed in further approaches to learning.

DRILLING AND PRACTICE

The first portion of learning is that of drilling and practice. Once the athlete thoroughly understands the skill and can perform a few completely, then she will need lots of practice. This practice is vitally important for later consistency. The gymnast should be given many hundreds of attempts to perform the skill in its finished stages so that she will become very familiar with all the subtle nuances of the skill. The skill should also be practiced in circumstances as close to those of a competition as is safe and practical. The gymnast will be rather inconsistent when she begins the drilling, but in time she will gain consistency and become more familiar with the fairly broad range of acceptable mechanics for the skill's performance.

This drilling allows her to see and feel many times the various parts of the skill that produce success and failure. It is important that the gymnast be allowed to fail on the skill safely. This is my principal objection to spotting. The gymnast who is spotted a lot will usually be successful in completing the skill even when she should not be (because the spotter is assisting her to completion). I believe that this is a grave error. The gymnasts must know what nuances of performance will bring success and what errors will bring failure. Of course, the failures in gymnastics can be painful in more ways than one, so it is important that failure does not mean injury, but simply not completing the skill. I believe that gymnasts learn faster and more thoroughly this way. It does require extreme care to always pick a good mat situation and the right time to perform the skill to avoid injury. The most critical time comes when the gymnast will do it "for real" the very first time. This is usually when it must be transferred from the pit to a hard mat, with the low bar in, on the high beam, and so on. If you are using a nonspotting approach, it will probably take longer to get your gymnasts to the high beam or the hard surface, but once they get there, they are generally successful right away.

Because the safety of the gymnast depends so much on how well the skill is performed, anything that can enhance the performance consistency of the athlete is well worth waiting for. The nonspotting approach forces a coach to create better learning drills and concepts. You must communicate in more precise terms instead of simply relying on kinesthesis and manipulating the gymnast through the skill. On the other hand, the gymnast is responsible for every execution of the skill. By outlawing spotting in our gym (with only a very few exceptions), I found that the use of drills and special mat situations became an integral part of learning. My ability to communicate in nonscientific terms got better, my ability to paint better word pictures became more multidimensional, and my ability to empathize with what the athlete saw and felt made me understand the skills and the athlete much better. There were few questions as to the gymnasts' understanding of the skill and of their ability to perform it, since I could always see clearly what each repetition produced without clouding the issue of whether the spotter helped and whether the gymnast could perform as well without the psychological crutch of a spotter.

DETERMINING READINESS

You must make decisions every day regarding the readiness of the athlete. Making determinations such as when an athlete is ready for a new, more difficult drill, or for the first-time execution without the pit or crash mat, is a critical part of understanding learning and the athlete. You are faced with hard decisions: Can she do it without getting hurt? Will she freak out and make an error that prevents her from progressing any further? Have we done all the drills and learning progressions so that the chances of getting hurt are practically negligible? In only a few other sports are athletes so susceptible to injury that could result from a mistake in judgment by the coach.

One of the best guidelines you can adopt is to ask yourself, "Can the gymnast do this skill even if she makes the worst possible mistake she is likely to make? If she really blows it, can she still complete the skill successfully enough to avoid injury or a fearful situation?" If the answer to this is "yes," then go ahead and try one. The gymnast's margin for error must be so large that no matter how stupid the mistake might be, she will complete the skill easily.

This approach gives both you and the gymnast enough confidence to go ahead and attempt the skill without high risk of getting hurt. If you follow this procedure, you will almost never go wrong, and the gymnast will be confident that you always know when she is ready. Therefore, she will be less likely to do all the balking and stalling that usually goes on during the first few attempts at any new skill. This respect is worth waiting for. The gymnast's confidence in her own ability to perform under pressure and the gymnast's and coach's faith in making the right decision will facilitate later learning.

TWO METHODS OF ENHANCING SKILL LEARNING

Method 1: Perceptual Equipment

I have noticed a continuing similarity among students of gymnastics over the past 17 years. The gymnasts have shown a marked tendency to learn gymnastics skills in one of three ways, and these consistencies led me to explore the phenomenon by keeping records and studying the literature. From this work I have developed a personal learning theory applicable to most skills in gymnastics. I doubt that it will withstand academic scrutiny, but I have found it to be very helpful in teaching skills to gymnasts. In watching gymnasts and studying films of twisting, I noticed that the gymnast often approaches learning twisting in one of two ways. She either will, or won't, tend to look for visual information while performing the skill itself. It became apparent with film analysis that some gymnasts appear to look all around during the twisting skills, while others do not seem interested in looking around at all. In fact, the ones who looked often looked in the silliest directions—often in opposition to sound mechanics. Then I began to notice other similarities within each group that were not shared by the other group. As I studied the literature I came across three words that I have corrupted to use in qualifying my observations: *haptic*, *optic*, and *analytic-plastic-synthetic* (Larson, 1971). The haptic learner is one who "boldly" approaches the skill by feeling or kinesthesis. The haptic is interested in body position rather than orientation with the outside environment. The optic appears to be more calculating as she approaches learning by using visual information. The optic uses visual checkpoints throughout the learning and performance of the skill. The analytic-plastic-synthetic is a subset of either the haptic or optic. The analytic-plastic-synthetic learner analyzes the skill intellectually, breaks it down into its component parts (which may not be natural), and then puts them back together again. Table 12-1 compares these two types of learning.

This theory has assisted my coaching well beyond its apparent simplicity. The consistency of these factors has been amazingly apparent over the last 17 years. The practical application of the idea shows up many times during training. An optic learner will often have difficulty doing a double twist off the balance beam even though she has done them for a long time on floor exercise. She will appear to go through the same learning steps that she did when she first learned the double twist on the floor. She will stop in all the same places and search for checkpoints. The haptic learner will usually transfer skills very easily. She will have very little difficulty moving the double twist to the balance beam from floor exercise, providing the cartwheel or round-off is correct. This helps us understand that although the biomechanical analysis of competent performers may show us a good technique for performing the skill, the gymnast may need to approach this technique in ways other than strict imitation. We have traditionally just put people in the belt, or spotted them until they "got the feeling." This method is probably useful for the haptics but not for the optics. The optic may need to have a teaching methodology that allows her to perform the skill with

TABLE 12-1   Haptic Versus Optic Learning

Haptic	Optic
1. Learns by feeling	1. Learns by seeing
2. Films show head is still	2. Films show head is moving
3. Tries to spin in the twist to the completion of the skill	3. Twists only as far as orientation will allow
4. Once she learns the skill, she can transfer it to any event with a similar take off	4. Must take short period to relearn skill for each new application
5. If she makes a mistake she will finish the twist but land on hands and knees	5. If she makes a mistake she never completes the twist but stops at some fraction
6. If you ask her, while she is learning, how far she twisted she does not always know	6. If you ask her, while she is learning, how far she twisted she can tell you to the 1/8 twist
7. She can pose the body position of take off or nearly any portion of the skill	7. She cannot tell what the exact position of her body is
8. She cannot report seeing anything during the skill learning	8. She can report seeing many things in rather good detail
9. Usually appears to "set" and spin	9. Twist appears "wobbly"
10. A somewhat faster learner	10. A somewhat slower learner
11. Never "loses" a skill	11. Will occasionally "lose" skills due to new environment, new technique, or interference from another skill with similar technique

safety while stopping at various points to gather the checkpoints for her perceptual equipment. This gymnast may have to be told what to look for rather than how it feels. One young gymnast having more difficulty than other gymnasts may simply need to be informed that it takes her perceptual equipment a little longer to assimilate the movements than some of her teammates but that she will be just as good as they are in short order. In fact, she will probably be a lot better at sticking landings.

Analytic-plastic-synthetic learning comes into play when, during the learning of some skills, the gymnast breaks the skill down into more palatable sections. These sections may not necessarily be natural divisions of the skill. For example, in the double twist, the learner may not divide a skill into two full twists, but may instead divide the skill into a one-quarter twist during take-off followed by a spin of one and three-quarters in the air. Both haptic and optic learners may do this to the skill, even as they apply their own peculiar perceptual equipment. Usually a gymnast will do this for safety and security reasons when she fears that "lost" feeling of total lack of orientation, and will always seek to return to a body position (for haptics) or a visual cue (for optics) to gain control. Because the loss of orientation is threatening, a gymnast will attempt to maintain orientation regardless of the skill and its technical requirements or seeming natural divisions.

Watch how your gymnasts learn and see if there are learning patterns similar to those I have described. If you notice consistencies like these, you can file each decision regarding learning in a new category coinciding with the apparent type of perceptual equipment the gymnast has. At the very least, you will have achieved a new appreciation for the learning process. The best way to learn about learning is usually to go to the learner. Watch the way the learner attacks the problem. In other words, teach the gymnast and not the skill. Simple imitation of a skill may be the place to start in determining methodology for teaching, but it is not the place to end. The skill, like multiplication tables, is the material to be taught, but to teach it the teacher must know something about the learner. Does the learner understand other concepts of a similar nature? Does the learner read from left to right or right to left? Can the learner see or feel the material clearly? It is amazing to me how often we engage in the teaching of skills without knowing much about the process we participate in.

Method 2: The Inner Game

A second most interesting approach to learning has been offered by Timothy Gallwey in his book, *The Inner Game of Tennis* (1974). Why would a gymnastics coach be interested in tennis? This book talks a lot about aspects that are important for all types of skill learning, not just tennis. This book should be in every coach's library and should be well dog-eared. The author makes some assumption that come more from Eastern religion than from science, but nevertheless, the message should be loud and clear to the teacher of skills:

1. The coach should help the learner avoid the emotional judgment that takes place during the trial-and-error portions of learning.

2. The coach should help the learner to use her own perceptions as accurate tools for discovering the proper technique for the skill.

3. The coach should help the athlete believe that the body being used to perform all these skills is really quite capable of learning almost anything we allow it to.

One of the most important things I learned from this book is a game. The game is called hit and bounce. The tennis version has the student say (out loud) "hit" when the ball hits the racket and "bounce" when the ball hits the ground. This is supposed to help the player concentrate. In trying to apply this game to gymnastics I found some amazing things. The gymnasts often do not have the foggiest idea when things are actually happening. I had the gymnast say "hit" when she punched the vaulting board for a take off and "bounce" when she hit the horse. A marvelous revelation occurred. The gymnasts who were most skilled could say the hit and bounce at the right times. Those who were in the early learning stages announced "hit" and "bounce" at the oddest times. Interestingly, those who were late in punching the board or hitting the horse were also late in announcing the appropriate words. Those who announced the words early were also early in their timing of technique for performing the skill.

This was a fascinating realization for me. How could the gymnast try to adjust her timing so that she was doing something at a different time if she did not really know when her feet were actually striking the board or her hands actually striking the horse? How could I ask her to be someplace else when she did not know where she was? The timing of many gymnastics skills is critical. The feet will be on the board for only a few hundredths of a second. The gymnast must initiate or complete many movements. If the timing is off even the tiniest amount she will realize less force for her use later in the skill.

I began asking the gymnasts other questions that have taught me a great deal about their learning patterns. The gymnast who is unskilled in some movement cannot report what her body position is during most phases of that skill. By asking her simply to pay attention to these, the skill will slowly improve as if she were watching herself on a videotape in her mind. During the game of hit and bounce the gymnast's timing will improve if I just ask her to pay attention to the sounds she makes upon striking the board, floor, or bar, as she announces the appropriate word. Sometimes simply asking her to look at the body part striking the surface or piece of equipment is enough. One of the greatest eye-openers for me came when I asked the gymnast to say "now" when she thought the bar would be there for her to catch on a Deltchev on uneven bars. Not only was she wrong but the bar was nowhere near where she thought it would be. By asking her to listen carefully and say "now" a little later we made some progress. Then I said "now" along with her. This helped her find the bar with ease. The activity was not a threat. She did not get lost and she even enjoyed this simple approach to learning about a skill she had seen done hundreds of times. I found that this works better than videotape.

This whole approach to learning I owe to a book on tennis. Learning skills is not only markedly faster using this "Inner Game" approach, but the learning is more fun, more productive, easier, and more alive. We have applied this approach to hundreds of circumstances. Ask the athlete to say "now" when she thinks she is split. Ask her to pose her position while twisting and then show her on videotape or pose her yourself. See if she can then find this position in the air. If you want to change it, she has to know where "it" is. The thoroughness and truly developmental approach that this provides us with also gives another multidimensional look at a portion of gymnastics training. Adding more dimensions will make us more able to cope with the wide variety of students that happen to come along by simply putting them into our system and adapting those facets that will be necessary to deal with them. We are therefore more consistent and systematic in our approach and have more control over the learning process.

PSYCHOLOGICAL PREPARATION FOR PERFORMANCE: ANXIETY CONTROL

Psychological preparation for competition touches many portions of training. Drilling skills, learning, practicing the routine, practice meets, and so on are all part of psychological preparation. Preparation for the pressure of the competition and the ability to hit the routine in the decisive moment can be enhanced by a definitive plan that includes a few simple techniques. The techniques do not provide a guarantee but will help the athlete cope with these pressures more easily.

The gymnast should practice her routines during the precompetitive stage of preparation on a "must-make" idea. That is, if she is assigned six routines, she must make all six without a major error. A major error consists of any deduction greater than two-tenths. If she must make six and she falls on the first two routines, then she will do a total of eight. This helps provide some consequences for making the routines. This may not be appropriate during the earliest phases of the precompetitive stage, because the gymnast might well be working until midnight trying to make six routines. In the early stages one might give the gymnast eight routines to make six. If the gymnast does not make six in a row she can only do a maximum of eight routines in trying to get her routine assignment finished. Another simple method is to ask the gymnast to make a certain number in a row and if she is successful she may stop and work on something else. If the gymnast fails to accomplish the set number in a row she must do some higher number of routines commensurate with her abilities and the time of the season. These are a few simple policies that help make the consistency factor of routines a more serious business.

Perhaps the best way to prepare for competition is to have mock meets during training. At mock meets each gymnast must perform a single routine or a series of routines with the coaches judging and the rest of the gymnasts watching. Scores are awarded and some reward is given upon successful completion of the routine. The gymnast should have to perform all of the pomp and ceremony necessary in actual competition. She should have a limited warm-up time, must acknowledge the superior judge at the beginning and end, must take her two vaults back to back, perform her own mental preparation prior to mounting, and so forth. This will help the athlete rehearse exactly the sequence of events that she will be likely to face when she must do it in front of real judges in competitions that mean a great deal to her. The coaches should attempt to make it as real as possible and all the rules of competition should apply.

One difficulty about these practice meets is that it is very hard for the gymnast to "get up" for them. The gymnasts will seldom perform in the practice meets the way that they do in a real competitive situation. The use of practice meets should still form a part of their training since this type of rehearsal is still better than no rehearsal at all. The meet cannot be won in warm-ups and the competition will not be decided in practice meets; they will merely help the athlete rehearse her approach to competing.

Each gymnast should have a set ritual for approaching each event prior to competing. The use of a set ritual and visual imagery has improved our gymnasts' consistency and confidence in facing a competition. The gymnast should practice this ritual and imagery during training and drilling routines. She begins by chalking the hands, setting the board, or standing at the runway or any specified place. Then she must go to a specific place each time for the beginning of the routine. The gymnast then stands and visually pictures herself doing the mount, first portion, or the entire exercise. Upon completing this she raises her hand to acknowledge the judge and mounts, runs, steps onto the mat, and so on. The gymnast should learn to approach the event as if it were in a bubble of concentration. The gymnast takes this little bubble with her to all competitions so that immediately prior to the event she is always in the same familiar state of concentration and readiness. Of course, there will always be some gymnasts who believe that this will make them nervous or mess up. With such gymnasts, don't let the bubble concept become a bone of contention. If athletes are brought up with the idea of creating a special place for competition that is practiced along with the physical practice of routines, they will feel a little more at home during the portions of competition that lead directly to the performance. Most good athletes have a set ritual of preparing themselves for competition anyway. This little ritual simply helps systematize this preparation for a young athlete who, because of her inexperience, may not have settled upon a ritual that works well for her. The gymnast must practice this ritual so that she can call upon it when she needs it.

A LOOK AT FEAR

Somewhat related to learning, and certainly a factor in the performance of gymnastics skills, is fear. This phenomenon is one of the most costly factors in training and perhaps the greatest deterrent to progress. Fear can be expressed in many ways. The child may be afraid of such things as landing on her head, losing orientation, failure, the coach, a parent, competition, or winning. We should understand a little bit about fear before it becomes a catch-all term and loses its significance.

Fear is a feeling of dread or extraordinary discomfort from perception of a threat. Gymnasts must deal with fear nearly every day. The most basic type of fear for them is the fear of falling. In Psychology 101 we learned that humans have two innate or inborn fears—a fear of falling and a fear of loud noises. All other fears are learned. This fear of falling is with gymnasts all the time. They must deal with falling in every training session and throughout the learning of almost every skill. Watching little children dive into the deep end of the pool for the first time can give tremendous insight into understanding the fear mechanism in children doing gymnastics. The child in gymnastics must jump into the deep end of the pool for the first time almost daily. The child in swimming only has to face it once. When a child has learned to deal with her fear she has learned one of the most important lessons in gymnastics.

Fear causes an avoidance reaction: the frightened person will tend to avoid the thing that causes fear. You must plan for fear in the gymnast and for means to deal with it. Often the best approach to deal with fear in the athlete is to talk about it. The ability to question the gymnast openly about the circumstances she is in, what it is about the skill that frightens her, and at what point she loses the ability to control her fear, is the first and perhaps most important step. You can simply ask the child who is balking or stalling at doing a skill, "What is scary about it?" and an honest answer might be that she is afraid of landing short and hurting her ankles. Then you should ask if this is a reasonable fear (*will* she hurt her ankles if she lands short, and is this likely to happen?). If the answer is yes, or probably, then the fear is quite legitimate and steps should be taken to avoid the circumstance that causes this fear. Perhaps the gymnast should do the skill in the pit longer, she should be spotted, or her ankles should be taped or strapped to prevent her from being hurt if she makes a mistake; or perhaps another progression might be tried. All too often we look at the gymnast and simply assume that she is "chicken." It would be a bit naive to say that the gymnast cannot be "chicken" but we should explore every other possibility before we draw this conclusion.

A coach once came to me and asked if I could look at her gymnast's double back somersault on the floor and tell me why she always over-rotated and landed on her seat. I watched a couple under spot, and by looking at the gymnast it was obvious that she was perfectly capable of doing the skill with ease. I asked the coach how long she had been doing them. Did she train it into a pit or always with spot? Did the gymnast ever crash hard and hurt herself? Everything seemed appropriate. Then the coach had the gymnast do one by herself and the answer was obvious. The gymnast did everything in her power to keep from landing short. I asked the gymnast if her ankles hurt on the front between the foot and the shin, and she said they did. I asked if she hurt this spot often when she tumbled, and she did not want to admit it but when I touched her ankle there she hit the roof. Eureka! The gymnast was frightened of hurting her ankles and therefore her margin for error was so small that she had to land her somersaults near her heels or risk a painful jolt in her ankles. I showed the coach a tape job that I saw done on Steffi Kraeker from East Germany and had tried with my own gymnasts. The gymnast went home to try it out. The coach talked to me at the next competition and reported that a miraculous change had occurred in the gymnast, who now seemed to come up with astounding courage when facing her skills because it did not crunch her ankles anymore. This true story shows that sometimes we are looking for a technical correction for skill errors that have nothing to do with technique. We have to search for all possibilities to remedy a performance problem and turn over every stone in the search.

If fear is suspected, a little questioning of the athlete will usually provide all the evidence needed to discover what the problem really is. Interestingly, at first most athletes will not admit to being frightened because it is "sissy." We should try to allow these athletes to simply report their fears without being judgmental. If it's scary during the early learning stages, it is natural, as they get more accustomed to the skill, that it won't be scary any longer. A little fear is even healthy. The kind of fear that makes gymnasts a little apprehensive about a skill may give them a little added respect for its inherent dangers and keep them from approaching the skill flippantly and getting hurt as a result.

Fear is such a multifaceted concept that full treatment of the subject here is impossible. Fear is a very powerful motivator. The gymnast who fears failure will tend to avoid it. The athlete who fears injury will tend to avoid it. The athlete who fears success may also tend to avoid it. Along with perhaps fearing loss of social acceptance by being too good, the athlete may fear accomplishment.

These facets are complex and difficult—and I want to warn you against attempting to make the 10-cent variety psychoanalysis of your gymnast, even though you may become a pretty good amateur psychologist through years of experience of dealing with young people. Although one would think that a good athlete would naturally be highly disciplined and psychologically fit, there are many who are not. Theoretically, a good athlete should be strongly determined to succeed, but many are so talented that they participate in the sport as a lark and do very well simply because they are so talented. Athletes sometimes change their attitudes toward discipline, goals, and so on. Therefore, you should be aware of the possibility of change so you can attempt to deal with it. Although we cannot be hamstrung by not making a decision, we must be open to new information indicated by the behavior and conversation of each athlete.

The athlete is a complex person, and you should not make too many assumptions in dealing with her. But you should trust your own instincts and your knowledge of the gymnast rather than look for miracle cures that will make her an instant success. As the public is often seduced by gimmicks, you are also subject to the same appeal of gimmicks in coaching. You may look around and see the most successful coaches and try to emulate and imitate their actions without understanding the multifaceted impact their actions may have. An experienced coach may be harsh at one time, fatherly at another, and yet be in perfect control of the circumstances. The American public is particularly interested in success, winning, and fast results. Coaches have grown up with this in mind and we are suffering for it. There is no fast way of producing an athlete, and anyone who believes he or she has a shortcut is dealing in self-delusion. We must take each athlete one step at a time through her learning in order to help her to achieve her goals safely and surely.

PSYCHOLOGICAL PREPARATION FOR INTERPERSONAL RELATIONS

The Gymnast

The relationship of the athletes to each other and to the coaching staff can either be a plus to the program or a source of problems. I believe that the following policies are paramount in dealing with the issues that arise in this facet of the program.

Treat everyone the same. No matter how painful, when the star is misbehaving, deal with her swiftly and unmercifully. Avoid accusations of favoritism like the plague! The sense of justice of young people is unbending. They must all be treated equally or some will feel that others are more privileged than they are, and there will be a concomitant loss of discipline and respect.

The gymnasts must feel important. They must all have the same opportunities to become better athletes; the only deterrent to progress should concern their willingness to work and their ability. You must carefully divide your time and attention among them to indicate to each athlete that you are genuinely concerned about her progress and well-being.

The gymnasts must treat each other and the coach with respect and concern. If you allow insubordination and the typical kinds of "cattiness" or gossipy behavior that surround most gymnastics schools, you are a fool. Gymnasts who participate in such behavior should be dealt with quickly and justly. A single warning and initial punishment should suffice; upon the next offense they should be dismissed, regardless of their talent. It is important that you try to enhance the self-concept of each athlete by encouraging them, pushing them, and so forth. Team members themselves should also try to encourage each other. A few promptings from you and the opportunity for the athletes to imitate your encouragement and enthusiasm should help keep everyone motivated and feeling part of the total program.

You must work hard to maintain the camaraderie that can be developed through a team approach to gymnastics. Orchestrating the interactions of all these various personalities to achieve a few singular goals is a process marvelous to behold. The expert at this kind of people-to-people work is really a genius. It requires multidimensional thinking and a great deal of caring. The coach who can perform this magic will always have gymnasts in contention for the top awards.

The Coach

You—as well as your gymnasts—must prepare yourself for dealing with competition. Many texts have shown some of the interesting applications of body language to communication. Some have reported that most communication is nonverbal. You read the gymnast by the variety of behavioral flags she uses to show fear, illness, happiness, apprehension, frustration, and so on. The gymnast can also read you by seeing certain behaviors related to mood, health, and mental state. If you study the books on body language, you will be able to make sure that when you would like the athlete to be confident, you are not using a gesture that shows apprehension. You can also watch the body language of the athlete to see whether she is really interested in the skill being taught, is really ready for the first attempt at a new skill, or feels confident about the upcoming event.

Nervousness, frustration, anger, happiness, enthusiasm, and so on are all pretty infectious. You can be a "carrier" of all these moods or feelings and infect your gymnast with them. It is important for you and the athlete to be a little optimistic about the activity. You should portray confidence, enthusiasm, desire, and determination in the hope that the athlete will follow your lead. In short, you can help the athlete maintain an even outlook, confidence, and enthusiasm by modeling the mood you want to see. And you must be a pretty good actor at times.

Sometimes you will be involved in a variety of high-pressure and somewhat risky situations. Should you gamble on trying a new skill in an important meet? The judging is going badly, and you would like to protest, but the athletes might look at the protest as bad sportsmanship. You may get upset by the failure of an athlete that costs a team championship or costs the athlete a well-deserved place on the award stand. All of the emotions the athletes go through you also feel. If the athletes are doing well, you usually feel pretty good; if they aren't, you may feel depressed. Often you can turn around the lethargic attitudes of the athletes by being a whirlwind of energy yourself. Now and then you should attempt to step out of your skin to try and observe what the effect of your behavior is on the gymnasts. If you are causing some bad attitudes through your own attitude, then it's you who should be straightened out, not the gymnasts.

Your ability to step outside of the situation and look at it from another perspective is a key secret to becoming a controlling influence on the training circumstance. You can then take control of the situation rather than simply become the victim of the mood of the day. It is most important that you not simply talk about these miracle changes in mood but actually portray them. The gymnasts will follow your lead.

DECIDING HOW TO MOTIVATE: WHERE TO LOOK

We all know that motivation goes along with learning. You have a certain amount of "clout" in getting the gymnast to perform well. Unfortunately, this clout has been expressed always as some kind of miracle or as Lombardi-ism toughness. The typical lay person seems to think that the miracle of the 1980 hockey team should be able to happen in all sport at least three or four times an hour. Somehow a coach with poor training or poor equipment, or a team with poor training or no talent, should be able to win simply because they are the good guys. "Rocky," "The Bad News Bears," and other popular fictional accounts of "going for it" are simply not the way it really happens.

There are no gimmicks in learning; you simply have to do the work. The role of motivation in learning is that of encouragement. When you detect lack of determination in the gymnast (usually when they are not progressing), you often feel obliged to punish the athlete verbally for not trying hard enough. You must be careful in applying this kind of motivation. Ask yourself the following questions before you ever punish an athlete verbally for not trying during learning: Is the athlete strong enough to perform this skill? Is the athlete flexible enough to perform this skill? Does the athlete really understand the skill? Is the athlete fresh enough to perform the skill? Does the athlete really want to do the skill? If all the answers are affirmative but the athlete still cannot perform the skill, then it may be time to scold her. It doesn't make much sense to scold the athlete if she is not strong enough to do the skill. (Certain strength exercises should be performed to increase her strength.) If the athlete really doesn't understand the skill (the type of questioning discussed earlier can provide this evidence), then new teaching progressions need to be designed. Scolding is a last resort, only when all else has been tried and exhausted. If every coach would go through those questions during each training session for each skill then there would be a significant amount of teaching going on and very, very little scolding. This approach will give you a means of testing your approach for any athlete for any skill. If the athlete really is capable of doing the skill, then a little scolding will usually put her right into gear; the skill should come in less than five attempts, and everything will be happy again. If it does not come quickly, then continue to look for another error in the teaching; there must be a hole someplace that needs to be plugged.

CONCLUSION

The coach, the athlete, and the system of training all have a role in the psychological preparation of the gymnast. You should look at this phase of preparation with great interest. A little old-fashioned study will help you learn about learning, motivation, and stress management, and you can then use these tools to assist the athlete.

My own goals for psychological preparation have always been to make the gymnast fully independent. The gymnast should be so well prepared that nothing will be a surprise and anything that comes up during the competitive experience can be dealt with strictly by the athlete, with no help from the coach. When the athlete arrives in this position, our preparation is complete. We should strive to obtain an independent functioning gymnast who can handle anything thrown at her with good judgment and informed action. This is one of the greatest services we can offer.

13

Technical Preparation

The technical preparation of the athlete is that portion of training that determines the specific performance parameters or actions for a skill. Getting the child to actually do the skill is part of physical and psychological preparation. Determining which technique to use or what specific actions of all the body parts to employ is technical preparation. The technical preparation is concerned with the best possible performance of the skill itself. It is skill directed, not child-directed, and its goals are more cerebral and scientific.

COLD SCIENCE

Technical preparation should determine the most mechanically efficient way of doing the skill: the means of getting the body higher, farther, faster, and more elegant should be determined exactly before proceeding in the teaching of any skill. In other words, the most critical parts of the skill (those that will make completion of the skill possible with the most elegance and dynamics) should be determined before designing the methodology. Technical preparation is concerned with forces, accelerations, trajectories, center of mass, velocity, gravity, angular and linear momentum, and inertia. All of these factors are well defined in modern science, and classical mechanics has been around for decades. There still are a few unsolved mysteries, but not as many as we might think. Appendix E includes a list of books on biomechanics. I assume that most coaches reading this text have already read some of these books and have a working knowledge of some mechanics that they can call upon in understanding the following paragraphs (see Sands, 1981, 1982, for a "how to" approach to skills in modern women's gymnastics).

In this chapter I hope I can convince you to identify your needs in technical preparation so that you can better prepare your athletes for the newer, more difficult and dangerous skills that gymnastics is forcing upon us if we want to remain competitive. I believe that we have a responsibility to our gymnasts to analyze these skills carefully before inflicting them on the gymnast. The shear forces, impact velocities, stress, and potential for injuries should be determined *before* we begin trying out new methodology to get the child to do the skill.

BIOMECHANICS

Biomechanics is the study of the body in motion. What we need to do is study the body as it performs gymnastics skills in order to learn exactly what is happening in each joint and muscle group. Unfortunately, this is an expensive process because of all the instrumentation required to make the analysis accurate and practical.

ANALYZING SKILLS

Gymnastics skills are really quite slow by most standards of sport. The trained eye of the coach can often provide considerable information about the performance of a skill. Good judgment and knowledge of mechanics will help you know where to look and determine what factors are important. However, the eyeball analysis of skills is not nearly so good as analysis of the skill with slow motion videotape or film. As the film is analyzed frame by frame, you will generally be surprised at the difference between what you had thought was going on and what was actually going on in the skill. This is the first and typical step used to analyze a skill: the coach uses a machine to record the skill and then slows it down so that the simple velocity of the movement does not blur the visual impressions and understanding of what happened. There are limitations to this method: the most important is that only one frame can be seen at a time. This limits your perspective to one portion or segment of the skill and you lose the relationship of a particular frame to the entire movement. The second limitation is the speed of the film itself. Videotape is shot at 30 frames per second, and most film of the super-8 variety is shot at 18 frames per second. Even gymnastics skills are often too fast to be captured clearly on each frame at such a slow frame rate and shutter speed, and there is also the problem of blurring. Serious study of film should be done at frame rates of 60 frames per second or faster.

The second step of analysis is to record a series of frames on one page so that the relationship of the frames and the individual frames can be discerned. This can be done with tracing paper and pencil, with overhead projector transparency acetate, or with the computer and a digitizer. Having performed many of these tracings I can testify to their being better than film alone, but they are highly inaccurate and very time-consuming. One skill often can take 6 to 8 hours of drawing with film that uses only 18 frames per second. The understanding gained from such work is better than with film alone but the time investment and the inaccurary make this impractical. Because of the time constraints of the typical gymnastics coach, such analysis is not a common practice, regardless of how good it might be.

The next step is to use some instrumentation to perform analysis that is more accurate and faster. The use of the modern microcomputer has provided the coach with an avenue to perform analysis that was previously unavailable. An example of how the use of this type of analysis made a difference in the practical application to a skill occurred when I was trying to teach a gymnast a giant-to-reverse hecht on the uneven bars. The first gymnast I taught this skill to is remarkably gifted and an exceptional swinger on bars. I learned enough from watching men perform the skill and talking to men's coaches to get this child to do one competently and safely. Actually, she almost taught herself as I stumbled through my attempts at identifying a methodology. Later I wanted to teach this skill to another girl who was not as good a swinger but was still very talented. We began working on the skill, following roughly the same progressions used with the first girl. The second gymnast did ultimately learn to perform the skill, but with considerably less height and safety. The first girl was able to perform the skill safely, since if she missed the high bar she would simply land sitting on the low bar. If the second girl missed the high bar then she would land on her back or neck on the low bar. Therefore, the margin for error was not large enough to justify using the skill in a routine for the second gymnast. So I began talking to other coaches to see if there were other nuances of the technique that I may have overlooked or whether it was simply the giftedness of the first gymnast that allowed her to perform the skill so easily. One of our finest coaches told me that he had acquired a Russian coaching book that said that the arch portion of the skill just prior to release was the most important part, so I went home and began designing drills and methods to emphasize this portion of the skill to gymnast number two. We didn't get anywhere. The same problem persisted.

At about this time my computer program and digitizer were finished to allow me to do film analysis of skills. So I filmed both skills and analyzed them on the computer. The computer analysis showed that the first gymnast went so high because she lifted her legs much harder and faster than gymnast number two. The first gymnast showed much greater angle at the hips and very little angle at the shoulders. The second gymnast showed just the opposite. Looking at the paths of the center of mass it was obvious that the second gymnast just fell after the release while the first gymnast rose quite high. So I went back into the gym and forgot about the arch and started working on the leg lift and, lo and behold, the progression worked and the second gymnast was able to perform the skill higher and with much more safety. Although I had looked at film and videotape prior to this the relationship of these factors had never made itself apparent until the computer could draw each frame and break down the relationship to understandable proportions.

A second example comes from tumbling. A very good gymnast was continually losing force on her round-off because of a misplaced landing leg that forced her knee to collapse inward. The path of the knee was markedly inward instead of parallel to the other knee. Because I was concerned about potential injury, I analyzed this problem and after the simplest, most incomplete calculation found a shear at the knee of 430 pounds. I showed the gymnast the calculations and elaborated on the fact that if she did 150 round-offs a day, times 430 pounds of force, times 6 days a week, times 50 weeks a year, she was likely to get herself injured. This was all the motivation necessary to convince her to change a technical problem that had bothered her tumbling for years. The numbers do not usually lie, and sometimes information processed by an expensive machine is easier to listen to than information processed by a little grey matter. You should be able to see, however, that the application of the computer to analyze performance and determine injury potential is one of the most important uses we could put to the computer. In fact, after this incident I began taking a more serious interest in other such occurrences of poor mechanics in skills to see if the computer could help me determine potentially dangerous techniques, like whipping the low bar from a handstand, putting the feet over the head on double somersaults, the arch technique of vaulting, and some jumping techniques.

DESIGNING NEW SKILLS

Perhaps the most exciting example of the value of my little computer is its assistance in designing new skills. The computer was largely responsible for the forward giant swing performed by Amy Koopman for the first time in 1982 at the International Invitational in Fort Worth. The computer helped me design a technique for a downswing that would allow her to do a forward giant to a handstand without hitting the low bar. This has helped revolutionize my approach to uneven bars, and I owe a large part of it to the computer.

GETTING STARTED WITH A COMPUTER

Every coach should take an interest in such equipment and learn how it can be applied to training. The computer may seem complicated, but so did a flip-flop at first. With no background in computers at all and little money to spend, I can now, after 5 to 6 years, perform analysis and work that was previously limited to universities. The computer necessary to perform the type of analysis that follows would cost less than $4000.00, excluding the programs. The process of analysis of skills begins with the film. We chose a super-8 camera that shoots 80 frames per second. The super-8 film is not very expensive and can be obtained in black and white (it can shoot your subject in low light). Then we got a behind-the-back screen to project the film on. A digitizer is connected to the screen to send the *x-y* coordinates of each body landmark to the computer for storage. The coach places the cursor of the digitizer on both feet, both ankles, both knees, both hips, both shoulders, both elbows, both wrists, both hands, the torso, and the head. The computer then stores these coordinates and performs some calculations based on the mass and the center of mass of each segment to determine the location of the entire body's center of mass. This is all stored on the computer's floppy disk and later fed back into the machine for further analysis. The computer can select any single frame or series of frames and provide a stick figure of the body. The computer can show any single segment or limb through any single frame or series of frames. The paths of each body part and the center of mass can be shown through any portion of the skill. The time duration of each graphic representation is also given so that the coach can judge relative times between athletes. This type of analysis is complete with forces, accelerations, moments of inertia, and so on. The diagrams shown as Figures 13-1 through 13-27 are those produced by my computer for a simple skill, the snap down to layout somersault. I selected the snap down to layout as an example because it is a familiar, well understood gymnastics skill.

A look at these diagrams will give you an idea of what the computer can do for you. I hope that every coach who looks at them will rush right out and get started using this type of instrumentation to gain a better understanding of what is actually occurring in gymnastics skills. The use of the computer and other related types of equipment will help gymnastics training enter the 20th century.

BIOMECHANICS GRAPHIC ANALYSIS

```
SUBJECT NAME = KATIE MCDIVITT      DATE OF ANALYSIS =  7 / 10 / 83
SUBJECT HEIGHT =  64  INCHES      162.56  CENTIMETERS
SUBJECT WEIGHT =  104  POUNDS   47.2727  KILOGRAMS

FILM SPEED =  80  FRAMES PER SECOND
FRAME INCREMENT =  1            TIME DURATION =  1.2375  SECONDS
NAME OF SKILL = SNAP DOWN TO LAYOUT      NAME OF EVENT = FLOOR EXERCISE
CAMERA DISTANCE =  39        CAMERA HEIGHT =  5
REFERENCE POINT =  669    317
SCALING FACTOR =  1
```

```
PHASES OF SKILL                    STARTING FRAME NUMBER
        FF HAND CONTACT                  1
        SNAP DOWN                        7
        HANDS DEPARTING                  14
        HANDS AIRBORNE                   17
        FOOT CONTACT                     23
        HEEL CONTACT                     27
        HEELS DEPART                     29
        FEET DEPART                      34
        PIKING                           46
        SEES FLOOR                       66
        LANDING PREPARATION              82
        FOOT LANDING CONTACT             94
        EOF                              99
```

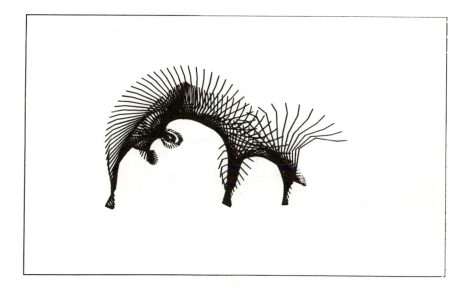

Figure 13-1

Figures 13-1 through 13-27   The snap down to layout somersault as shown by computer analysis. The diagrams of body parts are based on filtered data.

```
SUBJECT NAME = KATIE MCDIVITT
SKILL = SNAP DOWN TO LAYOUT     EVENT = FLOOR EXERCISE

SKILL PHASE DISPLAY

PHASE IN THIS DISPLAY = FF HAND CONTACT
FRAMES IN THIS DISPLAY ARE  1  TO  7
TIME DURATION = .0875  SECONDS        SCALING FACTOR =  1
```

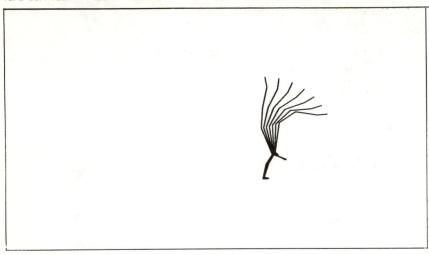

Figure 13-2

```
SUBJECT NAME = KATIE MCDIVITT
SKILL = SNAP DOWN TO LAYOUT     EVENT = FLOOR EXERCISE

SKILL PHASE DISPLAY

PHASE IN THIS DISPLAY = SNAP DOWN
FRAMES IN THIS DISPLAY ARE  7  TO  14
TIME DURATION = .1  SECONDS        SCALING FACTOR =  1
```

Figure 13-3

```
SUBJECT NAME = KATIE MCDIVITT
SKILL = SNAP DOWN TO LAYOUT     EVENT = FLOOR EXERCISE

SKILL PHASE DISPLAY

PHASE IN THIS DISPLAY = HANDS DEPARTING
FRAMES IN THIS DISPLAY ARE  14  TO  17
TIME DURATION =  .05  SECONDS        SCALING FACTOR =  1
```

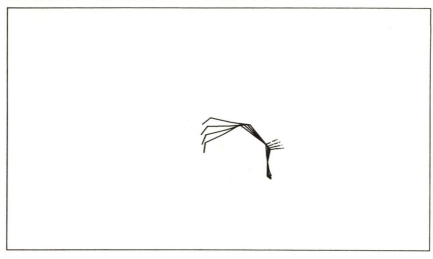

Figure 13-4

```
SUBJECT NAME = KATIE MCDIVITT
SKILL = SNAP DOWN TO LAYOUT     EVENT = FLOOR EXERCISE

SKILL PHASE DISPLAY

PHASE IN THIS DISPLAY = HANDS AIRBORNE
FRAMES IN THIS DISPLAY ARE  17  TO  23
TIME DURATION =  .0875  SECONDS        SCALING FACTOR =  1
```

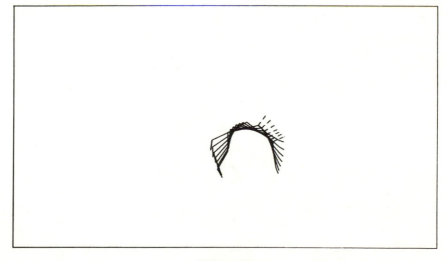

Figure 13-5

```
SUBJECT NAME = KATIE MCDIVITT
SKILL = SNAP DOWN TO LAYOUT      EVENT = FLOOR EXERCISE

SKILL PHASE DISPLAY

PHASE IN THIS DISPLAY = FOOT CONTACT
FRAMES IN THIS DISPLAY ARE  23  TO  27
TIME DURATION =  .0625  SECONDS        SCALING FACTOR =   1
```

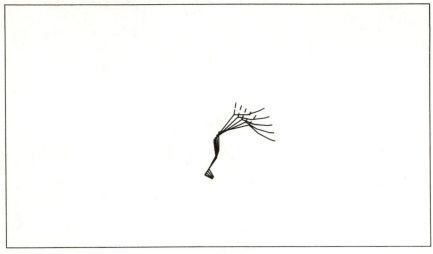

Figure 13-6

```
SUBJECT NAME = KATIE MCDIVITT
SKILL = SNAP DOWN TO LAYOUT      EVENT = FLOOR EXERCISE

SKILL PHASE DISPLAY

PHASE IN THIS DISPLAY = HEEL CONTACT
FRAMES IN THIS DISPLAY ARE  27  TO  29
TIME DURATION =  .0375  SECONDS        SCALING FACTOR =   1
```

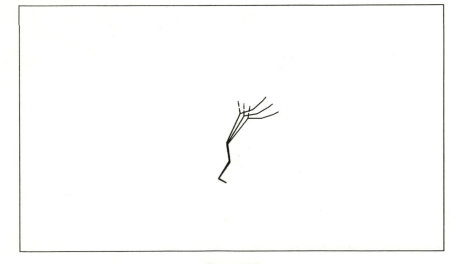

Figure 13-7

SUBJECT NAME = KATIE MCDIVITT
SKILL = SNAP DOWN TO LAYOUT   EVENT = FLOOR EXERCISE

SKILL PHASE DISPLAY

PHASE IN THIS DISPLAY = HEELS DEPART
FRAMES IN THIS DISPLAY ARE 29 TO 34
TIME DURATION = .075 SECONDS   SCALING FACTOR = 1

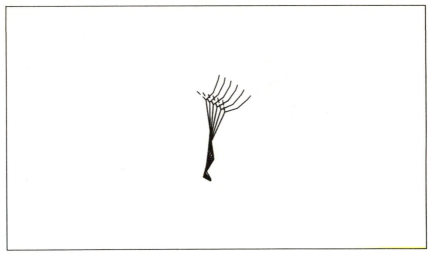

Figure 13-8

SUBJECT NAME = KATIE MCDIVITT
SKILL = SNAP DOWN TO LAYOUT   EVENT = FLOOR EXERCISE

SKILL PHASE DISPLAY

PHASE IN THIS DISPLAY = FEET DEPART
FRAMES IN THIS DISPLAY ARE 34 TO 46
TIME DURATION = .1625 SECONDS   SCALING FACTOR = 1

Figure 13-9

SUBJECT NAME = KATIE. MCDIVITT
SKILL = SNAP DOWN TO LAYOUT   EVENT = FLOOR EXERCISE.

SKILL PHASE. DISPLAY

PHASE IN THIS DISPLAY = PIKING
FRAMES IN THIS DISPLAY ARE 46 TO 66
TIME DURATION = .2625 SECONDS   SCALING FACTOR = 1

Figure 13-10

SUBJECT NAME = KATIE. MCDIVITT
SKILL = SNAP DOWN TO LAYOUT   EVENT = FLOOR EXERCISE.

SKILL PHASE. DISPLAY

PHASE IN THIS DISPLAY = SEES FLOOR
FRAMES IN THIS DISPLAY ARE 66 TO 82
TIME DURATION = .2125 SECONDS   SCALING FACTOR = 1

Figure 13-11

SUBJECT NAME = KATIE MCDIVITT
SKILL = SNAP DOWN TO LAYOUT   EVENT = FLOOR EXERCISE

SKILL PHASE DISPLAY

PHASE IN THIS DISPLAY = LANDING PREPARATION
FRAMES IN THIS DISPLAY ARE 82 TO 94
TIME DURATION = .1625 SECONDS   SCALING FACTOR = 1

Figure 13-12

SUBJECT NAME = KATIE MCDIVITT
SKILL = SNAP DOWN TO LAYOUT   EVENT = FLOOR EXERCISE

SKILL PHASE DISPLAY

PHASE IN THIS DISPLAY = FOOT LANDING CONTACT
FRAMES IN THIS DISPLAY ARE 94 TO 99
TIME DURATION = .075 SECONDS   SCALING FACTOR = 1

Figure 13-13

```
SUBJECT NAME = KATIE McDIVITT
SKILL = SNAP DOWN TO LAYOUT      EVENT = FLOOR EXERCISE

SKILL PHASE DISPLAY

PHASE IN THIS DISPLAY = FOOT CONTACT
FRAMES IN THIS DISPLAY ARE  23  TO  34
TIME DURATION =  .15  SECONDS        SCALING FACTOR =  1
```

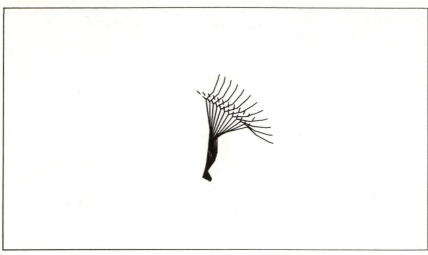

Figure 13-14

```
SUBJECT = KATIE McDIVITT
SKILL = SNAP DOWN TO LAYOUT       EVENT = FLOOR EXERCISE

LIMB PATH DISPLAY

LIMB IN THIS DISPLAY = LEFT LEG
FRAMES IN THIS DISPLAY ARE FROM  1  TO  23
TIME DURATION =  .2875  SECONDS        SCALING FACTOR =  1
```

Figure 13-15

```
SUBJECT = KATIE MCDIVITT
SKILL = SNAP DOWN TO LAYOUT        EVENT = FLOOR EXERCISE

LIMB PATH DISPLAY

LIMB IN THIS DISPLAY = LEFT LEG
FRAMES IN THIS DISPLAY ARE FROM   23  TO  34
TIME DURATION =  .15  SECONDS         SCALING FACTOR =  1
```

Figure 13-16

```
SUBJECT = KATIE MCDIVITT
SKILL = SNAP DOWN TO LAYOUT        EVENT = FLOOR EXERCISE

LIMB PATH DISPLAY

LIMB IN THIS DISPLAY = LEFT LEG
FRAMES IN THIS DISPLAY ARE FROM   23  TO  34
TIME DURATION =  .15  SECONDS         SCALING FACTOR =  1.2
```

Figure 13-17

SUBJECT = KATIE MCDIVITT
SKILL = SNAP DOWN TO LAYOUT   EVENT = FLOOR EXERCISE

LIMB PATH DISPLAY

LIMB IN THIS DISPLAY = LEFT LEG
FRAMES IN THIS DISPLAY ARE FROM 34 TO 94
TIME DURATION = .7625 SECONDS   SCALING FACTOR = 1

Figure 13-18

SUBJECT = KATIE MCDIVITT
SKILL = SNAP DOWN TO LAYOUT   EVENT = FLOOR EXERCISE

LIMB PATH DISPLAY

LIMB IN THIS DISPLAY = LEFT LEG
FRAMES IN THIS DISPLAY ARE FROM 94 TO 99
TIME DURATION = .075 SECONDS   SCALING FACTOR = 1

Figure 13-19

SUBJECT = KATIE MCDIVITT
SKILL = SNAP DOWN TO LAYOUT   EVENT = FLOOR EXERCISE

LIMB PATH DISPLAY

LIMB IN THIS DISPLAY = TORSO
FRAMES IN THIS DISPLAY ARE FROM   1   TO 23
TIME DURATION = .2875 SECONDS   SCALING FACTOR = 1

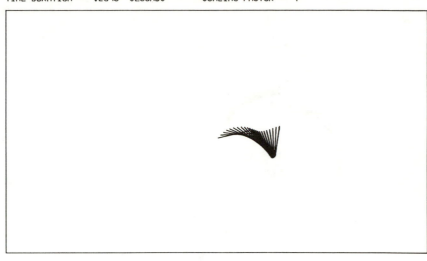

Figure 13-20

SUBJECT = KATIE MCDIVITT
SKILL = SNAP DOWN TO LAYOUT   EVENT = FLOOR EXERCISE

LIMB PATH DISPLAY

LIMB IN THIS DISPLAY = TORSO
FRAMES IN THIS DISPLAY ARE FROM 23 TO 34
TIME DURATION = .15 SECONDS   SCALING FACTOR = 1

Figure 13-21

```
SUBJECT = KATIE MCDIVITT
SKILL = SNAP DOWN TO LAYOUT        EVENT = FLOOR EXERCISE

LIMB PATH DISPLAY

LIMB IN THIS DISPLAY = TORSO
FRAMES IN THIS DISPLAY ARE FROM  34  TO  94
TIME DURATION =  .7625  SECONDS        SCALING FACTOR =  1
```

Figure 13-22

```
SUBJECT = KATIE MCDIVITT
SKILL = SNAP DOWN TO LAYOUT        EVENT = FLOOR EXERCISE

LIMB PATH DISPLAY

LIMB IN THIS DISPLAY = TORSO
FRAMES IN THIS DISPLAY ARE FROM  94  TO  99
TIME DURATION =  .075  SECONDS        SCALING FACTOR =  1
```

Figure 13-23

SUBJECT = KATIE MCDIVITT
SKILL = SNAP DOWN TO LAYOUT   EVENT = FLOOR EXERCISE
BODY PART PATH DIAGRAM

FIRST BODY PART = LEFT FOOT   SOLID LINE
SECOND BODY PART = LEFT KNEE   DOTTED LINE
TIME DURATION = 1.2375 SECONDS   SCALING FACTOR = 1
FRAMES DISPLAYED ARE FROM 1 TO 99

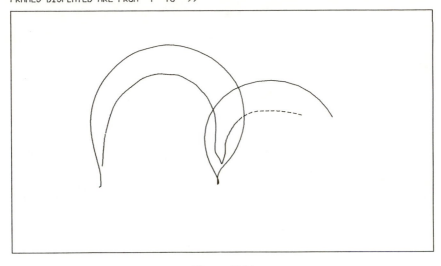

Figure 13-24

SUBJECT = KATIE MCDIVITT
SKILL = SNAP DOWN TO LAYOUT   EVENT = FLOOR EXERCISE
BODY PART PATH DIAGRAM

FIRST BODY PART = LEFT HIP   SOLID LINE
SECOND BODY PART = LEFT SHOULDER   DOTTED LINE
TIME DURATION = 1.2375 SECONDS   SCALING FACTOR = 1
FRAMES DISPLAYED ARE FROM 1 TO 99

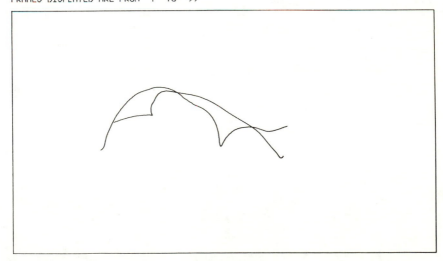

Figure 13-25

```
SUBJECT = KATIE MCDIVITT
SKILL = SNAP DOWN TO LAYOUT      EVENT = FLOOR EXERCISE
BODY PART PATH DIAGRAM

FIRST BODY PART = LEFT ELBOW    SOLID LINE
SECOND BODY PART = LEFT HAND    DOTTED LINE
TIME DURATION = 1.2375  SECONDS       SCALING FACTOR =  1
FRAMES DISPLAYED ARE FROM  1  TO  99
```

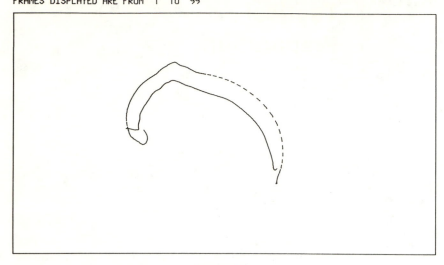

Figure 13-26

```
SUBJECT = KATIE MCDIVITT
SKILL = SNAP DOWN TO LAYOUT      EVENT = FLOOR EXERCISE
BODY PART PATH DIAGRAM

FIRST BODY PART = HEAD    SOLID LINE
SECOND BODY PART = CENTER OF MASS   DOTTED LINE
TIME DURATION = 1.2375  SECONDS       SCALING FACTOR =  1
FRAMES DISPLAYED ARE FROM  1  TO  99
```

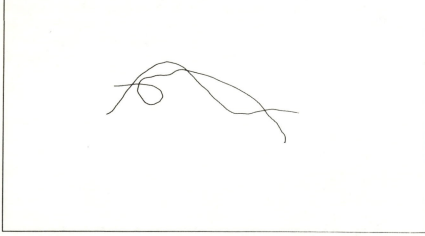

Figure 13-27

14

Tactical
Preparation

Tactical preparation is the strategic preparation of the athlete. Strategy does not come up in coaching discussions very often since it is a part of preparation that gets little emphasis. The strategy of gymnastics is not immediately apparent to the uninitiated. There are strategic ways of looking at gymnastics that go beyond those present in other sports (the surprise play, a new player on the field, holding out until you see the whites of their eyes, etc.). Gymnastics strategy usually gets underemphasized because of the concern with the technical portions of gymnastics preparation.

The tactics of gymnastics include the selection of skills and their timing in the learning sequence of the gymnast. A second aspect of tactics is the selection of competitions and their importance to the development and rank of the gymnast. And then there is a strategy within competitions that involves team order for development of team score, all-around score, or individual event medals. Playing strategy in gymnastics is like a poker game. Each facet of gymnastics is given a certain card with a suit and value. The coach and athlete then must play these cards in the best possible fashion to achieve the finest results. The results may or may not win but the tactical presentation of the cards at the right time and in the right order can enhance or detract from the process of reaching for and attaining the goal.

SKILL SELECTION

The tactical area of skill selection includes several subcategories: the tactics of learning skills, the tactics of routine construction, and the tactics of routine composition. Skill learning has a tactical side because of the inherent movement concepts present in skills.

Learning psychology has told us that it is very difficult to learn a new response to an old stimulus. For example, a gymnast who is accustomed to doing her twisting in a certain fashion from a round-off flip-flop may be very competent. The gymnast may want to learn an Arabian for her floor exercise. In the learning of the Arabian one should probably try to learn twisting for fulls and double fulls before attempting the Arabian from a flip-flop so that the two take-off techniques are not confused and the gymnast (especially if she is optic) tries to learn two different but similar take-off techniques from the same skill. It would be wiser, or more tactically sound, to learn the Arabian from the round-off so that the gymnast will not confuse the two. Furthermore, the Arabian usually leads to another round-off through to another somersault. The gymnast who must perform the Arabian from the flip-flop will use up a lot of space for the flip-flop and therefore cannot run very far to the hurdle. This does not leave much room for the remainder of the tumbling pass to be performed within the limits of the diagonal. This example of the use of the Arabian is an example of tactical preparation regarding that particular skill and its use.

There are many examples of skill selection that can have a bearing on the progress and potential of our gymnast. The use of tinsicas in compulsories and learning is a grave error, in my opinion. These skills are done with inherent crookedness and since the gymnast will be forced to drill them to achieve a level of consistency and perfection, the gymnast is enhancing the imbalanced development of her shoulder flexibility. If the gymnast must do tinsicas, it would be wise for her to perform many tinsicas on her weak side to avoid crookedness resulting from drilling the same qualities on both sides.

The selection of vaults is important, not only from the standpoint of the gymnast's learning, but from the standpoint of acceptability of the judges. For example, I remember well a national championship competition in which I had a gymnast performing a handspring with a double twist on vaulting. This vault is extremely difficult—much more difficult than a Tsukahara or handspring front. This gymnast had flight and distance and she finished the twist. In fact, in 17 years of coaching I have never seen anyone else ever do a handspring with a double twist. She got a 9.2 for the vault that stuck. Tucked Tsukaharas and other vaults of considerably less difficulty beat her. She could do a good pike Tsukahara but we elected to perform the double twisting handspring. It was a big mistake. The judges simply did not appreciate the immense difficulty of this vault. They are more interested in vaults that somersault. A somersaulting vault looks difficult, no matter who looks at it. The idea of risk is supposed to embody the concept of risking a fall, not risking an injury, but the appreciation of the judge and perhaps most everyone else indicates that you had better somersault in vaulting if you want to win.

Tactical selection of skills should answer some of the following questions.

- Will the skill be useful for the learning of other skills, or will it interfere?
- Will the technique selected allow the gymnast to transfer the learning to more difficult skills, or is it a "dead end?"
- Can the gymnast perform this skill at the end of her routine as well as the beginning?
- Will the judges appreciate the difficulty or the elegance of the skill?
- Does the gymnast need it to satisfy a composition requirement or is it simply "overkill" because the gymnast already satisfies all the requirements?
- Is the skill necessary—even though it does represent "overkill"—because this gymnast will be in contention for medals on that particular event, or will it make the routine so relentless in difficulty that it will force some form errors that would not be there if the gymnast could do an easier skill?
- Will the skill fit the structure of the routine?
- Will the gymnast have to dismount onto the board of the beam routine or need to use several connections to face the right way to dismount?
- Will the dismount be easy to land (in other words, can the gymnast see the floor)?
- Is the skill attractive when viewed from all directions?
- Will the skill make the gymnast susceptible to injury because of the number of repetitions that must be performed in order to become consistent?

Our national escalation of difficulty at the expense of technical excellence, and of elegance, has shown that we do not understand tactical preparation of skills.

TACTICS FOR VAULTING

I believe that every gymnast should be able to perform several different vaults. In the learning stages we try to get each gymnast to perform a handspring to front somersault type of vault and a Tsukahara type of vault. In the beginning the gymnast will be immediately successful at the Tsukaharas because of their simplicity. I always have my gymnasts learn the handspring front vaults also, since they often become valuable later when the gymnast is accomplished and needs an ultradifficult vault. The drilling of the handspring helps further refine the run and hurdle for the young gymnast. The use of some statistics can show the types of vaults that receive the highest scores. I scouted the 1981 European championships in Madrid and kept some extensive statistics on the type of work done. The top six nations performed only a handful of vaults: the layout Tsukahara, tuck Tsukahara with a full twist, Cuervo, handspring front tuck, pike Tsukahara, and layout Tsukahara with a full twist. Table 14-1 shows the distribution of scores and number of vaults as shown at this competition.

TABLE 14-1   Vault Distribution

Type	Number Performed	% Total	Average Score	Range
Layout Tsukahara	20	55.55	9.53	9.4 –9.65
Tsukahara full tuck	6	16.66	9.74	9.65-9.8
Cuervo	4	11.11	9.73	9.65-9.8
Handspring front tuck	3	8.33	9.50	9.45-9.55
Pike Tsukahara	2	5.55	8.85	
Layout Tsukahara full twist	1	2.77	9.65	

This table shows us that the most popular vault was the layout Tsukahara, and it seems to be a pretty good scoring vault, with a range of 9.4-9.65. If you want to get higher scoring vaults, then you might look to the Cuervo or the tuck Tsukahara with a full twist. They are done about 25% less often and show a range of scores from 9.65-9.8, indicating that you could win with these vaults. The tuck Tsukahara with a full twist looks to be the best "bread and butter" vault, because it has a slightly higher average score than the others and we know that it's a little easier to learn than the Cuervo. Note that there were none of the full-on types of vaults done or handspring fronts with a half twist. This is interesting, but may require further study. You could look at these statistics and see which vaults to aim for when you are making tactical decisions prior to designing training curriculums and determining skill drills. It's a good idea to keep such statistics on each event during the different competitions of the year; it will soon become apparent what level of work is required to win at each level of competition. This can help you design a training curriculum that will get you to a competitive stature quickly and surely.

The advent of the new round-off to the board and flip-flop or Arabian dive to the horse will throw a wrench in the above statistics, because these vaults were not being performed competitively at that time. Watch carefully the outcome of certain skills, since there seems to be a ceiling level to the scores attached to these skills. The best gymnasts should not be training skills that have this score ceiling attached; they should be working on skills that will always open doors to higher difficulty, execution, and scoring potential.

Vaulting is the only event in which the gymnast gets two attempts. The gymnast should always use the second attempt to make a better vault than the first attempt. Furthermore, the gymnast should not foul up the first one if she is going to perform two in a row, because the judges seem to attach a ceiling to the second vault score. The gymnast should try to perform her best vault twice in preliminary or competition I-B so that she has two opportunities to stick it; then if the second one is better than the first, she will have the first score to build from.

TACTICS ON UNEVEN BARS

The uneven bars should utilize skills that are easy to connect and allow the gymnast the opportunity to cover up an error without anyone noticing. To promote learning routines and ease the composition problems of the youngest gymnasts, I made a major tactical decision to avoid whipping skills, teach as many of the large swing skills as possible (late dropping, free hips, stalders, etc.), and keep the dismount simple. The categories of skills that the young gymnast must perform are a somersault skill, a twisting skill, a large swing skill to handstand on the high bar, and a dismount with a somersault. These can be satisfied in a variety of ways and many skills fit into these categories. You simply must select those that fit and have the appropriate connections.

The more advanced gymnast should look to men's high bar for clues as to the probable direction of the event. Women's uneven bars usually lags about 3 years behind men's horizontal bar. The increased prevalence of releases on high bar in men's gymnastics brought about a similar increase in releases on women's uneven bars—but later. The gymnast should attempt to get the elements in her routine accomplished with a minimum number of connections, and as close as possible to the necessary total number of skills required under composition. The gymnast should always have a plan for covering up a mistake if something goes wrong. The only times that these plans usually break down is on release skills. If the gymnast misses a release she is usually in for a fall, so the releases should be selected carefully to ensure consistency. The gymnast will usually feel more confident with a routine constructed so that it is difficult to fall.

Constructing a routine that makes consistency a simple matter will aid in performance and score. The ultradifficult skills that the gifted bar worker will perform should be drilled for a long time, and their consistency should be demonstrated before they are placed in the routine. I have often seen the very talented uneven bar worker using a routine that is simply too complex to be consistent, and she frequently makes errors or has form problems. Complexity for its own sake is not a sound compositional goal.

The uneven bars should be carefully planned for each gymnast so that no one learns a skill that cannot be used because she can't connect it. The gymnast should not be performing a routine that is so complex and difficult that there is no time during the routine for her to collect herself before major difficulties. The gymnast should have a variety of dismounts at her disposal so that she can get off the bars safely when she has made an error and is fatigued at the end of the routine. The coach should plan carefully to cover for every eventuality in performance.

AN EXAMPLE OF TACTICAL PREPARATION: MY COMPULSORY-OPTIONAL

Consideration of these categories led me to construct a "compulsory-optional" routine that each young gymnast of mine must learn on uneven bars as her first routine. The routine allows for easy connections, it is safe, it allows for easy addition of new skills, and the gymnasts can perform it without need for exact bar settings. The mount consists of a glide kip on the low bar facing the high bar. Then there is an immediate cast to somersault over the low bar and catch the high bar. This is followed by a half turn to drop glide to the low bar. Then a kip with a half turn to catch the high bar is followed by a long hang kip and immediate cast to two free hip circles in a row. The gymnast then straddles onto the high bar, performs a sole circle to underswing with a half turn and swings down to tap the low bar with her thighs. After tapping her thighs on the low bar she swings backward and upward to release to a front somersault tucked to landing facing the high bar. The routine is performed during the early education of the gymnast; only rarely will she use it to compete. Individual differences and strengths and weaknesses soon channel the gymnast into other skills, but this routine forms a consistent way of beginning. Changing the routine (by adding new skills) is very easy so that progress is unimpeded.

The typical changes to the routine that occur as the gymnast progresses can be inserted at any time. Instead of the kip half turn catch, the gymnast can do a kip catch, sit on the low bar, and kip to the high bar and cast to handstand. The handstand is followed by a pirouette and whip to the low bar. The two free hips can be substituted for by inserting a toe on and off, stalder, or giant swing as the skills are accomplished. Instead of the underswing with a half turn into the dismount the gymnast can do a toe on front or Comaneci dismount. The two free hips could lead to a Deltchev or a reverse hecht without upsetting the structure of the routine. This "compulsory-optional" routine also serves a variety of educational and safety functions.

Each skill and routine should continually open more doors for higher difficulty or better execution. The over-the-bar somersault mount was chosen because it is safer than a Brause and more directly simulates the types of regrasps done from a Deltchev. The over-the-bar somersault is usually missed safely as the gymnast will land on her seat or feet if she should miss her grip on the high bar. The Brause usually has the gymnast landing on her back if she misses the high bar. The Brause also seems to allow the gymnast to confuse the cast and land on her back on the low bar. The half turn to drop glide was selected simply because it is hard. This forces the gymnast to drop efficiently, straight, and have a strong kip for the next skill. The kip half turn catch was selected because it forces the gymnast to kip strongly. This is usually the first skill to change as the gymnast will soon do a handstand pirouette on the high bar to turn around. The two free hips are used so that the gymnast must perform two large swinging skills to handstand on the high bar. The dismount is performed from a straddle onto an underswing half turn and swing down to tap the low bar with the thighs. The gymnast then swings backward and upward with a "hecht beat" to release and a front somersault to a stand. The principal reason for selecting this dismount is because it is pretty easy to understand, the gymnast does not fall from great heights, if she misses she will land on her seat rather than her head or back, and it provides some learning about landing forward rotating dismounts with greater safety. A related tactical decision for dismounts is that we try never to do dismounts or vaults that are essentially a forward somersault. This is because I have witnessed a few injuries caused by landing on a straight leg and injuring the knee through hyperextension. The uneven bar dismount chosen for the compulsory-optional routine does rotate and land forward, but it is moving backward. In other words, even though the gymnast is rotating forward she is swinging backward or away from the direction of the impact of straightening legs. This adds a measure of safety since the gymnast can land with nearly straight legs but avoid injury by simply sitting down. The routine is not very long and allows the young gymnast to perform a routine quickly that will not close doors to her later development.

TACTICS ON BALANCE BEAM

The balance beam is the great equalizer of women's gymnastics. The skills on balance beam are not inherently difficult; most gymnasts can perform them easily on the floor. The difficulty comes from the narrowness of the supporting surface and the very nerve required to complete the event without falling. Gymnasts usually look at balance beam as a threat and an event to be "conquered." Many an all-around championship has been decided by the balance beam—especially at the highest levels, where the gymnasts are not so easily differentiated on the basis of the other three events. This puts a significant amount of pressure on the one event that can produce large deductions in score very quickly. The gymnast can be moved from contention to a position far from placing with one fall from the beam. This would indicate that the tactics of balance beam are particularly crucial to performance.

The balance beam requires the most time in training to achieve competence and the most dogged determination to avoid learning poor habits. Gymnasts who have a good dance background generally do better on balance beam than those who do not. The alignment of the gymnast is of paramount importance in determining her ability to stay on the balance beam. This means that the young gymnast should have extensive dance training along with her gymnastics training. I am not convinced that the older and more accomplished gymnasts really reap much benefit from continued dance training. The pattern seems to be set when they are younger and the older gymnasts simply work with the habits gained during early training. I believe that dance training is even more important than the learning of tricks for the young gymnast. The young gymnast must be familiar with tricks on the balance beam, but it does not appear to take nearly as long to teach her how to perform the skill on the balance beam as it does to keep her alignment through the variety of dance and gymnastics skills that she will have to be competent at.

The tactical decisions involved with routine composition on balance beam are similar to those of uneven bars in principle. The routine should not be of relentless difficuty, and should avoid complexity for complexity's sake. A few statistics in balance beam are also somewhat easy to keep. At the 1981 European Championships I kept statistics on balance beam for analysis of the types of skills being performed. Table 14-2 gives an indication of the types of skills performed by the top six nations at the 1981 European Championships and a ratio of how many of these skills were performed per routine of these nations.

The top six nations included 18 gymnasts. The mounts broke down into 50% a jump or press handstand, 12% from a round-off to the board for takeoff, 5% headsprings, and 33% were other miscellaneous mounts. The dismounts consisted of 27% a round-off to a double somersault, 5% cartwheel to double somersault, 5% flip-flop to double somersault, 12% flip-flop to a double twist, 16% were a double twist from anything else, and 33% were other types of dismounts. Interestingly, the dance skills on

TABLE 14-2   Skills Performed at 1981 European Championships

Type of Skill	Number Performed	Number/Routine
Layout step out	12	.65
Flip-flops	31	1.89
Aerials	15	.82
Back somersaults	11	.61
Front somersaults	2	.10

balance beam were not well developed. There was only one turn in the entire meet that was more than the simple full turn required under composition.

A coach could look at these statistics and see that a good tactical decision for high-level athletes might be to encourage them to learn a dismount that is a double somersault, since the top six nations in the world are using a double somersault dismount almost a third of the time. The coach might see that dance is being deemphasized and therefore opt for a more trick-oriented routine and concomitant training. These types of decisions must be made frequently; you should always keep one ear to the ground to determine the pattern and direction of training to keep the athletes learning the skills and techniques that will keep them in contention.

In my opinion, the path international gymnastics is taking on balance beam is not in keeping with a very artistic approach. The balance beam should be theatre on a stick. It should be floor exercise elevated above the floor. It should be a question of elegance, art, creativity, and movement. What we are developing on balance beam is a wooden tightwire act that has no redeeming characteristics other than risk. After all, if the gymnast were to perform a single tuck back on the floor in her floor exercise routine, everyone would be sick. The only redeeming characteristic of a tuck back on balance beam is its risk. I may have allowed a tactical blunder by allowing gymnasts to perform skills that are more dance-oriented and easily more difficult and fall-producing than a tuck back, but I do not believe that balance beam should continue on the path it is going. Elegance has been sacrificed in the name of difficulty, crucified on the cross of "risk."

One of the most important tactical coaching approaches for balance beam is in how the event is observed. You have eight places from which to evaluate each routine. You should stand at each end, both sides, and all four corners: from the ends you will be able to see alignment problems, from the side you can detect technical problems, and from the four corners you can see what the judge will likely see. This helps you do a better job. Sometimes the long hours of training engender a sort of complacency that allows you to become lethargic about seeing as much as possible. The usual problems of balance beam performance are easy to see if you watch carefully. Move around the beam area in a pattern that will allow you to watch the routines and skills from all these positions. You'll find that this will help you be a better judge of existing and potential problems.

In constructing the routine, you should include certain categories of skills. For instance, the gymnast should have a two- or three-trick combination that includes a somersault. She should have at least one aerial skill, a handstand, a turn that is more than a full, a leap or jump with a turn, and a dismount with more than one twist or more than one somersault. These guidelines can help you and the gymnast begin training skills that will ensure variety. The skills should remain as symmetrical as possible. (Skills that are not symmetrical are most likely to produce balance errors and falls.)

The routine should last only a short period past the minimum time requirement to allow the gymnast to spend less time at risk of making mistakes, and—if she should fall—to retain a relatively relaxed pace through the remainder of the routine without having to worry about going overtime. The gymnast should have a choreographed set-up for each major difficulty. This set-up is a natural position and a short pause that allows the gymnast to make any last-minute corrections necessary to ensure alignment.

The balance beam is well recognized as the most threatening event. Because the event is so devastating in determining placings a conservatism has covered the event and caused it to become just plain boring. Although some difficult skills are being performed, the event has ended up being mostly tumbling on a small surface. Careful coaching of the event through long and thorough preparation of each skill and combination can make balance beam an artistic event. Unfortunately, in our zeal to create champions fast we cannot perform this type of preparation. The preparation of a complete balance beam worker who can perform her skills with alignment and elegance is the most challenging part of balance beam coaching. It is not the most glamorous, however. It is not as spectacular as the full-in. It takes an educated and artistic person to appreciate the work. But, in my opinion, it is worth it.

TACTICS FOR FLOOR EXERCISE

The tactical decisions in floor exercise include: choice of tumbling, choice of dance skills, choice of music, and choice of structure. The choice of tumbling can again be helped with some statistics. Most routines contain three tumbling passes with a fourth tumbling sequence that might be called simple tumbling (such as an aerial walkover, or backwalkover pirouette). Table 14-3 shows the types of tumbling included by the gymnasts of the top six nations at the 1981 European Championships.

You can quickly see that first passes should contain a double somersault if possible. The second pass is usually twisting and the third pass is more than a third double somersaulting but 50% use a double twist. The young gymnast should see that a double twist can go a pretty long way in helping to satisfy the tumbling requirements. The more advanced gymnast should seek a double somersault. The gifted gymnast should use a variation of a double somersault that is not of the typical round-off flip-flop double somersault sequence by using a combination to the double somersault or twisting the double somersault. Finally, the gymnast should try and select some kind of stationary tumbling skill that will be eye-catching and enhance the general appearance of the routine without gathering deductions or increasing fatigue.

TABLE 14-3   Breakdown of Tumbling Types at 1981 European Championships

First Pass

Type of Pass	Percent
Round-off flip-flop double tuck	27.77
Round-off flip-flop double pike	27.77
Round-off flip-flop full-in	16.66
Whip backs through to double salto	11.11
1½ step out to double salto	5.55
Round-off flip-flop triple twist	5.55
Round-off double twist	5.55

Second Pass

Type of Pass	Percent
Round-off flip-flop double twist	22.22
Round-off flip-flop triple twist	11.11
Round-off flip-flop 1½ through to tuck	11.11
Round-off flip-flop full	5.55
Handspring front layout round-off full	5.55
Round-off flip-flop full flip-flop full	5.55
Round-off Arabian round-off tuck	5.55
Front step out round-off flip-flop double twist	5.55
Round-off full twisting flip-flop	5.55
Round-off flip-flop double tuck	5.55
Round-off flip-flop Arabian round-off double twist	5.55
Round-off flip-flop 1½ twist punch front	5.55
Round-off flip-flop full flip-flop full twist flip-flop	5.55

Third Pass

Type of Pass	Percent
Round-off flip-flop double twist	44.44
Round-off flip-flop double pike	22.22
Round-off flip-flop double tuck	16.66
Round-off flip-flop full	5.55
Round-off flip-flop Arabian round-off flip-flop double twist	5.55
Round-off flip-flop Arabian round-off layout	5.55

The dance, music, and structure of the routine is very much determined by the personality of the gymnast and her personal tastes. The music should inspire her. The dance should exaggerate her strengths and hide her weaknesses. The structure should allow her to perform the entire routine with ease so that hard dance skills and difficult tumbling can be performed with safety and consistency.

Since dance occupies the most time in the routine, it must have audience appeal and no deductions. Each gymnast has particular strengths and weaknesses in dance. The strong-legged tumblers should also be able to leap, run, and jump well. The elegant dancers who might not tumble powerfully can perform axle turns, multiple turns, spins, and illusions from skating to gain their score by artistry. The most important tactical decision a coach can make about the dance in floor exercise is that gymnastics has not even scratched the surface of what dance has to offer floor exercise. Our approach to the dance of floor exercise is largely two-dimensional: score and consistency. Only a few gymnasts have stepped into the realm of actually dancing in floor exercise rather than simply executing the movements they were taught. Again, the climate of gymnastics is to produce gymnasts fast and assembly-line the champions. The extensive and intensive training necessary to perform the dance portions of floor exercise take many years. We should all increase our knowledge about the dance areas that are so important to floor exercise. Increased appreciation of the subtle nuances of the dance should improve floor exercise as an event. In this country there are few people knowledgeable about the dance of floor exercise. We should encourage them and emphasize this portion of our floor exercise routines to enhance all facets of the event.

The structure of the routine usually consists of a short dance sequence so as not to fatigue the gymnast prior to her first tumbling run. The first tumbling run is the most difficult because of the constraints of fatigue present in later portions of the routine. The second tumbling pass is done quickly so that the gymnast still has some energy left. The major portion of dance is performed next with a slowdown of the pace near the end of the dance sequence so the gymnast can rest a little before the last tumbling run. After the last tumbling run the gymnast usually dances for a short time to the ending. It does not take long for someone to see that this structure is very wise when the gymnast is performing difficult tumbling. The only way to do it much differently is by extraordinary conditioning to avoid the fatigue problems. You should try to vary this pattern when possible to make it more interesting and draw attention to the routine. And in the routine, use a tumbling pass with something other than a double salto or a double twist. There are many unusual tumbling skills the gymnast can perform, such as full and a half twisting dive rolls, twisting aerials, butterflies, barrel turns, and so on.

TACTICS FOR TEAM COMPETITION

The tactical decisions that surround team competition may not be immediately apparent to you if you've never taken a team into competition that was in contention to win or had a placement of significance at stake. The gymnastics team entering competition usually consists of six members, although there are team competitions with less. The six-member team competes on eight events (four compulsory and four optional). There are six scores available for each event and five of these six scores usually count for the team score. The competing team is allowed to drop the lowest score from the total. Therefore, five gymnasts have to complete their routines without error for the highest score available for that particular team. The event scores are added together for the total team score which determines the winner and the team placement. The coach must tactically choose the six best athletes on each event through instinct, statistics, past experience, and consistency in training and previous competitions. The decision of which athletes will compete is usually not very difficult. You go with the best people. The question may arise as to whether to go with the flashy gymnast who may gain a high score but lacks consistency, or to go with the gymnast who may not score as high but is usually more consistent and will be less likely to fall. This is often the greatest gamble of all. There are many other factors associated with this decision. Can the team win with a mediocre score? Are individual medals important as well as the team score? Will the all-around be sacrificed due to a fall and the concomitant loss of score-building by a particular gymnast? These additional factors are all important for you to consider in setting the team lineup.

Once you establish the team personnel, you can then begin to determine the order of competition. The order of competition of the athletes is important for score building. It is traditional in gymnastics that the gymnasts will compete in their order of competence on the team, from least competent to most competent. The judges and officials will expect this to happen. It is even logical from a performance standpoint to save the best for last. This sets up a peculiar format for the awarding of scores to the gymnasts as they perform their exercises. Each score is usually a tenth or two higher than the previous score in succession as the athletes perform. This is traditional, everyone expects it to work that way, and in fact it does. You can take advantage of this tradition by simply knowing it is likely to happen. When a team has a very significant all-around performer who is in contention to win, and the team goal is to have her win, she should go up last on every event to ensure that she will get the score traditionally attached to being last on the event. If the team has a weak performer then this performer should probably not go up first. If the weakest performer goes up first then the scores might go 8.8, 9.0, 9.1, 9.3, 9.4, 9.6. The 8.8 is thrown out and the total is calculated. If the weak gymnast goes up third then the scores might go 9.0, 9.1, 9.1, 9.3, 9.4, 9.6. This is a natural building of scores as everyone expects but the team score has been increased by a tenth because instead of counting a 9.0 the team is counting a 9.1. All the gymnasts did the same routines but the placement of the gymnasts in the order has affected the scores awarded. If all the gymnasts are of similar ability then one might best choose to play the order of competition straight. There is a gamble in all this because if any of the middle gymnasts fall then the building process begins from a lower score and the later gymnasts in the order will have difficulty building their scores from the preceding scores.

Here's an example of how this phenomenon works—it happened to me in college while competing. My coach planned a "trick" on the judges and reversed all the normal orders of competition. I won floor exercise when I was clearly the worst one on the team. The judges finally caught on by the fourth event. This underscores the point that in team competition the order of competition of the athletes will have a great bearing on the outcome of the scores. So you should carefully study the order of competition before submitting the list to the meet officials. The gymnasts should understand how the order of competition works so that there are no misunderstandings of the goals involved. If the team, not an individual, comes first, then a few gymnasts may have to be sacrificed to hide a weaker gymnast in the middle. If the all-around is most important, then the all-around contender should go up last on every event to assure that she gets the scores that will build to help her all-around total. If individual event medals are most important then the best athlete on that event must go up last so that this gymnast will get the necessary score.

It is vitally important that the gymnasts understand this tactic. Often a gymnast who might be a better beam worker than another will go up earlier in the lineup to help start the building of scores at a higher place. The stronger gymnast might also go up earlier so that a weaker gymnast can be hidden in the middle. The only times when these tactics are inappropriate are when the team is an easy winner or not in contention. Then the order can be used to promote the all-around or individual event medals, or played straight to simply rank the gymnasts in their order of competence.

Of course, all these tactics rely on the ability of the gymnast to hit her routines. If any of the gymnasts do not hit then the tactics for order of competition fall apart. The compulsory section of competition is usually where these tactics are played with most success. The optional portion of competition usually dictates an order that depends partly on how the compulsories went. If a gymnast has fallen in compulsories, then she is usually out of contention for the all-around, so she can be used earlier in the lineup to help build the scores of the gymasts who still have a chance of winning or being in contention. If you have a gymnast who is likely to fall, then you should decide if it would be better to put her up first and take it on the chin right away (to build scores with only five gymnasts) or to put her up last so that if she falls she will not unnerve any gymnast who would otherwise have to follow her, knowing that her score *must* now count.

CONCLUSION

Study the rules of gymnastics very carefully. If you are smart and play your cards right, you can enhance the scoring potential of your team through many avenues. You are being a little naive about the process and tactics of gymnastics if you are simply relying on the gymnasts to hit their routines. If you select skills carefully, promote skills that will lead to other skills without generating bad habits, and become street-wise about some competitive circumstances, you can help the young gymnast realize her goals with greater ease.

15

Theoretical Preparation

Theoretical preparation is attitude and spirit preparation. The attitude of the gymnast toward herself, her coach, significant others, competition, gymnastics, politics, and so on must be identified and defined. Theoretical preparation is a sort of athletic version of values clarification that should help each gymnast better understand herself, her abilities, her goals, and her relationships with others through gymnastics.

Many things will come up during the years of training that will have a potentially profound effect on the athlete's attitudes and self-concept. The gymnast must come to deal with long hours of hard work with little early recognition; she may be injured, she will face failure and success, she will face people who do not want her to do well, and she will face many perceived injustices. The spirit of the gymnast must be sturdy and determined. You must nurture and inform this spirit in gymnastics-related matters and you must exemplify the qualities of justice, truth, and consistency. The serious young gymnast is growing up as she continues her training, and as coaches, we can help her become more adult and independent. We can teach the gymnast a lot more than how to do a flip-flop.

Theoretical preparation is really *applied* philosophy. The philosophy included in Part I will give you a good idea of what I believe is an appropriate philosophy for the coach of gymnastics. The theoretical preparation of the gymnast involves a few specific concepts: handling success and failure, understanding the inequities and the injustices of gymnastics, and understanding the achievement motive. These three concepts are those most often faced by the inquisitive young gymnast. As the gymnast grows through sport and other life activities she will become puzzled at double standards and her role in the total gymnastics and sport picture.

SUCCESS AND FAILURE

A difficult concept for young gymnasts to understand is that the value of a person does not depend upon her ability as a gymnast. An athlete can be a valuable person and still not place first in a particular competition. In other words, the worth of a human being is not determined by her competitive rank. This has become a little clouded in western sport where winning is not only everything, but if you do not win you are nothing. Although no one likes to lose, the child must understand her realistic ability and potential to win. Although she need not be satisfied with her placement at every competition she should be happy that she struggled as hard as she could. Even in a loss there are significant things to be learned.

The successful gymnast cannot come to believe that she is indestructible and the failing gymnast cannot come to believe that she is unsalvageable. Very few people understand the mental agony an athlete must go through to give her best. This is a factor that I have tried to communicate to media people with little success. Take a child who is performing a sport in which everyone expects her to act like an adult: she should not cry, should not fail, and should always be goal-directed. The fact that many of our young athletes can do this is remarkable, considering the pressure they are under. Time and again I have seen the character of a gymnast questioned by the media as they try to drum up some human interest. We must do everything we can to encourage athletes to understand that success and failure are simply two sides of the same coin. Neither will make them happy or unhappy automatically. The gymnast must be prepared to understand where success and failure belong in her striving for achievement.

Success and failure are both powerful teachers and motivators for achievement. Real victory may be won by the gymnast who places tenth rather than first. Rank 10 may have stretched her abilities to the absolute limit: she may have come to understand that she is worthwhile and that she has much to offer herself and others. Most importantly, rank 10 may make her understand that she can do whatever she sets her mind and ability to. She may not be the best, but she can be one of the best. Winning may not be everything, but striving and struggling to win is. This can bring success or failure, depending upon how she would like to label it. The gymnast must be taught to understand and trust her instincts enough to know the difference between success and failure for her. This lesson takes a long time to learn.

THE INJUSTICES

There are many injustices in gymnastics. The very first competition will raise many questions regarding the competence of the judging and the favoritism that may apply to certain name gymnasts or teams. Sadly, favoritism and inequities do exist in gymnastics. There are some name gymnasts from time to time who get carried when they make mistakes. There are some teams who stand a better chance than other teams do of getting the benefit of the doubt. I believe that over time these inequities are somewhat balanced out for most gymnasts, but nevertheless, the sense of justice of young people is inviolable. You must teach the gymnast how to handle and understand these inequities when they occur.

The attention showered upon some gymnasts by the media may not necessarily be based on performance alone. A gymnast may see herself being overlooked by the media and by the selection process for national and international competition. It is important that she have other means of measuring her ability and performance than by the expectations and whims of the media or the judges. The gymnast is likely to suffer as a "have not" before she is accomplished enough and proven enough to automatically receive the benefit of the doubt. The key to it all seems to be that the gymnast should be the very best she can be. There must be no possibility of doubt in the judges' minds as to who is the best. It is faith in the concept that the best will always rise to the top that keeps many in the sport through thick and thin. Fortunately, this is still the general mode of gymnastics. Unfortunately, some corruption and some favoritism exist. We must prepare our athletes to understand some of its inevitability and encourage them to fight such injustices by deed as well as word. Cheating and favoritism are never acceptable. The gymnast must understand that it can be lived with as long as we always strive to eliminate it.

It's up to you to help the gymnast understand that these injustices are not right, not acceptable, but not worth giving up over. The gymnast should prove that her courage is far above reproach and her ability to accept a defeat or an injustice is simple testimony to her sportsmanship and concern for following rules. Two wrongs do not make a right; the gymnast cannot correct an injustice by poor sportsmanship. Our gymnasts must maintain their dignity and honor in a world often barren of the qualities.

Each gymnast must understand herself and her fellow gymnasts. You are responsible not only for seeing that all the gymnasts get along but that each holds the other in a web of mutual respect and dignified interaction. The typical cattiness of childhood, the teasing and sarcasm cannot exist unchecked in the training situation. The gymnast should be prepared to conduct all social interactions in a friendly manner. The atmosphere need not be militaristic and you should not be placed in the role of policeman. I do believe, however, that there is no room for insubordination between gymnasts. At the first occurrence of such a manner our gymnasts are dealt with swiftly and harshly. You are the model for such behavior and should always foster respect by your own relationships with the young gymnasts.

ACHIEVEMENT

The young gymnast should use gymnastics as an opportunity to practice the achievement motive in microcosm. The struggle is the important thing. We usually do not see that the struggle is the goal. The struggle is the teacher. The gymnast can come to learn that struggling for something worthwhile is essential for human dignity. As with anything we want to get good at, we have to practice it. Gymnastics is the practice time for struggles that will face the gymnast for a long time after she hangs up her grips. Medals and trophies are like grades in school that measure how well you have learned the subject matter of achievement. The subject matter of gymnastics is the life experience of meeting a challenge and struggling to solve it.

Our culture has so lost sight of the beauty of the struggle. Anything is okay as long as you don't get caught. Being mediocre is the easy way to do it. Being really good is very uncomfortable. The circle of friends of achievers are usually other achievers as well. We need to encourage our achievers, not convince them that the cards are so stacked against them that they cannot win. Gymnastics can give them the wings of determination and confidence to see any problem through to the end and attack any goal and achieve it. In short, gymnastics can and must give them the courage and the tools to become the best person that they can become.

Theoretical preparation is preparation of the spirit. The gymnast can do her flip-flops and other skills day after day and the various other categories of preparation will help her. The spirit of the gymnast is where the artist comes from, and where the decision is made to go for it or stand and watch it. We must give them the tools to choose wisely and confidently.

IV

APPLICATIONS

In Part IV, I will give you a few examples of how the principles and concepts discussed in previous chapters can be applied in your program.

No concept is worth much unless the student or practitioner can apply it in the real world. In giving clinics and symposia I have learned that I must tailor the material so that the coaches could take it home that very day and apply it in their own gymnasium situation. I have stepped away from this idea somewhat in earlier portions of this text in the hopes of laying a foundation that will help you do your own problem solving. The following examples illustrate some problem solving I've done using the principles covered in previous sections. Often, an example is worth a thousand theoretical explanations.

This part begins with two film analyses of skills (a Cuervo vault by an East German and a full-in performed by a Romanian). The second section is my methodology for teaching the full-in somersault. Then, two short chapters are concerned with somewhat more nebulous facets of gymnastics — the warm-up and overtraining. Finally, two chapters comment on aspects of the 1981 American Cup: one is an analysis of uneven bar composition, and the other includes some observations of the training of female athletes at this competition.

I hope that the informal nature of these short sections will encourage you to begin writing down your own observations and ideas. We need this kind of documentation. Gymnastics is a peculiar sport in that when one generation of coaches leaves the sport no written documentation of their successes and failures exists to pass along to later generations. It would be a tremendous help to our sport to document all our actions so that we can adopt and adapt what works and avoid what doesn't. Failure to do this forces each succeeding generation of coaches to make the same silly errors the previous generation made. At present our history is passed on strictly by word of mouth through clinics and symposia. Our sport will not approach adult stature until our history is kept intact for later generations to study and build upon.

The examples I've included in the following short chapters are not designed to give you instant solutions to the problems that show up in the training gym. They should give you an overall idea of my own search for answers in my own training program, and what I found out. Often, I have gone down the wrong path in looking for answers to questions and problems that have plagued my training program — but even this was helpful, since I now know where *not* to look.

16

Looking
at Two Skills

I have analyzed the following two skills by tracing each frame onto paper. You can use this method of analyzing mechanics and skill technique if you don't have a computer and if you have enough time to do the drawing. It would be a little bold to say that these are biomechanical analyses, considering what actually goes into a biomechanical analysis. You are simply encouraged to look at the following two skills and at the sort of knowledge that can be gained from such analysis. I firmly believe that it is well worth the effort.

SKILL NUMBER 1: THE CUERVO VAULT

The gymnast performing this vault is Birgit Senff from the German Democratic Republic. The tracings shown as Figure 16-1, positions 1-28, are made of selected frames from a film I took at the 1981 American Cup. Only selected frames were used, since the film speed of 80 frames per second provides about 160 frames for this vault, and the variation between these frames is so small that it is impractical to include them all. The high film speed does ensure that the figure is not blurred so that drawings can be more accurate relative to exact body positions and position in space.

The first frame represents the first full figure available for tracing. The notes and angles were included for your interest but are not highly accurate because I'm a pretty lousy artist. The film was taken at 90 degrees to the motion of the gymnast.

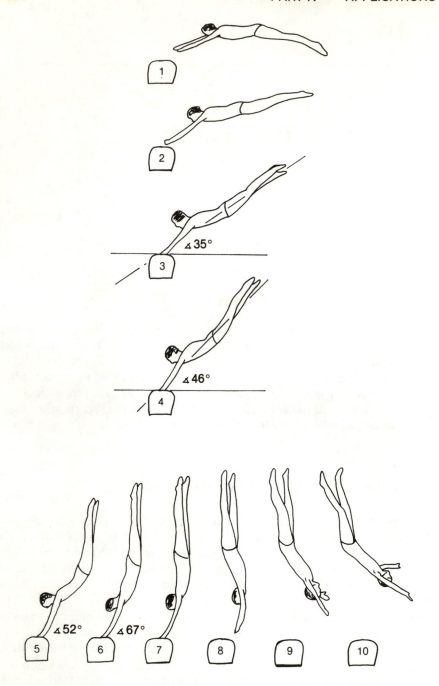

Figure 16-1 The Cuervo Vault performed by Birgit Senff at the 1981 American Cup. Positions 1-28 are tracings of selected film frames.

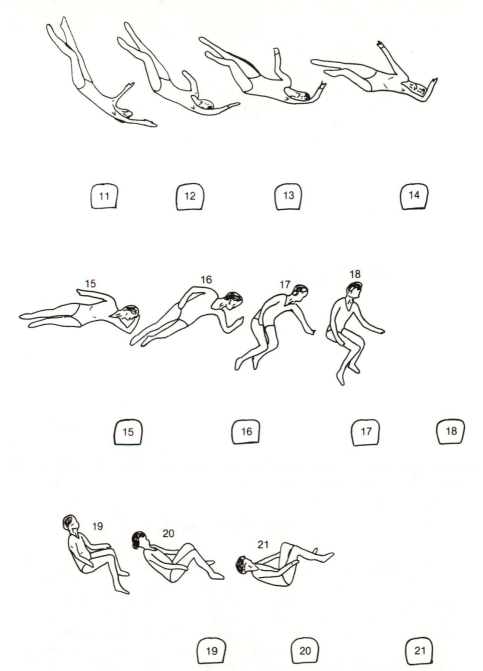

11   12   13   14

15   16   17   18

15   16   17   18

19   20   21

19   20   21

Figure 16-1 (continued)

Figure 16-1 (continued)

Of particular interest is the separation of the gymnast's legs during the end of the compression phase of the impact on the hands at the horse. This occurs in frame 3 and is critical to the outcome of the turn about the long axis of the body. This separation indicates that the gymnast is applying some force to the horse to initiate the twist of the body prior to leaving the horse. Increasing the speed of the left leg relative to the right leg during the support phase and then stopping it quickly to accomplish the transfer of momentum just prior to release will give the left lower segment of the body more rotational momentum once airborne. This means that the left side of the body is moving into the somersault faster than the right side of the body. The subtlety of this initiation is important to the overall appearance of the vault. This allows the twist to appear to be accomplished while airborne.

A second contribution to the turn appears to be accomplished by the typical method of lowering one arm to the side to create unequal radii of rotation about the somersault axis. The unequal radii of the two sides of the body will cause the body to tilt or turn about the longitudinal axis and contribute to a form of the "cat" type of twist. This tilt was confirmed by filming the same gymnast from the end on another attempt. The type of cat twist referred to here has been referred to in other gymnastics circles as the "conical tilt twist," hula hoop twist, etc.

The gymnast also uses a slight pike at the hips as she leaves the horse. This slight pike in the hips in frames 9 and 10 creates the potential for the use of the more standard cat type twist by skillfully using the moments of inertia of various body segments to accomplish additional turn. The gymnast twists by using the relatively larger moment of inertia of the lower segment of the body by twisting the upper body segment against it. This is shown in frame 11 as the gymnast has the deepest pike at this point and she is turning the upper body against the long moment of inertia of the lower body during this frame. During frames 12, 13, and 14 the gymnast straightens or extends the hips (particularly the right side) and thus the lower segment catches up with the upper segment to change the airborne position.

The extension of the lower segment forms a second portion of the cat type twist similar to the opening of pike we see in the Yamashita half turn. The legs are now twisting or using the upper body as the segment holding the largest moment of inertia. The bending of the legs during this phase in frames 15 and 16 at the knee but not at the hip (until frame 17) encourages this type of turn and also encourages the continued speed of the somersault, since a relatively shortened radius of rotation is maintained about the somersault axis.

These small "squirms" of the gymnast allow her to twist by skillfully using her different body segments and their relative inertias to turn the body. The most important concept for the coach is that she is using many methods of twisting at once to accomplish this vault. Most gymnasts actually use many methods to do skills—so it's a good idea to look for *all* the methods, not simply at the most popular or most obvious technique at the moment. Many subtle things are happening during most skills. They are fascinating to study and what we learn by our analyses of these skills often gives us new insight into what is actually going on.

The score received for this vault was 9.65. The panel consisted of a Canadian superior, USA, Czechoslovakia, Japan, and the People's Republic of China. The 9.65 was the second ranking score for preliminaries on vaulting.

SKILL NUMBER 2: THE FULL-IN

The tracings shown as Figure 16-2, positions 1-43, are from the warm-ups of the preliminary competition for the March 1981 American Cup. The analysis was performed in April 1981. Lavinia Agache did one full timer before this performance. Her left ankle was taped heavily and short landings brought grimacing from her so I would assume that her left ankle was quite sore. None of her work was hesitant, however, and I remember seeing her miss only one throughout the training and competition.

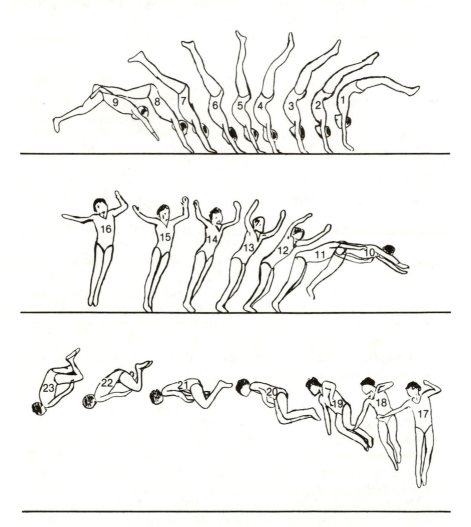

Figure 16-2   Full-in performed by Lavinia Agache at the 1981 American Cup. Positions 1-43 are tracings of selected film frames.

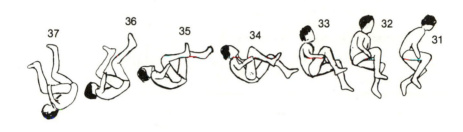

Figure 16-2 (continued)

Of perhaps more interest than the full-in actually is her flip-flop. She does not use the typical collapse in the shoulders as seen in most other gymnasts. This shoulder collapse as seen in Figure 16-3 is present in other full-ins such as those of Canary, Mateja, Schwandt, Gnauck, Moukihina, and Zakarova. The collapse is distinguished by the shoulders of the gymnasts moving in front of her hands. This straight shoulder technique has been shown before in Maria Filatova and Leslie Pyfer and presents an interesting contrast from the type of hand contact phase normally seen in the flip-flop prior to the take-off for tumbling skills. The straight-shoulder technique as

(a)   **(b)**

Figure 16-3   The two types of hand support phases for the flip-flop.
(a) Schematic of the type of technique used by Agache; (b) Schematic
of the position used by most other gymnasts. Finer analysis of this
difference will be done in the future.

described here consists of keeping the shoulders slightly behind the hands
during hand contact of the flip-flop. The girls using the flip-flop without
the shoulder collapse do not seem as strong as the girls listed above and
perhaps must use this technique because they do not have the strength in the
shoulders to collapse and push in time to realize enough force in the snap
down. The outcome of the technique from crude observation is that the
distance from hands to feet in the snap down from the flip-flop appears farther. Whether this technique is advisable for execution remains for further
analysis. The coach should note the positions here and study film closely for
judgment of the efficacy of this shoulder action during the flip-flop.

The film was shot at 80 frames per second and the interval between
tracings here is approximately nine frames. I attempted to keep this consistent, but any estimates of time cannot be made with any assurance of
accuracy.

Agache keeps her knees bent throughout the twist and pikes, putting
her feet over her head at the end of the second somersault. The fact that the
legs come apart is partly due, I believe, to the hard and early turn of the
gymnast into the twist at take-off. The leg appearing to lag behind is consistent with the Chinese and Romanian techniques in that the gymnast who
twists to the right lands with her left leg behind and the gymnast who twists
to the left lands with her right leg behind.

Figure 16-2, positions 1-43, is provided to give you another look at
information-gathering in skill analysis. Although few definitive answers can
be discerned from such analysis, your awareness of the actual positions and
movements during the skill will help you make better word pictures in
describing to the gymnast exactly what the skill should look like. In some
cases, even knowing what the skill should not look like is an aid to teaching.
You can only teach what you know. Anything that enlarges your sphere of
knowledge can only help you teach the skills.

17

The Full-in:
A Methodology

INTRODUCTION

The following look at a methodology for teaching the full-in is strictly from experience, not from science. I have had the pleasure of working with two young gymnasts who have performed the full-in double somersault in floor exercise successfully. The first, Christa Canary, was the first in our country when she performed the skill at the 1979 World Championship Trials. The second gymnast was Kim Mateja who performed the skill successfully in five competitions. Kim also did the skill from the balance beam without aid, onto a crash mat.

I have learned a fair amount about the methodology through the school of hard knocks as have these gymnasts, and I have also learned from the observations of Rhonda Schwandt and Laurie Kaiser, who pioneered the skill in our country. The need for our gymnasts to be working this skill is a high priority since this is one of the "feathers" that should be in the cap of the elite international caliber gymnast. At the past American Cup a Romanian and a Chinese gymnast performed this skill in floor exercise and a Chinese gymnast also performed the skill as a dismount from the balance beam.

The time necessary for assuring safe performance of the full-in is 9 to 12 months after learning to perform the double somersault in pike or tuck consistently and safely. This is an overview of the way that two gymnasts learned the skill; it is not the only way. In fact, the two girls learned the skill in different ways since a pit was not available when Christa was learning but one was available throughout Kim's learning period.

THEORY

As with all approaches to learning, and especially in the case of blazing a trail (as with Christa), learning must proceed from a theory of what one wants the final product to look like. Also, there must be a theory of what portions of the skill or methods of executing the skill are critical.

The full-in consists of a full twist in the first somersault and then a back somersault to complete the two somersaults and return to the feet. Asking the question of what is critical to the execution of the skill one should look at the twisting, because the gymnast probably already does the double somersault in pike or tuck if the coach is even considering the full-in. What do we need to know about the full twist in the first somersault? Or, what is it about the full that makes this skill so difficult? After doing the double somersault many times most gymnasts do not complain of loss of orientation when they perform full-ins. Usually, they know exactly where they are in space but may report difficulty in accurately predicting when they should expect the mat to strike them. This simply requires many repetitions and therefore is not critical to our understanding.

The most critical thing about the full twist is that the gymnast must elongate her body to perform the full quickly enough so that it doesn't decrease her total somersault speed for the duration of the two somersaults. This elongation may be in the form of a layout full twist followed by the second somersault in pike or tuck, or the tucked full twist followed by the second somersault in pike or tuck, or a piked full twist followed by the second somersault in pike or tuck. This lengthening of the body to shorten the twist radius is the costly part of the skill in that the gymnast must be able to lengthen her body enough to get the twist done quickly and efficiently without slowing down the somersault so much that she does not have enough airborne time to complete the two somersaults. Interestingly, the two gymnasts I am familiar with performed the full in various ways. When they first learned the skill the full was slightly tucked; after some time the full got straighter and straighter. My theory of why this occurred follows later.

I assumed that the gymnast must be able to do a somersault with an open body position in the first somersault and a closed or tighter body position in the second somersault. In order to receive permission to begin learning the full-in, a gymnast (a) must have been doing the double somersault in competition; (b) must have been able to do the double pike somersault; and (c) must have been able to do an efficient round-off flip-flop. She also had to know how to do the method of somersaulting that I would call a "whip-pike" (in other words, she had to know how to straddle pike and put her feet over her head slightly before landing).

I had heard the trampolinists telling how easy it was to execute the full-out somersault, and we tried this first on their recommendation — and failed dreadfully. There definitely did not appear to be enough time in the air for the gymnast to turn over once and then extend her body for the twist in the second somersault with even the smallest of safety margins. We soon gave up the full-out.

APPLICATION

In the early learning stages the girls did not learn the entire skill. In keeping with a theory I had of what was important for the skill, we began doing layout-tuck and layout-pike somersaults. The layout-tuck and layout-pike are a bit misnamed in that few are actually done fully stretched for the entire first somersault. The gymnast usually performs the layout position for the first half somersault and then pikes or tucks to facilitate the somersault and rotates one and a half somersaults or slightly less to her feet. This procedure of learning the layout-pike before beginning to insert the twist happened from the desire to be extra careful (in Christa's case) since we did not have a pit to simply "go for it," and I wanted to have a usable skill for her if she proved incapable of performing the full-in.

The layout-pike somersault proved to be a blessing in disguise. All the girls working on it reported that the layout pike was easier to land than the double pike and that it felt remarkably like a Tsukahara. With this information I began using words that approximated the feeling that they reported to me. It seems that it feels to them as though they do a very high and fast flip-flop to a handstand on an imaginary horse and then when they see the ground for a moment while in this "airborne handstand" they do an aerial snap-down to the somersault to rotate the remaining one and a half somersaults to their feet. We later found that the ability of the girl to pike quickly from the arched "airborne handstand" to the pike was critical for her ability to realize the fullest rotational speed available for the second somersault.

My adaptation of the performance theory into a learning theory was that the elongated body in the first half somersault of the layout pike was where the full twist would be inserted. I also knew that by adding some twist we would subtract some of the somersault force in the very act of inserting the twist. The loss of somersault force by putting in the twist could be regained by bending the knees and hips slightly (this would do little harm to the twist and could greatly facilitate the somersault).

The gymnast also knew how to put her feet over her head by performing the straddle pike in the second somersault, and she knew how to pike quickly from the arched body position. The straddle pike would allow her to land on her feet, performing only about 65% of the second somersault. This should give the gymnast a larger margin for error and more capability of landing on her feet if her ability to produce raw power was somewhat limited.

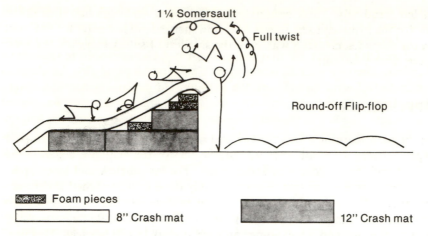

Figure 17-1   Diagram of mat situation for full-in.

The progression paused here for Christa. Since we did not have a pit, we built a mat situation that would allow her to feel the transition from the full to the snap down back somersault without having to "go for it." Figure 17-1 shows this mat situation. It consists of performing a round-off, flip-flop, full in a tuck position to the top of the hill created by the mats. The gymnast lands on her back or shoulders and rolls backward down the hill. The measurement of steps is critical to making this drill practical. After a little experience the gymnasts all got used to tumbling to a spot. I believe this skill alone is vitally important. Considerable time was spent on this with young gymnasts so that they could later take advantage of elaborate mat situations for their learning. The ideal execution of the drill was performed when Christa did the round-off, flip-flop, and tucked full, and she landed on her back on the inclined mat and rolled down the hill by straddle piking her feet over her head. The progress of the learning was controlled by the steepness of the incline; the steeper the incline the faster she flipped the second somersault and the more "authentic" the feeling became. When it appeared that she would soon turn over the second somersault by accident, we went to the next stage.

For Christa, all that was left was some courage and a little spotting. The interesting part of this episode of her learning came after the first execution when she reported that it felt "exactly like a layout-tuck." Kim avoided the special mat situation in her progression, as an experiment on my part, and took the skill directly to the pit where she turned over easily into the foam. Out of curiosity, we did later take her to this drill of rolling down the hill. It appeared here that once Kim knew how to "flip" the second somersault she did not need the mat situation since she turned over so quickly that the hill appeared dangerous. The hill ended up being in the way of her head when she piked her feet over head. Therefore, we left this drill and used it only for the young gymnasts in their early learning stages.

Once we had the pit in our gym we simply did the skill into the foam until we felt comfortable that the gymnast had enough room to make it to her feet. Then we would place very soft mats in the pit at first for them to begin to feel some firmness to the landing. Harder and harder mats were placed in the pit until the mats were fairly solid, and a 4-inch mat was placed on the top. The key to the mat level seemed to be that after the mats and the pit had compressed from the landing impact the gymnast's feet were at floor level. This meant that the mats had to be slightly higher than the floor when they were placed in the pit prior to the landing impact.

Christa did her learning (and therefore her competition warm-ups, and so on, with spot). Kim was never spotted once on her full-in and refused a spot most strenuously when she did it out of the pit for the first time. Before acquiring Kim as a gymnast we had vowed to end spotting altogether in our gym and the addition of the pit made this a practical and safe doctrine. Kim went through her learning without spotting and did not want a spot when the skill was taken out of the pit. Of course, Kim had done hundreds into the pit. This learning process had taken about seven months.

As the gymnasts gained experience in the skill they began performing the skill less frequently in practice. They began the combination and routine regimen, and interestingly, the complexion of the execution of the full-in changed as they became more comfortable. The gymnasts both displayed increasingly straight body fulls prior to the tuck or pike in the second somersault. I believe this is due to their increased efficiency through repetition and I believe that their ability to pike their feet over their head quickly is the most important phase of the skill. The ability to get from the twist quickly to the pike was enhanced through repetition and the straighter body full allowed them to get the full finished more quickly and therefore get to the phase of the quick pike earlier in the execution of the skill.

CONCLUSION

The full-in is a vital skill in our quest for international competitive success. It is my estimation that Americans are clearly behind in this type of skill and that in the next few years we will be further behind if we do not begin preparing our gymnasts in earnest for these types of skills.

18

The Gymnast
and the Warm-up

It is not uncommon in warm-ups to watch a gymnast suddenly become disoriented on a skill that she has been doing for months or perhaps years. It is not rare to see a gymnast become completely demoralized because the beam shakes, the bars are stiff, or the take-off board is dead. It is highly likely that an early morning warm-up will be very different from a late afternoon or evening warm-up.

In the past, and still occasionally today, the general stresses and strains of the warm-up on both coaches and gymnasts are obvious. The preparation of the gymnast immediately prior to competition is a delicate process that can spell disaster or triumph. Systematic preplanning can help alleviate many warm-up problems and make for a generally calm, confident, and consistent approach to the preparation of the gymnast. Many factors go into the preplanning, but they fit nicely into the following five criteria: physical, technical, psychological, tactical, and theoretical.

PHYSICAL

Physical criteria refer to the body of the gymnast and the biochemistry of the physical activity. It is a popular contention that the warm-up, whether active (running, calisthenics, skill rehearsal) or passive (hot bath, shower) is beneficial to the postwarm-up activity. Controlled research does not shed much light on the real effect, beneficial or not, on subsequent performance. A survey of the research literature by Peter V. Karpovich showed that 14 investigations indicated a positive effect; 15 indicated no effect, and 2 indicated harmful effect (Karpovich, 1971). This would seem to indicate that the benefits of warm-up activity are uncertain, at best.

Study of the actual effects of a warm-up activity on body processes yields the following information. A warm-up will raise the body core temperature 1 to 2 degrees Farenheit (deVries, 1966). Core temperature refers to deep body temperature. Research has shown that warm muscles contract and relax faster, are more extensible (stretchable), and that the increased temperature helps blood carry and release oxygen more efficiently. Since gymnastic activity is largely anaerobic, the oxygen-carrying capacity of the blood may have little effect on performance but could help speed recovery times between bouts of routines. The body of the gymnast will change temperature naturally throughout a daily cycle, with low temperature in the early morning hours and high temperature late in the afternoon or early evening. This will vary from individual to individual. The lower temperature in the morning can account for the possible experience of having difficulty getting going in the early morning warm-ups and competitions, since the lowered body temperature may inhibit the muscle from doing its job most efficiently. On the other hand, those performance times in the afternoon or early evening may be benefited by the higher natural circadian cyclic temperature.

It takes about 5 minutes of moderate work (like jogging) to raise the core temperature 1 to 2 degrees (deVries, 1966). This increase in temperature is indicated when the athlete begins to perspire. Various sources indicate that the warm-up effect will last from 45 to 80 minutes. Therefore, to be on the safe side, the gymnast should not sit inactive for more than 45 minutes between the cessation of warm-up activity and the beginning of performance. In some competitions this may present a problem. It may be necessary for the gymnast to warm up several times through a competition from one event to the next. Of course, the competitive event can serve as the warm-up for the next event.

The state of training may have an effect on the physical part of warm-ups. A nonconditioned or deconditioned athlete will be more easily fatigued by long warm-ups or by being forced to warm up several times due to long waits between events. In planning for this possibility it may be necessary to remove dangerous skills for safety or not attend the competition if it has a history of poor administration. A very experienced gymnast will require much less physical warm-up than will the inexperienced gymnast because of differences in their confidence, familiarity with meet formats, and knowledge of past history of their performances.

TECHNICAL

The technical facet of the preparation of the gymnast in warm-ups refers to that short rehearsal of skills before competition. During this rehearsal prior to competition the gymnast is likely to encounter some technique errors and problems that she may be able to handle herself or that will require you to step in and take care of. Stepping in to handle the various problems requires that you be very knowledgeable and well-prepared. The small amount of time available to fix a performance problem forces you to make quick judgments, and your judgment must be based on knowledge of the gymnast, of problems likely to occur, and of the means to eliminate them quickly.

Some technical or execution problems will occur because of differences in equipment. The timing of some gymnastics skills is highly critical and any change in the performance environment directly related to skill execution actually forces the gymnast to relearn the skill during warm-ups. The sensory information used in some skills on the uneven bars, for example, depends upon the flexibility or springiness of the rail. When using unfamiliar equipment the gymnast is faced with a whole new set of force requirements and timing changes. This is most likely to occur in skills that are new enough not to be firmly entrenched or those with critical timing requirements. Therefore, those skills requiring consistency of equipment should be considered critical, and back-up skills that do not require consistent equipment should be designed into the choreography of the exercise to be available when needed.

Back-up skills are vitally important with the escalation of difficulty, higher performance standards, and the increased need for safety of the gymnast. A gymnast performing a very difficult skill may encounter performance problems in the warm-up before competition from fatigue, new equipment, overtraining, poor attitude, and other factors. A back-up skill or sequence should be designed so that it can be used or substituted for a more difficult sequence when the safety of the gymnast or completion of the exercise is at stake.

Another use of back-up skills is when the preparatory or "set-up" skills used to prepare for the difficult movement did not come off properly and the gymnast must substitute a less difficult skill for the ill-prepared more difficult one.

PSYCHOLOGICAL

The psychological side of warm-ups is easily the most critical, most talked about, most devastating, and the least understood. This is where the true artistry of coaching comes to the front, and where, unfortunately, a lot of witchcraft also emerges. It is very difficult to be scientific and systematic about the psychological aspect of warm-ups because of a lack of scientific tools.

It is often nearly impossible to predict on the basis of her warm-up behavior how the gymnast will compete. However, there are some tools and criteria that can be at least helpful. Your best tool is keen observation. Each gymnast is providing a wealth of information to you through her body language. The gymnasts will use various gestures and gesture clusters to indicate their moods, reactions to stress, anticipation, level of readiness, and many other traits. We react to each other's body language often unconsciously, but with a little study and practice you can use this knowledge to help deal with the moods and personality of the gymnast. Some gestures indicate frustration, some fear, others defensiveness, and some thoughtfulness. By paying close attention to these signal flags shown by the gymnast, you can gain an understanding of the wordless message the gymnast may be communicating. You can use these signals to gain insight into the feelings of the gymnast at that moment. Then, of course, it will be up to you—on the basis of your instincts and experience—to alter these moods and feelings of the gymnast, possibly by using body language yourself. Your own body language can influence the mood of the gymnast, since she can react to your body language just as easily as you can react to hers.

Another helpful psychological tool is music. Often the airborne "electricity" of warm-ups is like a morgue. Music of the proper type can do much to change the mood of the gymnast. The music can be used to perk them up, calm them down, cheer them, distract them, or encourage them. How you use these tools is much like the way an artist uses paint and canvas. It is important that you be consistent and confident in your approach; without confidence and empathy, no approach will work.

TACTICAL

The tactical side of warm-ups deals with the general game plan or strategy to be applied to the competition. This facet can be divided into four parts: rules, composition, appearance, and general administration. The rules category applies to those things dictated by the governing body and the meet director (such as the order of events, time schedule, inquiry and protest procedures). The rules should be well understood. Inquiries should be written out in advance in a skeleton format so that only the appropriate information need be added on the spot, to save time. Any questionable skills should be cleared through the meet referee prior to the competition so that they will be evaluated justly.

Tactical composition refers to the choice of skills and the effect of that choice on scoring potential. This should be done before warm-up time unless there is a new technical development in a particular skill during the warm-ups. If a skill is found to be unsalvageable (because of many mistakes in warm-ups), then a replacement skill that will do little harm to the composition and scoring potential should be used. A new piece of equipment— generally the vaulting board—may cause problems with the gymnast's skills.

If the gymnast suffered an injury that is not incapacitating and will allow her to compete, then all the limitations must be determined and alternate skills must be used to prevent further injury and not damage scoring potential.

The appearance of the gymnast is very important, and it can often be reflected in her score. The selection of her hairstyle, leotard cut and color, and footwear can have an effect on her appearance. The gymnast should not warm up in the same leotards she will later perform in (to prevent the perspiration stains and chalk marks on the fabric). Although hairstyles are very individual, it's important to remember that hairstyles that may be acceptable in everyday life can become a mess in movement. The use of too many articles to keep it in place can be distracting.

General administration aspects of warm-ups include such factors as selecting the gymnasts' particular competitive order on each event (unless this has been done by a draw) and taping of the floor around the apparatus so that the position of the apparatus during warm-ups can be duplicated during competition. Uneven bar warm-up order should be planned to minimize changing bar settings. First aid and training supplies must be kept available, and time must be allowed for taping ankles or hands.

THEORETICAL

The theoretical part of warm-ups refers to the philosophy or purpose of the competition. Each competition is a little different in this regard. Some competitions are for team placement, qualification to another meet, fun, experimenting with new skills for the first time in competition, and adding experience. Each girl may have a different outlook as to why she is there, and this should be understood by each competitor before competition begins. Furthermore, the goal of the competition should be spelled out so that each gymnast can monitor her progress toward that goal.

The gymnasts need to know what is expected of them in winning or losing. They need to know what is expected of them when they face an injustice or two. The goals need to be set and understood by all, and then you have to maintain the direction toward these goals.

The warm-up is the last opportunity for the coach and athlete to interact before the decisive moments of each event. This last-moment preparation should be planned carefully so that no loose ends interfere and no new loose ends are created.

19

Overtraining

In the effort to train athletes to the highest levels, we can find an affliction of excellence. Only the highly and intensively trained can suffer from it. The general term for this problem is *overtraining*. Historically, this phenomenon has been referred to as peaking and troughing, the slump, staleness, or the loss of athletic form. Overtraining is the loss of that particular quality or energy that makes the athlete especially able to compete and perform well.

Overtraining is a general run-down condition of the athlete or a type of chronic fatigue resulting from the accumulation of many remnants of residual and uncancelled fatigue factors from previous training. Our purpose and interest in this phenomenon is in developing training schedules and regimes to cause the maximum training effect without training to the point of overtraining. The athlete must always be able to handle the accumulation of fatigue by not depleting the reserves of the body, thereby avoiding "staleness," "slumping," or loss of "momentum." In directing the training process the coach, physician, trainer, and physical therapist must guide and work with the gymnast to maintain a balanced training schedule.

Overtraining is a very general, nonscientific term used to describe many sport stress fatigue problems. Because overtraining is such a general term, each aspect of overtraining should be identified and categorized so that it may be more easily dealt with.

STRESS

Overtraining is considered to be excess stress. Stress is defined in a number of ways, varying from "all the nonspecific changes within the biological system," to "disturbances in the homeostatic balance of the organism" (Larson, 1971). For our purposes, let us consider stress to be anything that causes the organism (gymnast) to react. It is this reaction of the organism (amount, quality, and duration) that can cause fatigue. The uncancelled and accumulated fatigue states produce overtraining when they pass the threshold of the organism's ability to adapt and accommodate to them.

Many types of stressors can accumulate to produce fatigue and run down the organism. Exercise, disease, sleep disturbances, poor eating habits, fear, anxiety, frustration, temperature, altitude changes, mental conflicts, monotony, and major changes in life style are examples of stressors that affect all athletes.

Hans Selye, perhaps the world's foremost authority on what stress can do to the organism, theorized that every stressor causes a nonspecific reaction in the organism to that stress or accumulated stress. Selye's theory, the "General Adaptation Syndrome" (GAS), describes the stress reaction process (Sheehan, 1972). The GAS consists of three stages:

1. the alarm stage, when the organism recognizes a stressor and warns the body to prepare for action;
2. the resistance stage, when the organism makes the actual adaptation to the stress;
3. the exhaustion stage, when the adaptation energy is used up and the organism fails.

This theory fits well into Russian training literature, which describes the training process as a period of acquisition of athletic form, followed by a relative stabilization of athletic form, and then ending the cycle with the temporary loss of athletic form.

Although the three stages that the organism must endure in stress adaptation are the same, the characteristics of the stages may vary widely. The GAS of disease and exercise are somewhat different, although athletics may test the reserves of the body similarly. Athletic stress is intermittent and voluntary, whereas disease stress is constant and more devastating on many body systems.

The direction of the training process, then, must be to prevent the gymnast from entering a severe exhaustion stage at the wrong time (near meet time). Unfortunately, it is near meet time that the gymnast is usually forced to work harder and therefore is more likely to neglect her rest. The overwork near meet time places the gymnast in greater risk of slipping into fatigue that will harm performance. We must consider that the direction of the training process consists of working the gymnast optimally with loads heavy enough to ensure progress and not so heavy that the gymnast slips into overtraining.

TYPES OF OVERTRAINING

Alfonz Kereszty (Larson, 1971) has described four types of fatigue and overstress for the athlete. All of these categories must be considered in directing the training process and planning for the gymnast. The first category of *overstress* includes all the factors other than the athletic activity. Among the factors in this category are infections, disease, poor nutrition, and poor personal conduct (staying out late, poor personal hygiene, and so on). This category must be eliminated first in determining where an overtraining problem might come from. These factors can interfere with training and planning for training cycles, and may sabotage the analysis of a fatigue problem because you may not always be aware of them; and even if you are, you cannot measure their intensity.

The second type of overstress is *chronic fatigue*. This is the sum total of small and neglected remnants of tiredness that only by their accumulation become noticeable and problematic. The characteristics of this category are elevated basal metabolism, high resting and exercise pulse rates, and prolonged, delayed return to resting pulse rates. This category is the one most likely to be encountered by the highly trained gymnast and in looking further at overtraining this will be the type of overtraining we will be referring to. It is interesting to note that only athletes who have reached a sufficient level of training may fall victims to this category of overtraining, which occurs most frequently during the periods of form conservation *between competitions*.

The third type of overstress is called *overstrain*. This type usually develops in those athletes who must put out excessive amounts of energy (for instance, long-distance runners, swimmers, and skiers). This category is unlike the previous one in that the stress is specific and need not be added to other stressors—perhaps unrelated—to produce overtraining.

The fourth type of overstress is called *indisposition*. This refers to decreases in performance lasting a few hours to a day or two. This category encompasses the premenstrum and the general circadian cyclic nature of the athlete in her general daily body rhythms. Such events that cause indisposition are changes in time zone, mental conflicts, poor sleep, frustration, and an overzealous desire to win.

SYMPTOMS

A closer look at some of the symptoms of overtraining may be helpful. There are documented physiological effects shown in the athlete by stages. During the alarm and resistance stages, the pituitary gland secretes adrenocorticotropic hormone, which stimulates the secretion of corticoids by the adrenal cortex to help the body adapt to stress. The adrenal cortex secretes cortisone and cortisol, which are anti-inflammatory corticoids. The adrenal medulla secretes adrenalines, which are pro-inflammatory, and the pituitary also releases thyrotropic hormone, which activates the thyroid to increase metabolism. Physiological symptoms of the exhaustion stage of the GAS are: weight loss, higher resting and exercise heart rates, higher systolic blood pressure, elevated body temperature, elevated blood sugar, and altered electrocardiogram.

Overtraining can exist in mild, moderate, and severe form. You will be able to observe some of the symptoms of overtraining in your gymnasts at different times in the training cycle.

Mild symptoms include excessive weariness after a typical or regular training load. The tiredness lasts longer than usual, perhaps to the next day. Actions are slower and less accurate, and there is an accompanying loss of strength and balance coordination. Progress stops and scores will fall.

Moderate overtraining symptoms are primarily those of emotional and motivational problems. The gymnast may be unusually irritable, argumentative, provocative, apathetic, sleepy, and slow to respond. The gymnast may lose self-confidence and appear to try and rest more often to save her energy. The gymnast perspires easily and profusely and may report sleep disturbances.

Severe overtraining symptoms may cause the gymnast to feel pain in the chest area, aching under the ribs, a new awareness of heart action, palpitation, and shortness of breath. Bowel movements may lose regularity and legs will feel dead and heavy. Of course, athletes in any of the stages of overtraining are more susceptible to injury.

HOW TO PREVENT OVERTRAINING

Although there are a few medications that can help deal with overtraining once it occurs, a preventive rather than a curative approach is far more desirable. Prevention consists of the elimination of unnecessary stress, the control and moderation of necessary stress, and the careful selection of stressors to prevent wasting energy on nonessential actions. Eliminating the outside and unnecessary stressors can be vitally important to maintaining the stress load below overtraining levels but is beyond the scope of this chapter.

Determining the necessary stressors and monitoring them to keep them within tolerance levels is within the reach of most coaches and their training situations. Eastern Europeans have used training diaries of the number of elements performed and other factors in the athletes' daily lives. The items are usually written in a diary and then monitored by the coach and gymnast to learn about the effects of training on the gymnast, the loads undertaken, and their apparent results. These are usually kept in chart form and with other records on sleep, health, enthusiasm for training, quality of work performed, number of elements, weight, and heart rate.

As the gymnast progresses through her training schedule you can get a good indication of how she's doing by watching her records closely. Sleep disturbances, health, desire to practice, weight, heart rate, hours of sleep, and so on can give a good data base for analyzing the effects of training on the gymnast by simply graphing the numbers of the gymnast's responses (see Appendix A).

Runners have used some of the following criteria for determining peaking. As the prepractice and postpractice weight get closer and closer together (the gymnast should lose a little weight during training because of water loss through perspiration) the runner is nearing a peak. In contrast, if the runner is continually losing weight, this is a sign of overtraining because of catabolism, and may necessitate slowing the training process. The pulse rate should be fairly consistent from day to day. If the prepractice heart rate consistently rises, the gymnast may be overtraining. Runners take their heart rate immediately upon awakening and before getting out of bed and compare this to that of the previous day. If the heart rate is significantly higher than it was the previous day, then the athlete may have trained too hard and will therefore train lighter that day. Although all of these methods are loaded with scientific holes they are at least administratively feasible, inexpensive, and better than nothing. The use of medical techniques (often invasive) of measuring blood and muscle chemistry are not available to the typical gymnastics gym situation, and until they are, the techniques I've just mentioned are useful substitute measures.

The results of such records and data can help determine attendance at some competitions and use of particular skills in competition if these skills are on the fringes of the ability of the gymnast and she is not in peak condition. It may be appropriate to avoid difficult skills when the physiological data indicates that the athlete may be facing a fatigue problem.

Directing the training process to allow the gymnast to train throughout the year without risk of undue fatigue and the problems associated with it should be a goal of every coach. Too often, coaches see only the immediate and specific rather than the panoramic picture of the training program and its effects on the athlete over many months. If you monitor the training progress and carefully control the stress factors you should be able to help the gymnast realize her potential.

20

Compositional Analysis: Uneven Bars

Analyzing the composition of routines (particularly those performed in high-level competitions) can help you understand where an event is at the moment and where it is going; it can also motivate you and the athlete to develop compositions of your own routines that will be on a par with those of the top gymnasts. It is probably most helpful when you perform the analysis at the composition level your program is aspiring to so that you can design plans to reach the level of composition demonstrated in the meet being analyzed. In a sense, compositional analysis is a type of scouting report.

The uneven bar event has changed dramatically through the past couple of years, and this change is typified by the types and number of skills performed in the routines of national and international competition. The following look at uneven bars comes from the 1981 American Cup, in which the countries of Japan, People's Republic of China, German Democratic Republic, Federal Republic of Germany, Mexico, Canada, Romania, Italy, Bulgaria, Czechoslovakia, and Hungary took part, each with one or two gymnasts. The United States provided three gymnasts used in this analysis. Elaine Thompson recorded the routines, and I am greatly indebted to her for transcribing the routines from the judging shorthand so that they might be used for this analysis.

The analysis covered six major areas: mounts, large-swing skills, release and somersault skills, twisting skills, uprises, and dismounts. Tables 20-1 through 20-6 show how many of these skills were performed and give the number and percentage or average per routine values.

TABLE 20-1   Mounts

	All Gymnasts	
Skill	Number	Percentage
Glide variations	11	55
Straddle low bar with hands	3	15
Front salto sit low bar	2	10
Free straddle low bar	2	10
Jump free hip	1	5
Stem rise handstand	1	5

	Top Eight Gymnasts	
Skill	Number	Percentage
Glide variations	3	37.5
Front salto sit low bar	2	25
Straddle over low bar with hands	1	12.5
Jump free hip	1	12.5
Stem rise high bar	1	12.5

TABLE 20-2   Dismounts

	All Gymnasts	
Skill	Number	Percentage
Toe on front tuck	3	15
Comaneci full twist	3	15
Clear hip hecht	2	10
Snap down back tuck	2	10
Hecht back tuck	2	10
Comaneci tuck	2	10
Toe on front half	1	5
Double twist flyaway	1	5
Toe on front full	1	5
Full twist flyaway	1	5
Clear hip front pike half	1	5
Double flyaway tuck	1	5

	Top Eight Gymnasts	
Skill	Number	Percentage
Comaneci full	2	25
Snap down back	2	25
Clear hip hecht	1	12.5
Clear hip front pike half	1	12.5
Toe on front half	1	12.5

TABLE 20-3   Large Swing Skills

Skill	All Gymnasts Number	Average per Routine
Clear hip	31	1.55
Stalder	13	.65
Giant	6	.33
Endo shoot handstand	3	.15
Endo shoot release	2	.10
Toe on toe off	1	.05
Toe on blind change	1	.05

Skill	Top Eight Gymnasts Number	Average per Routine
Clear hip	11	1.37
Stalder	13	1.625
Giant	6	.75
Endo shoot handstand	3	.375

TABLE 20-4   Release and Somersaults

Skill	All Gymnasts Number	Average per Routine
Straddle back over low bar	3	.15
California hop	3	.15
Brause	3	.15
Keiskehre	2	.10
Peach	2	.10
Front over low bar to high bar	2	.10
Janz front	2	.10
Hop to eagle grip	2	.10
Whip to handstand on low bar	1	.05
Underswing half over low bar	1	.05
Endo shoot brause	1	.05
Deltchev	1	.05
Clear hip half to high bar	1	.05
Shaposhnikova	1	.05
Hop to eagle grip	1	.05

TABLE 20-4   Cont'd

Skill	Top Eight Gymnasts Number	Average per Routine
Straddle back over low bar	3	.375
Hop to eagle grip	2	.25
Endo shoot to brause	1	.125

Note: The Chinese had one underswing to catch the high bar and no other releases to speak of. The USA clearly led the field in number and variety of releases.

TABLE 20-5   Twisting Skills

Skill	All Gymnasts Number	Average per Routine
Pirouette to immediate swing	4	.20
Underswing one and a half	1	.05
Whip full on low bar	1	.05
Cast full on high bar	1	.05

Top Eight Gymnasts

The top eight gymnasts occupied this category with pirouette to immediate swing. These were one free hip blind change, pirouette to stalder, and Julianne McNamara who pirouettes to everything.

TABLE 20-6   Uprise Skills

Skill	All Gymnasts Number	Average per Routine
Uprise to high bar	4	.20
Uprise to handstand	3	.15
Vault over high bar	2	.10

Top Eight Gymnasts

One of the top eight gymnasts did a vault over the high bar; one did the uprise to handstand, and a third did the uprise to the high bar.

21

Observations of Training: Female Foreign Gymnasts at the 1981 American Cup

Gymnasts began arriving in Fort Worth for the American Cup on Tuesday, March 17 for a competition to begin with women's preliminaries on Saturday, March 21. Finals would be held on Sunday, March 22. These observations, compiled by viewing training on Wednesday, March 18, included the following teams: People's Republic of China, German Democratic Republic, Hungary, Bulgaria, and Czechoslovakia. Romania and the United States had not arrived by the Wednesday training session. I later observed that Romania used a rather similar system regarding the numbers of repetitions. There were some striking similarities and differences among these nations and their approach to immediate preparation for competition.

Each country arrived for training at different times (mostly because of their airline schedules). Two training times were available for them, and every country took part in both sessions. The morning training time was occupied with very light work and the afternoon training consisted of full routines and many repetitions. The morning training began with an organized (or at least preplanned) warm-up. Every country began by running 2 to 5 minutes, either around the floor exercise mat or around the arena. After this jogging, each country had a preplanned series of stretching exercises done in unison or near unison as the athletes worked on the floor exercise area. Japan was the only country that had men and women warming up together. The German Democratic Republic had both men and women doing many of the same exercises, but the two groups did them separately. During the morning training all countries except one began on balance beam after their warm-ups (which lasted a minimum of 10 and a maximum of 20 minutes). The German Democratic Republic began their training on uneven bars.

During the morning training session no country did much high-intensity work at all. The balance beam consisted of dance elements after their complexes of walking, running, and so on. Bars consisted of kips, casts, and free hips. Floor exercise saw round-offs and flip-flops with most gymnasts not even turning a somersault. Vault consisted of handsprings. The entire morning training session lasted 2 hours for China, the hardest working country.

After the morning session, the delegations had lunch following a short walk back to the hotel from the Convention Center. The gymnasts all returned sporadically from lunch. As the countries returned they all began with the same warm-up ritual used in the morning training. Each country wore heavy, thick warm-up suits. Again, each country took from 10 to 20 minutes for their warm-up. During the afternoon session, each country happened to come in at approximately equal intervals, and every country began on balance beam. The gymnasts performed a short warm-up and then each country did from 6 to 10 full routines. Variation was shown in mounts and dismounts; some countries did the mount and dismount for every routine and some chose to include the mount or dismount only on selected routines. After the routine portion of balance beam each gymnast went over trouble spots (which generally included a few more mounts and dismounts). There were few falls and little evidence of personal idiosyncracies; the gymnasts were very businesslike in their approach. The work was completed rather quickly, with little or no time wasted between routines.

During balance beam all the coaches were present in the beam area and a great deal of "coaching" or teaching took place. During this training some skills that were still in the early learning stages were included. Those skills that had some danger were done as timers or set-ups to be used in the competition or left out depending upon their consistency. The Chinese Jiang Wei did full-in timers from the beam but did not turn any over.

After balance beam each country moved on to bars for its next event. The bar work consisted of longer and more thorough preparation of skills before beginning routines. Each country did 4 to 6 routines, and all included the mount and dismount. (All these routines were performed without a major break.) If the routine contained a major error, fall, or other mishap, then the routine did not count and was repeated. After the uneven bar training the gymnasts covered a few trouble spots but not so thoroughly as during the postroutine portion of balance beam. Only those skills that were going to be used in competition were practiced on the bars. I could not determine any skills being trained that were of doubtful consistency.

The next event chosen by the delegations was usually vaulting. This event provided some interesting problems because the coaches and gymnasts had some problems accommodating to the springy vaulting boards, particularly on the first day. By the second day of training all the countries had adapted and were vaulting very well. Each country began vaulting by taking some runs toward the horse that veered off to the side as they neared the board. Then followed handsprings and half-ons to get accustomed to the board and prepare for their vaults. The only girl who was spotted on vault was Senff from GDR. She was performing a Cuervo and had a little problem with the board for a while. The other countries did no spot vaulting at all and performed such vaults as the layout Tsukahara, Tsukahara with a full twist, and the handspring front somersault. The number of vaults performed by the different gymnasts varied greatly throughout the week. Egervaris from Hungary did two layout Tsukaharas total and one Chinese girl did handspring fronts for 45 minutes straight because her coach was visibly angry at her. The most popular vault was the layout Tsukahara.

At floor exercise on Wednesday gymnasts from every country performed two floor exercise routines with variations of less intense tumbling. The countries began with tumbling passes the gymnast was going to use in her routine. During the routines the gymnasts did less intense tumbling by doing tucks and layouts instead of their twisting and double somersaults. Later in the week the gymnasts performed two complete routines with full tumbling. The gymnasts' dance work was rather unambitious and no one spent much time preparing her dance skills.

After floor exercise the Chinese were the only country to do conditioning exercises. They began with running for 5 minutes. After running they did a series of three sets of 50 repetitions of two exercises. In the first exercise, the gymnast was lying on her stomach on the floor with her hands clasped behind her head. The gymnast then raised her legs and her head and shoulders off the floor. Each gymnast was careful not to arch her lower back. The gymnast then returned to lying flat on the floor. The exercise was repeated 50 times and was performed quickly. Although the first set contained 50 repetitions, the gymnasts seemed to lose count on subsequent sets when their coach was not looking and they did a few less. The second exercise was similar to the first except the gymnast lay on her side and sort of "side arched" upward to raise her legs and shoulders. These were also done 50 times for three sets.

After the lying exercises the gymnasts went to bars and did 20 pull-ups. The next exercise was interesting, as I believe the intent was to imitate the upswing of free hips. The gymnast began by pulling to an inverted hang with a straight body. The gymnast adopted a body position of a slight pike with a chest contraction and then the gymnast extended her hips and pulled upward until the legs were about 4 inches from the bar which was about 6 inches past the knee toward the hip. The gymnasts never extended to an arch. They were very careful to maintain the slight pike and the chest contraction throughout the exercise. The gymnasts did 20 repetitions of this exercise.

After uneven bars the gymnasts went to their coach who held their feet as they kicked to a handstand and held the handstand for 1 minute. After this conditioning period the coaches spent about 5 minutes bundling them up for the rather chilly weather outside. The Chinese worked the hardest during the training session. They were the third country into the arena and the last country to leave.

The female gymnasts at the American Cup were prepared significantly differently from the male gymnasts at this competition. In fact, I did not see one single full routine from a male gymnast during the entire training period prior to the competition.

There are some interesting consistencies in the training approaches all these countries used in the period of preparation immediately prior to the competition. This brief look at precompetition preparation can give you a valuable clue as to how much work is expected from the female gymnast in international, invitational-type competition. If you are going overseas for the first time, you may need some rules of thumb for determining how much work is normally expected from teams during training. This preparation period can contribute to success or failure at the competition.

Epilogue

There are no schools for gymnastics coaches. There are no universally accepted curricula. Certification of coaches is usually looked upon as another hassle and opportunity for someone to take our money without providing anything of substance. The best coaches look at their job as something only the talented and experienced can do. There is little respect among the most productive coaches and lots of jealousy, miscommunication, and misunderstanding. Every four years we continue to reinvent the wheel. We cannot continue to train athletes for 1984 and 1988 with 1960 methods. Other nations often laugh at our ineptitude and remarkable ability to make good athletes despite so little organization and education. At times our coaches and administrators are amazed that we do as well as we do, considering our limitations in program and knowledge.

Progress in gymnastics is in the hands of its coaches. Gymnastics cannot evolve as a sandlot sport because it is too dangerous and the equipment is heavy and expensive. Only the energy, character, and determination of the coaches can make and keep gymnastics a wholesome, honest enterprise for all who participate. The purpose of this text is to acquaint gymnastics coaches with dimensions of philosophy, program, and preparation they may not have considered. Robert Frost said, "I am not a teacher but an awakener." I hope that you have stumbled into a few ideas that raise questions, cause wonder at our inadequacies, bolster your determination, and encourage your commitment.

Much of the learning and character of the young people involved in gymnastics can be enhanced by our careful and concerned teaching of gymnastics and other life skills; every decision, action, event, activity, exercise, and project should be planned with the best interest of these athletes at heart. If we can set this criteria as a final measure of worth for every aspect of our programs, then our progress is assured and our value to young people enhanced.

Coaching involves a great deal more than simply being a walking, talking, spotting, skill analyzer. I believe that our greatest limitation as a profession is in our failure to define our goals, concepts, and principles within our own sphere of contribution. So let's document what we do and what we think. There's no way we can remove the "art" or "individualism" of good coaching, but every art has some rules and some axioms. Write it down. Let everyone know where we stand. The only issues that can be improved are those open for analysis and comment. Our progress and longevity as a sport may well be determined by our courage in exposing our ideas. This exposure will help sift through the misunderstandings. The problems that perpetuate themselves will be seen more clearly and steps will be taken to remove them.

A

Daily Training Diary

Name _____ **Starting Date** _____

Class Level _____

Resting Heart Rate for 15 Seconds

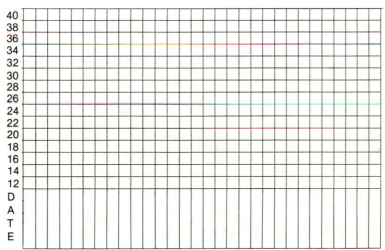

Weight Records

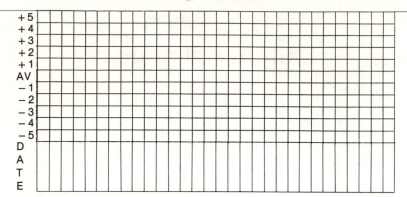

Illness Records

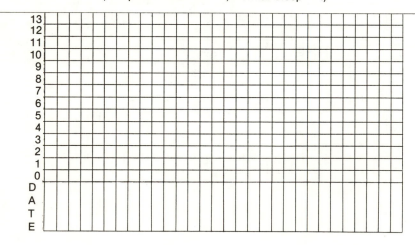

Length of Sleep—Number of Hours
(Sleep Disturbance = *, Normal Sleep = .)

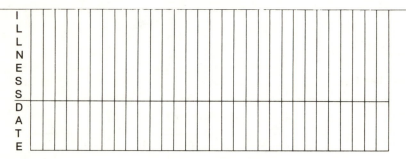

Date	Body Part	Event	Injuries Skill	Treatment	Limitations
1					
2					
3					
4					
5					
6					
7					
8					
9					
10					
11					
12					
13					
14					
15					
16					
17					
18					
19					
20					
21					
22					
23					
24					
25					
26					
27					
28					
29					
30					

B

Computer
Programs

In this section I have included four computer programs, a brief description of each program, and a variety of charts and printouts produced by these programs. Even if you know little about computers, take a look at the print-outs of the daily records to see the types of information being stored and the ease with which the computer handles such information and makes it understandable to the coach.

The programs are written in MicroSoft BASIC for the Apple II Plus with 64K memory, two disk drives, and CPM card. The printer is a Microline 84 by Okidata. The computer graphics capability, some of the codes for line feed, and other features are peculiar to this printer. I wrote the computer programs, and have developed my skills sufficiently over the past 6 years to be able to do the jobs I need done.

You can modify these programs to work on a variety of machines. The CPM operating system and MicroSoft BASIC are rather common denominators in computers. Conversion to other languages is left to your discretion.

PROGRAM NUMBER 1

I call this program (Figure B-1) "Log.bas"—it is the program that the athletes face prior to beginning training. An athlete stands at the computer and answers the questions put to her by the computer. This program knows the gymnast's name and records all the data by storing it on a floppy disk. The gymnast has the opportunity to correct any mistakes at the end of the program and the coach has the option of having the information stored or receiving daily printouts of each day's records.

Figure B-1   Program 1: Log.bas.

```
100 HOME:PRINT TAB(10)"INITIALIZATION OF DAILY INFORMATION":PRINT
110 INPUT"ENTER TODAY'S DATE (MM/DD/YY) ";DT$
120 PRINT:INPUT"ENTER THE DAY ==) ";DA$
130 PRINT:PRINT"OUTPUT TO LINE PRINTER (Y)ES OR (N)O?"
140 LP$=INKEY$:IF LP$="" THEN 140
150 GOTO 200
200 HOME:PRINT TAB(20)"DAILY TRAINING LOG":PRINT:PRINT
205 TU=0:TE$="":HE$="":CH=0
210 PRINT "PRESS THE LETTER BESIDE YOUR NAME"
220 PRINT:PRINT"A = LEAFMAN","B = LEDERER","C = LINDHOLM","D = MCDIVITT",
    "E = MILLS"
225 PRINT
230 PRINT"F = KUROWSKI","G = SOBOTKA","H = LABUY","I = JAKOPIN","J = TRAVLOS"
235 PRINT
240 PRINT"K = KIPKA","L = HAMILTON","M = SCHAFFNER","N = TREWITT"
245 PRINT
250 PRINT"O = ROETHLISBERGER":PRINT
255 PRINT:PRINT
260 PRINT"X = COMPILE","Z = ELEMENTS":PRINT
270 N1$=INKEY$:IF N1$="" THEN 270
280 IF N1$="A" THEN NA$="LEAFMAN":FI$="LORI":GOTO 500
290 IF N1$="B" THEN NA$="LEDERER":FI$="LYNN":GOTO 500
300 IF N1$="C" THEN NA$="LINDHOLM":FI$="IKA":GOTO 500
310 IF N1$="D" THEN NA$="MCDIVITT":FI$="KATIE":GOTO 500
320 IF N1$="E" THEN NA$="MILLS":FI$="PHOEBE":GOTO 500
330 IF N1$="F" THEN NA$="KUROWSKI":FI$="SHERYL":GOTO 500
340 IF N1$="G" THEN NA$="SOBOTKA":FI$="SANDY":GOTO 500
350 IF N1$="H" THEN NA$="LABUY":FI$="TAMMY":GOTO 500
360 IF N1$="I" THEN NA$="JAKOPIN":FI$="JENNIFER":GOTO 500
370 IF N1$="J" THEN NA$="TRAVLOS":FI$="TINA":GOTO 500
380 IF N1$="K" THEN NA$="KIPKA":FI$="GINNY":GOTO 500
390 IF N1$="L" THEN NA$="HAMILTON":FI$="GAIL":GOTO 500
400 IF N1$="M" THEN NA$="SCHAFFNER":FI$="PAULA":GOTO 500
410 IF N1$="N" THEN NA$="TREWITT":FI$="NICOLE":GOTO 500
420 IF N1$="O" THEN NA$="ROETHLISBERGER":FI$="MARIE":GOTO 500
430 IF N1$="X" THEN HOME:RESET:RUN "COMPILE"
440 IF N1$="Z" THEN HOME:RESET:RUN "ELEMENTS"
450 GOTO 200
500 HOME:PRINT TAB(20)"SLEEP RECORDS":PRINT
510 PRINT "HELLO ";FI$;", WHAT TIME DID YOU GO TO BED LAST NIGHT?":PRINT
520 PRINT"PLEASE, USE THE LETTER NEXT TO THE TIME.":PRINT
530 PRINT"A - 7:00 PM","B - 7:15 PM","C - 7:30 PM","D - 7:45 PM":PRINT
540 PRINT"E - 8:00 PM","F - 8:15 PM","G - 8:30 PM","H - 8:45 PM":PRINT
```

```
550 PRINT"I - 9:00 PM","J - 9:15 PM","K - 9:30 PM","L - 9:45 PM":PRINT
560 PRINT"M - 10:00 PM","N - 10:15 PM","O - 10:30 PM","P - 10:45 PM":PRINT
570 PRINT"Q - 11:00 PM","R - 11:15 PM","S - 11:30 PM","T - 11:45 PM":PRINT
580 PRINT"U - 12:00 AM","V - 12:15 AM","W - 12:30 AM","X - 12:45 PM":PRINT
590 PRINT"Y - 1:00 AM","Z - 1:15 AM","1 - 1:30 AM","2 - 1:45 AM":PRINT
600 PRINT"3 - 2:00 AM","4 - 2:15 AM","5 - 2:30 AM","6 - 2:45 AM":PRINT
610 SL$=INKEY$:IF SL$="" THEN 610
620 IF SL$="A" THEN TI$="7:00PM":TJ$="46":GOTO 990
630 IF SL$="B" THEN TI$="7:15PM":TJ$="46":GOTO 990
640 IF SL$="C" THEN TI$="7:30PM":TJ$="45":GOTO 990
650 IF SL$="D" THEN TI$="7:45PM":TJ$="45":GOTO 990
660 IF SL$="E" THEN TI$="8:00PM":TJ$="44":GOTO 990
670 IF SL$="F" THEN TI$="8:15PM":TJ$="44":GOTO 990
680 IF SL$="G" THEN TI$="8:30PM":TJ$="43":GOTO 990
690 IF SL$="H" THEN TI$="8:45PM":TJ$="43":GOTO 990
700 IF SL$="I" THEN TI$="9:00PM":TJ$="42":GOTO 990
710 IF SL$="J" THEN TI$="9:15PM":TJ$="42":GOTO 990
720 IF SL$="K" THEN TI$="9:30PM":TJ$="41":GOTO 990
730 IF SL$="L" THEN TI$="9:45PM":TJ$="41":GOTO 990
740 IF SL$="M" THEN TI$="10:00PM":TJ$="40":GOTO 990
750 IF SL$="N" THEN TI$="10:15PM":TJ$="40":GOTO 990
760 IF SL$="O" THEN TI$="10:30PM":TJ$="39":GOTO 990
770 IF SL$="P" THEN TI$="10:45PM":TJ$="39":GOTO 990
780 IF SL$="Q" THEN TI$="11:00PM":TJ$="38":GOTO 990
790 IF SL$="R" THEN TI$="11:15PM":TJ$="38":GOTO 990
800 IF SL$="S" THEN TI$="11:30PM":TJ$="37":GOTO 990
810 IF SL$="T" THEN TI$="11:45PM":TJ$="37":GOTO 990
820 IF SL$="U" THEN TI$="12:00AM":TJ$="36":GOTO 990
830 IF SL$="V" THEN TI$="12:15AM":TJ$="36":GOTO 990
840 IF SL$="W" THEN TI$="12:30AM":TJ$="35":GOTO 990
850 IF SL$="X" THEN TI$="12:45AM":TJ$="35":GOTO 990
860 IF SL$="Y" THEN TI$="1:00AM":TJ$="34":GOTO 990
870 IF SL$="Z" THEN TI$="1:15AM":TJ$="34":GOTO 990
880 IF SL$="1" THEN TI$="1:30AM":TJ$="33":GOTO 990
890 IF SL$="2" THEN TI$="1:45AM":TJ$="33":GOTO 990
900 IF SL$="3" THEN TI$="2:00AM":TJ$="32":GOTO 990
910 IF SL$="4" THEN TI$="2:15AM":TJ$="32":GOTO 990
920 IF SL$="5" THEN TI$="2:30AM":TJ$="31":GOTO 990
930 IF SL$="6" THEN TI$="2:45AM":TJ$="31":GOTO 990
940 GOTO 500
990 IF CH=1 THEN 10000 ELSE 1000
1000 HOME:PRINT TAB(20)"SLEEP RECORDS":PRINT
1010 PRINT"NOW I NEED TO KNOW WHEN YOU AWOKE.  PLEASE USE THE LETTER.":PRINT
1020 PRINT"A - 5:00 AM","B - 5:15 AM","C - 5:30 AM","D - 5:45 AM":PRINT
```

```
1030 PRINT"E - 6:00 AM","F - 6:15 AM","G - 6:30 AM","H - 6:45 AM":PRINT
1040 PRINT"I - 7:00 AM","J - 7:15 AM","K - 7:30 AM","L - 7:45 AM":PRINT
1050 PRINT"M - 8:00 AM","N - 8:15 AM","O - 8:30 AM","P - 8:45 AM":PRINT
1060 PRINT"Q - 9:00 AM","R - 9:15 AM","S - 9:30 AM","T - 9:45 AM":PRINT
1070 PRINT"U - 10:00 AM","V - 10:15 AM","W - 10:30 AM","X - 10:45 AM":PRINT
1080 PRINT"Y - 11:00 AM","Z - 11:15 AM","1 - 11:30 AM","2 - 11:45 AM":PRINT
1090 PRINT"3 - 12:00 PM","4 - 12:15 PM","5 - 12:30 PM","6 - 12:45 PM"
1100 SM$=INKEY$:IF SM$="" THEN 1100
1110 IF SM$="A" THEN AW$="5:00AM":AX$="26":GOTO 1490
1120 IF SM$="B" THEN AW$="5:15AM":AX$="26":GOTO 1490
1130 IF SM$="C" THEN AW$="5:30AM":AX$="25":GOTO 1490
1140 IF SM$="D" THEN AW$="5:45AM":AX$="25":GOTO 1490
1150 IF SM$="E" THEN AW$="6:00AM":AX$="24":GOTO 1490
1160 IF SM$="F" THEN AW$="6:15AM":AX$="24":GOTO 1490
1170 IF SM$="G" THEN AW$="6:30AM":AX$="23":GOTO 1490
1180 IF SM$="H" THEN AW$="6:45AM":AX$="23":GOTO 1490
1190 IF SM$="I" THEN AW$="7:00AM":AX$="22":GOTO 1490
1200 IF SM$="J" THEN AW$="7:15AM":AX$="22":GOTO 1490
1210 IF SM$="K" THEN AW$="7:30AM":AX$="21":GOTO 1490
1220 IF SM$="L" THEN AW$="7:45AM":AX$="21":GOTO 1490
1230 IF SM$="M" THEN AW$="8:00AM":AX$="20":GOTO 1490
1240 IF SM$="N" THEN AW$="8:15AM":AX$="20":GOTO 1490
1250 IF SM$="O" THEN AW$="8:30AM":AX$="19":GOTO 1490
1260 IF SM$="P" THEN AW$="8:45AM":AX$="19":GOTO 1490
1270 IF SM$="Q" THEN AW$="9:00AM":AX$="18":GOTO 1490
1280 IF SM$="R" THEN AW$="9:15AM":AX$="18":GOTO 1490
1290 IF SM$="S" THEN AW$="9:30AM":AX$="17":GOTO 1490
1300 IF SM$="T" THEN AW$="9:45AM":AX$="17":GOTO 1490
1310 IF SM$="U" THEN AW$="10:00AM":AX$="16":GOTO 1490
1320 IF SM$="V" THEN AW$="10:15AM":AX$="16":GOTO 1490
1330 IF SM$="W" THEN AW$="10:30AM":AX$="15":GOTO 1490
1340 IF SM$="X" THEN AW$="10:45AM":AX$="15":GOTO 1490
1350 IF SM$="Y" THEN AW$="11:00AM":AX$="14":GOTO 1490
1360 IF SM$="Z" THEN AW$="11:15AM":AX$="14":GOTO 1490
1370 IF SM$="1" THEN AW$="11:30AM":AX$="13":GOTO 1490
1380 IF SM$="2" THEN AW$="11:45AM":AX$="13":GOTO 1490
1390 IF SM$="3" THEN AW$="12:00PM":AX$="12":GOTO 1490
1400 IF SM$="4" THEN AW$="12:15PM":AX$="12":GOTO 1490
1410 IF SM$="5" THEN AW$="12:30PM":AX$="11":GOTO 1490
1420 IF SM$="6" THEN AW$="12:45PM":AX$="11":GOTO 1490
1430 GOTO 1000
1490 IF CH=1 THEN 10000 ELSE 1500
1500 HOME:PRINT TAB(20)"SLEEP DISTURBANCES":PRINT
1510 PRINT"DID YOU SLEEP RESTLESSLY ?":PRINT:PRINT"(Y)ES OR (N)O":PRINT
```

```
1520 RES=INKEYS:IF RES="" THEN 1520
1525 PRINT RES:PRINT
1530 IF RES="Y" THEN 1600
1540 IF RES="N" THEN 1600
1550 GOTO 1520
1600 PRINT"DID YOU AWAKEN BEFORE YOUR ALARM ?":PRINT
1610 PRINT"(Y)ES OR (N)O":PRINT
1620 PAS=INKEYS:IF PAS="" THEN 1620
1625 PRINT PAS:PRINT
1630 IF PAS="Y" THEN 1990
1640 IF PAS="N" THEN 1990
1650 GOTO 1620
1990 IF CH=1 THEN 10000 ELSE 2000
2000 HOME:PRINT TAB(20)"WEIGHT RECORDS":PRINT
2010 PRINT"NOW I NEED YOUR WEIGHT":PRINT
2020 PRINT"PLEASE ENTER YOUR WEIGHT FROM THE SCALE IN KILOGRAMS":PRINT
2030 INPUT"YOUR WEIGHT ?=====)";WT
2035 WG=WT*2.2:PRINT:PRINT:PRINT
2036 IF WG>120 THEN PRINT"PLEASE, REENTER YOUR WEIGHT":PRINT"YOU CAN'T WEIGH
     THIS MUCH !!!!":PRINT CHRS(7):PRINT CHRS(7):FOR X=1 TO
1500:NEXT X:GOTO 2000
2040 IF WG<40 THEN PRINT"PLEASE, REENTER YOUR WEIGHT":PRINT"YOU MUST BE
     AWFULLY  SKINNY !!!!!":PRINT CHRS(7):PRINT CHRS(7):FOR X=1 T
0 1500:NEXT X:GOTO 2000
2050 PRINT:PRINT:PRINT"YOUR WEIGHT IN POUNDS IS ==) ";WG
2060 WGS=STRS(WG)
2070 FOR X=1 TO 1000:NEXT X
2080 IF CH=1 THEN 10000 ELSE 2500
2500 HOME:PRINT TAB(20)"RESTING HEART RATE":PRINT
2510 PRINT"PLEASE, ENTER YOUR HEART RATE.":PRINT
2520 INPUT")))=====) ";HR
2530 IF HR<50 THEN HR=HR*4
2540 HRS=STRS(HR)
2550 IF CH=1 THEN 10000 ELSE 3000
3000 HOME:PRINT TAB(20)"DIETARY INFORMATION":PRINT
3010 PRINT"PLEASE, INCLUDE ALL THE FOODS THAT YOU HAVE EATEN IN THE LAST"
3020 PRINT"24 HOURS.":PRINT
3030 PRINT:PRINT"BE AS BRIEF AS POSSIBLE":PRINT
3040 LINE INPUT;FOS
3050 IF CH=1 THEN 10000 ELSE 3500
3500 HOME:PRINT TAB(20)"HEALTH INFORMATION":PRINT
3510 PRINT"PLEASE, USE THE LETTER OF THE ONE BELOW THAT APPLIES":PRINT
3520 PRINT"A -GOOD      B -STOMACH ACHE","C -HEADACHE","D -SORE THROAT":PRINT
3530 PRINT"E -RUNNY NOSE","F -NAUSEA","G -COLD","H -COUGH":PRINT
```

```
3540 PRINT"I -EAR ACHE":PRINT:PRINT:PRINT
3550 DE$=INKEY$:IF DE$="" THEN 3550
3560 IF DE$="A" THEN HE$="GOOD":GOTO 3990
3570 IF DE$="B" THEN HE$="STOMACH ACHE"
3575 IF DE$="C" THEN HE$="HEADACHE"
3580 IF DE$="D" THEN HE$="SORE THROAT"
3590 IF DE$="E" THEN HE$="RUNNY NOSE"
3600 IF DE$="F" THEN HE$="NAUSEA"
3610 IF DE$="G" THEN HE$="COLD"
3620 IF DE$="H" THEN HE$="COUGH"
3630 IF DE$="I" THEN HE$="EAR ACHE"
3640 HOME:PRINT TAB(20)"LET'S TAKE YOUR TEMPERATURE":PRINT
3650 PRINT HE$:PRINT:PRINT
3660 INPUT ")))====) ";TE$
3670 TU=VAL(TE$)
3680 IF TU)100.4 THEN PRINT:PRINT"PLEASE NOTIFY THE COACHES WITH THIS":PRINT
     "INFORMATION BEFORE STARTING TRAINING":PRINT
3685 IF TU(100.4 THEN 3990
3690 FOR X=1 TO 1500:NEXT X
3990 IF CH=1 THEN 10000 ELSE 4000
4000 HOME:PRINT TAB(20)"INJURY INFORMATION":PRINT
4010 PRINT"DO YOU HAVE AN INJURY TO RECORD ?":PRINT
4020 PRINT"(Y)ES OR (N)O"
4030 T$=INKEY$:IF T$="" THEN 4030
4040 IF T$="Y" THEN 4100
4050 IF T$="N" THEN 4060
4055 GOTO 4030
4060 N1$="NONE":BP$="NONE":EV$="NONE":SK$="NONE":TR$="NONE":LI$="NONE":GOTO
     4995
4100 HOME:PRINT"IS THIS INJURY (N)EW OR (O)LD"
4110 N$=INKEY$:IF N$="" THEN 4110
4120 IF N$="N" THEN N1$="NEW":GOTO 4150
4130 IF N$="O" THEN N1$="OLD":GOTO 4150
4140 GOTO 4110
4150 PRINT:INPUT"ENTER THE INJURED BODY PART --) ";BP$
4155 PRINT
4160 INPUT"ENTER THE SKILL --) ";SK$
4165 PRINT
4170 PRINT:PRINT"ENTER THE EVENT":PRINT
4180 PRINT"A-VAULTING","B-UNEVEN BARS","C-BAL BEAM","D-FLOOR EXERCISE"
4190 PRINT"E-TUMBLING","F-TRAMPOLINE","G-ALL EVENTS","H-OUTSIDE OF GYM"
4200 PRINT"I-UNKNOWN","J-BEAM DISMOUNTS":PRINT:PRINT
4210 JK$=INKEY$:IF JK$="" THEN 4210
4220 IF JK$="A" THEN EV$="VT":GOTO 4300
```

```
4230 IF JK$="B" THEN EV$="UB":GOTO 4300
4240 IF JK$="C" THEN EV$="BB":GOTO 4300
4250 IF JK$="D" THEN EV$="FX":GOTO 4300
4260 IF JK$="E" THEN EV$="TU":GOTO 4300
4270 IF JK$="F" THEN EV$="TR":GOTO 4300
4280 IF JK$="G" THEN EV$="AE":GOTO 4300
4285 IF JK$="H" THEN EV$="OT":GOTO 4300
4286 IF JK$="I" THEN EV$="UN":GOTO 4300
4287 IF JK$="J" THEN EV$="BD":GOTO 4300
4288 GOTO 4210
4300 PRINT:PRINT:INPUT"ENTER THE TREATMENT TAKEN --> ";TR$
4310 PRINT:INPUT"ENTER ANY LIMITATIONS TO PERFORMANCE --> ";LI$
4990 IF CH=1 THEN 10000 ELSE 4995
4995 GOTO 10000
5000 HOME:PRINT TAB(30)"WORKING":PRINT
5005 SN$=LEFT$(NA$,8)
5010 OPEN "R", 1, "B:"+SN$+".DAT",128
5020 FIELD 1, 5 AS A$,2 AS B$,7 AS D$,2 AS E$,7 AS F$,2 AS G$,1 AS H$,1  AS
     I$,7 AS J$,6 AS K$,10 AS L$,4 AS M$,3 AS N$,9 AS O$,2 AS P$,9 AS Q$,9
     AS R$,15 AS S$,25 AS T$
5030 LSET A$=LEFT$(DT$,5)
5040 LSET B$=DA$
5060 LSET D$=TI$
5070 LSET E$=TJ$
5080 LSET F$=AW$
5090 LSET G$=AX$
5100 LSET H$=RE$
5110 LSET I$=PA$
5120 LSET J$=WG$
5130 LSET K$=HR$
5140 LSET L$=HE$
5150 LSET M$=TE$
5160 LSET N$=N1$
5170 LSET O$=BP$
5180 LSET P$=EV$
5190 LSET Q$=SK$
5200 LSET R$=TR$
5210 LSET S$=LI$
5215 LSET T$=FO$
5220 I9=LOF(1)+1
5230 PUT 1,I9
5240 CLOSE 1
5250 IF LP$="Y" THEN 6000 ELSE 200
6000 LPRINT STRING$(80,199)
```

```
6010 LPRINT CHR$(255)
6020 LPRINT"DATE = ";DT$;"          DAY = ";DA$
6030 LPRINT"NAME","TO BED","AWAKE","RESTLESS","PRE AWAKE"
6040 LPRINT NA$, TI$, AW$, RE$, PA$
6050 LPRINT"WEIGHT","HEART RATE","HEALTH","TEMP","INJURY"
6060 LPRINT WG$, HR$, HE$, TE$, MI$
6070 LPRINT"BODY PART","EVENT","SKILL","TREATMENT"
6080 LPRINT BP$, EV$, SK$, TR$
6090 LPRINT"LIMITATIONS = ";LI$
6100 LPRINT"FOODS IN LAST 24 HOURS"
6110 LPRINT FO$
6120 LPRINT STRING$(80,199)
6130 GOTO 150
10000 CH=0:HOME:PRINT TAB(20)"ARE ALL YOUR ANSWERS CORRECT ?":PRINT
10010 PRINT:PRINT"(Y)ES OR (N)O"
10020 P9$=INKEY$:IF P9$="" THEN 10020
10030 IF P9$="Y" THEN 5000
10040 IF P9$="N" THEN 10060
10050 GOTO 10020
10060 PRINT:PRINT"WHAT WOULD YOU LIKE TO CHANGE ?":PRINT
10070 PRINT"A = TIME TO BED"
10080 PRINT"B = TIME AWAKE"
10090 PRINT"C = SLEEP DISTURBANCES"
10100 PRINT"D = WEIGHT"
10110 PRINT"E = HEART RATE"
10120 PRINT"F = DIETARY INFORMATION"
10130 PRINT"G = HEALTH INFORMATION"
10140 PRINT"H = INJURY INFORMATION"
10150 PRINT:PRINT
10160 P8$=INKEY$:IF P8$="" THEN 10160
10170 IF P8$="A" THEN CH=1:GOTO 500
10180 IF P8$="B" THEN CH=1:GOTO 1000
10190 IF P8$="C" THEN CH=1:GOTO 1500
10200 IF P8$="D" THEN CH=1:GOTO 2000
10210 IF P8$="E" THEN CH=1:GOTO 2500
10220 IF P8$="F" THEN CH=1:GOTO 3000
10230 IF P8$="G" THEN CH=1:GOTO 3500
10240 IF P8$="H" THEN CH=1:GOTO 4000
10250 GOTO 10160
```

PROGRAM NUMBER 2

This program (Figure B-2) is titled "Access.bas" — it performs the data read-outs from information stored by the gymnasts prior to practice every day. This program allows the coach to look up any gymnast and see any individual category of records at a glance. The program is not designed to use the graphics capabilities of the computer but rather the printer, since I find that paper copy is more important for my purposes. I need to push the buttons, then go back out to the training gym and watch practice while it prints out, then return and take the paper back into the gym so that I can study it.

Figure B-2   Program 2: Access.bas.

```
100 CLEAR ,,10000
110 HOME:PRINT TAB(15) "DATA ACCESS FILE MENU":PRINT
120 X=0
130 PRINT"A-LEAFMAN      B-LEDERER      C-LINDHOLM      D-MCDIVITT"
140 PRINT"E-KUROWSKI     F-SCHAFFNER    G-SOBOTKA       H-JAKOPIN"
150 PRINT"I-TREWITT      J-LABUY        K-TRAVLOS       L-MILLS"
160 PRINT"M-ROETHLISBERGER              N-HAMILTON      O-KIPKA"
180 PRINT
190 B$=INKEY$:IF B$="" THEN 190
200 IF B$="A" THEN SN$="LEAFMAN":GOTO 380
210 IF B$="B" THEN SN$="LEDERER":GOTO 380
220 IF B$="C" THEN SN$="LINDHOLM":GOTO 380
230 IF B$="D" THEN SN$="MCDIVITT":GOTO 380
240 IF B$="E" THEN SN$="KUROWSKI":GOTO 380
250 IF B$="F" THEN SN$="SCHAFFNER":GOTO 380
260 IF B$="G" THEN SN$="SOBOTKA":GOTO 380
270 IF B$="H" THEN SN$="JAKOPIN":GOTO 380
280 IF B$="I" THEN SN$="TREWITT":GOTO 380
290 IF. B$="J" THEN SN$="LABUY":GOTO 380
300 IF B$="K" THEN SN$="TRAVLOS":GOTO 380
310 IF B$="L" THEN SN$="MILLS":GOTO 380
320 IF B$="M" THEN SN$="ROETHLISBERGER":GOTO 380
330 IF B$="N" THEN SN$="HAMILTON":GOTO 380
340 IF B$="O" THEN SN$="KIPKA":GOTO 380
350 IF B$="P" THEN SN$="TRAVLOS":GOTO 380
360 IF B$="Q" THEN SN$="HAMILTON":GOTO 380
370 GOTO 190
380 HOME:PRINT:PRINT:PRINT:PRINT
390 PRINT"                 WORKING"
395 RN$=LEFT$(SN$,8)
400 OPEN "R", 1, "B:"+RN$+".DAT",128
410 GOSUB 2880
```

```
420 DIM DT$(17%),DA$(17%), SN$(17%), TI$(17%), TJ$(17%), AW$(17%), AX$(17%),
    RE$(17%), PA$(17%), WG$(17%), HR$(17%), HE$(17%), TE$(17%), NI$(17%),
    BP$(17%),EV$(17%), SK$(17%),TR$(17%), LI$(17%), RT(17%), AX(17%), TJ(17%)
430 DIM WG(17%), HR(17%), TE(17%), RW(17%), Y(17%), FO$(17%)
440 FIELD 1, 5 AS A$, 2 AS B$, 7 AS D$, 2 AS E$, 7 AS F$, 2 AS G$, 1 AS H$,
    1 AS I$, 7 AS J$, 6 AS K$, 10 AS L$, 6 AS M$, 3 AS N$, 9 AS O$, 2 AS P$,
    9 AS Q$, 9 AS R$, 15 AS S$, 25 AS T$
450 FOR X=18% TO 17%
460 GET 1, X
470 HOME:PRINT:PRINT:PRINT:PRINT"READING RECORD NUMBER ";X;"FILE NAME - ";SN$
480 DT$(X)=A$
490 DA$(X)=B$
500 SN$(X)=C$
510 TI$(X)=D$
520 TJ(X)=VAL (E$)
530 AW$(X)=F$
540 AX(X)=VAL (G$)
550 RE$(X)=H$
560 PA$(X)=I$
570 WG(X)=VAL (J$)
580 HR(X)=VAL (K$)
590 HE$(X)=L$
600 TE(X)=VAL (M$)
610 NI$(X)=N$
620 BP$(X)=O$
630 EV$(X)=P$
640 SK$(X)=Q$
650 TR$(X)=R$
660 LI$(X)=S$
665 FO$(X)=T$
670 NEXT X
680 CLOSE
690 HOME
700 PRINT TAB(20);"MENU":PRINT:PRINT
710 PRINT"CHOOSE ONE OF THE FOLLOWING":PRINT
720 PRINT"   1 ONE COMPLETE RECORD AT A TIME"
730 PRINT"   2 SLEEP RECORDS"
740 PRINT"   3 WEIGHT RECORDS"
750 PRINT"   4 HEART RATE RECORDS"
760 PRINT"   5 HEALTH RECORDS"
770 PRINT"   6 INJURY RECORDS"
780 PRINT"   7 DIETARY RECORDS"
785 PRINT"   8 RETURN TO MAIN MENU"
790 INPUT A
```

```
800 ON A GOTO 820,1140,1650,2060,2400,2620,3000,100
810 HOME:PRINT"      SINGLE RECORD NUMBER ";X
820 FOR X=18% TO 17%
830 HOME:PRINT"      SINGLE RECORD NUMBER ";X
840 PRINT:PRINT:PRINT"DATE","DAY","NAME"
850 PRINT;DT$(X),DA$(X),SN$
860 PRINT"TO BED","AWAKE","RESTLESS","PRE AWAKE"
870 PRINT;TI$(X),AW$(X),RE$(X),PA$(X)
880 PRINT"WEIGHT","HEART RATE","HEALTH","TEMP"
890 PRINT;WG(X),HR(X),HE$(X),TE(X)
900 PRINT"INJURY","BODY PART","EVENT","SKILL"
910 PRINT;N1$(X),BP$(X),EV$(X),SK$(X)
920 PRINT"TREATMENT","LIMITATIONS"
930 PRINT;TR$(X),LI$(X)
940 PRINT:PRINT
950 PRINT"(L)PRINT (N)EXT (R)ETURN"
960 CH$=INKEY$:IF CH$="" THEN 960
970 IF CH$="L"THEN 1020
980 IF CH$="N"THEN 1010
990 IF CH$="R"THEN 690
1000 GOTO 960
1010 IF X=17 THEN 690 ELSE NEXT X
1020 LPRINT"       DAILY RECORD ":LPRINT CHR$(255)
1030 LPRINT"DATE","DAY","RECORD NUMBER","NAME"
1040 LPRINT;DT$(X),DA$(X),X,SN$
1050 LPRINT"TO BED","AWAKE","RESTLESS","PRE AWAKE"
1060 LPRINT;TI$(X),AW$(X),RE$(X),PA$(X)
1070 LPRINT"WEIGHT","HEART RATE","HEALTH","TEMP"
1080 LPRINT;WG(X),HR(X),HE$(X),TE(X)
1090 LPRINT"INJURY","BODY PART","EVENT","SKILL"
1100 LPRINT;N1$(X),BP$(X),EV$(X),SK$(X)
1110 LPRINT"TREATMENT","LIMITATIONS"
1120 LPRINT;TR$(X),LI$(X)
1130 GOTO 950
1140 HOME:PRINT TAB(10)"SLEEP RECORDS":PRINT
1150 PRINT"(L)IST OR (G)RAPH OF SLEEP PERIODS"
1160 B$=INKEY$:IF B$="" THEN 1160
1170 IF B$="L" THEN 1200
1180 IF B$="G" THEN 1370
1190 GOTO 1160
1200 HOME:PRINT"IN BED";TAB(12)"AWAKE";TAB(20)"RSTLS";TAB(26)"PRE AW";TAB
     (35)"HOURS";TAB(42)"DATE";TAB(49)"DAY"
1210 FOR X=18% TO 17%
1220 PRINT;TI$(X);TAB(12)AW$(X);TAB(21)RE$(X);TAB(27)PA$(X);TAB(35)
     (TJ(X)-AX(X))/2;TAB(40)DT$(X);TAB(49)DA$(X)
```

```
1230 NEXT X
1240 GOSUB 1560
1250 PRINT"(L)PRINT OR (R)ETURN TO MENU"
1260 D$=INKEY$:IF D$="" THEN 1260
1270 IF D$="L" THEN 1290
1280 GOTO 690
1290 LPRINT CHR$(255):LPRINT TAB(29)"SLEEP RECORDS":LPRINT CHR$(255)
1300 LPRINT "FILE NAME ="SN$:LPRINT CHR$(255)
1310 LPRINT"IN BED";TAB(10)"AWAKE";TAB(20)"RESTLESS";TAB(30)"PRE AWAKE";TAB
     (40)"DAY";TAB(45)"HOURS";TAB(50)"DATE"
1320 FOR X=18% TO 17%
1330 LPRINT TI$(X);TAB(10)AW$(X);TAB(20)RE$(X);TAB(30)PA$(X);TAB(40)DA$(X);
     TAB(45) (TJ(X)-AX(X))/2;TAB(55)DT$(X)
1340 NEXT X
1350 LPRINT"AVERAGE SLEEP TIME = ";JK;" HOURS"
1360 GOTO 690
1370 HOME:PRINT TAB(10)"SLEEP PERIOD GRAPH":PRINT
1380 PRINT"NUMBER OF HOURS OF SLEEP":PRINT"  1 2 3 4 5 6 7 8 9 1 1 1 1 1"
1390 PRINT"                        0 1 2 3 4"
1400 FOR X=18% TO 17%
1410 PRINT STRING$((TJ(X)-AX(X)),"*")
1420 NEXT X:GOSUB 1560
1430 PRINT"(L)PRINT OR (R)ETURN TO MENU"
1440 E$=INKEY$:IF E$="" THEN 1440
1450 IF E$="L" THEN 1470
1460 GOTO 690
1470 LPRINT CHR$(255):LPRINT TAB(30)"SLEEP PERIOD GRAPH":LPRINT CHR$(255)
1480 LPRINT"FILE NAME =";SN$:LPRINT CHR$(255):LPRINT TAB(36)"HOURS";TAB(45)
     "SLEEP DISTURBANCES":LPRINT CHR$(255)
1490 LPRINT"7 8 9 1 1 1 1 1 2 3 4 5 6 7 8 9 1 1 1 "
1500 LPRINT"      0 1 2                 0 1 2"
1510 FOR X=18% TO 17%
1520 LPRINT CHR$(199);:LPRINT TAB(ABS(TJ(X)-46));STRING$(ABS(AX(X)-46)-(ABS
     (TJ(X)-46)),199);TAB(36)(TJ(X)-AX(X))/2;TAB(45)RE$(X);","
;PA$(X);" ";DA$(X);" ";DT$(X)
1530 NEXT X
1540 LPRINT"  AVERAGE SLEEP TIME = ";JK;" HOURS":LPRINT CHR$(255)
1550 GOTO 690
1560 Q=0:N=0:T=0
1570 FOR T=18% TO 17%
1580 Q=N
1590 RT(T)=(TJ(T)-AX(T))/2
1600 N=Q + RT(T)
1610 NEXT T
1620 JK=N /(T-1)
```

```
1630 PRINT"AVERAGE SLEEP TIME = ";JK;" HOURS"
1640 RETURN
1650 HOME:PRINT TAB(10) "WEIGHT RECORDS":PRINT
1660 PRINT"(L)IST OR (G)RAPH
1670 GH$=INKEY$:IF GH$="" THEN 1670
1680 IF GH$="L" THEN 1700
1690 IF GH$="G" THEN 1920 ELSE 1670
1700 HOME:PRINT TAB(10) "WEIGHT RECORDS":PRINT"FILE= ";SN$
1710 PRINT"WEIGHT","DATE","DAY"
1720 FOR Q=I8% TO I7%:SS=SS+1
1730 PRINT WG(Q),DT$(Q),DA$(Q)
1740 NEXT Q
1750 FOR X=I8% TO I7%
1760 UI=MM
1770 MM=UI+WG(X)
1780 NEXT X
1790 NN=MM/(X-1)
1800 PRINT"AVERAGE WEIGHT OVER RECORD PERIOD = ";NN
1810 PRINT:PRINT"(L)PRINT OR (R)ETURN TO MENU"
1820 QW$=INKEY$:IF QW$="" THEN 1820
1830 IF QW$="L" THEN 1850
1840 IF QW$="R" THEN 690 ELSE 1820
1850 LPRINT CHR$(255):LPRINT TAB(20) "WEIGHT RECORDS LIST":LPRINT CHR$(255)
1860 LPRINT"FILE NAME =";SN$:LPRINT"WEIGHT","DATE","DAY"
1870 FOR X=I8% TO I7%
1880 LPRINT WG(X),DT$(X),DA$(X)
1890 NEXT X
1900 LPRINT CHR$(255):LPRINT"AVERAGE WEIGHT OVER RECORD PERIOD = ";NN
1910 LPRINT CHR$(255):GOTO 690
1920 PRINT"(L)PRINT WEIGHT RECORDS GRAPH OR (R)ETURN"
1930 NM$=INKEY$:IF NM$="" THEN 1930
1940 IF NM$="R" THEN 690
1950 IF NM$="L" THEN 1960 ELSE 1930
1960 LPRINT CHR$(255):LPRINT TAB(20)"WEIGHT RECORDS GRAPH":LPRINT CHR$(255)
1970 LPRINT"FILE NAME = ";SN$:LPRINT CHR$(255)
1980 LPRINT TAB(23) NN
1990 LPRINT TAB(10) "+5";TAB(13)"+4";TAB(16)"+3";TAB(19)"+2";TAB(22)"+1";
     TAB(25)"AV";TAB(28)"-1";TAB(31)"-2";TAB(34)"-3";TAB(37)"-4";TAB(40)"-5"
2000 FOR X=I8% TO I7%
2010 RW(X)=WG(X) - NN
2020 Y(X)=25-RW(X)
2030 LPRINT TAB(Y(X)) CHR$(199);TAB(40) WG(X);TAB(50) DA$(X);" ";DT$(X)
2040 NEXT X
2050 LPRINT CHR$(255):GOTO 690
```

```
2060 HOME:PRINT TAB(10)"HEART RATE RECORDS":PRINT
2070 PRINT"LIST OF RECORDS"
2080 PRINT"FILE NAME = ";SN$:PRINT
2090 PRINT"HEART RATE","DATE","DAY"
2100 FOR X=18% TO 17%
2110 GP=RQ
2120 IF HR(X)<20 THEN HR(X)=HR(X)*10
2130 RQ=GP+HR(X)
2140 PRINT HR(X),DT$(X),DA$(X)
2150 NEXT X
2160 GB=RQ/(X-1)
2170 PRINT"AVERAGE HEART RATE OVER RECORD PERIOD =";GB
2180 PRINT"(L)PRINT,  (R)ETURN, OR (G)RAPH"
2190 VB$=INKEY$:IF VB$="" THEN 2190
2200 IF VB$="L" THEN 2340
2210 IF VB$="G" THEN 2230
2220 IF VB$="R" THEN 690 ELSE 2190
2230 LPRINT CHR$(255):LPRINT TAB(20)"HEART RATE GRAPH":LPRINT CHR$(255)
2240 LPRINT"FILE NAME = ";SN$:LPRINT CHR$(255)
2250 LPRINT"1 1 1 1 1 1 1 1 1 1 2 2 2 2 2 2 2 2 2 2 3 3 3 3 3 3 3 3 3 3 4":
     LPRINT"0 1 2 3 4 5 6 7 8 9 0 1 2 3 4 5 6 7 8 9 0 1 2 3 4 5 6 7 8 9 0"
2260 FOR X=18% TO 17%
2270 IF HR(X)<20 THEN HR(X)=HR(X)*10
2280 IF HR(X)>40 THEN 2290 ELSE 2300
2290 HR(X)=HR(X)/4
2300 LPRINT TAB(2*HR(X)-20)"*";TAB(60)DA$(X);" ";DT$(X);" ";HR(X)
2310 NEXT X
2320 VB$="":GOTO 2180
2330 NEXT X
2340 LPRINT "FILE NAME = ";SN$:LPRINT TAB(20)"HEART RATE RECORDS LIST":
     LPRINT CHR$(255):LPRINT "HEART RATE   DATE     DAY"
2350 FOR X=18% TO 17%
2360 LPRINT HR(X);TAB(10);DT$(X);"       ";DA$(X)
2370 NEXT X
2380 LPRINT "AVERAGE HEART RATE OVER RECORD PERIOD = ";GB
2390 VB$="":GOTO 2180
2400 HOME:PRINT TAB(10)"HEALTH RECORDS LIST":PRINT
2410 PRINT "FILE NAME = ";SN$
2420 PRINT"HEALTH","TEMP","DATE","DAY"
2430 FOR X=18% TO 17%
2440 PRINT HE$(X),TE(X),DT$(X),DA$(X)
2450 IF HE$(X)<>"GOOD       " THEN PP=PP+1
2460 NEXT X
2470 PRINT"NUMBER OF ILLNESS RECORDS = ";PP
```

```
2480 PRINT "(R)ETURN TO MENU OR (L)PRINT"
2490 G6$=INKEY$:IF G6$="" THEN 2490
2500 IF G6$="R" THEN 690
2510 IF G6$="L" THEN 2530
2520 GOTO 2490
2530 LPRINT CHR$(255):LPRINT TAB(20)"HEALTH RECORDS LIST":LPRINT CHR$(255)
2540 LPRINT"FILE NAME = ";SN$
2550 LPRINT"HEALTH","TEMP","DATE","DAY"
2560 FOR X=I8% TO I7%
2570 LPRINT HE$(X),TE(X),DT$(X),DA$(X)
2580 IF HE$(X)<>"GOOD       " THEN PO=PO+1
2590 NEXT X
2600 LPRINT"NUMBER OF ILLNESS RECORDS = ";PO
2610 GOTO 690
2620 HOME:PRINT TAB(10)"INJURY RECORDS LIST":PRINT
2630 PRINT"FILE NAME = ";SN$
2640 FOR X=I8% TO I7%
2650 IF NI$(X)<>"NON" THEN 2660 ELSE 2720
2660 PRINT"DATE = ";DT$(X);"    DAY = ";DA$(X)
2670 PRINT"INJURY","BODY PART","EVENT","SKILL"
2680 PRINT NI$(X),BP$(X),EV$(X),SK$(X)
2690 PRINT"LIMITATIONS = ";LI$(X)
2700 PRINT"TREATMENT = ";TR$(X)
2710 PRINT
2720 NEXT X
2730 PRINT"(L)PRINT OR (R)ETURN TO MENU"
2740 G8$=INKEY$:IF G8$="" THEN 2740
2750 IF G8$="L" THEN 2770
2760 IF G8$="R" THEN 690 ELSE 2740
2770 LPRINT CHR$(255):LPRINT TAB(20)"INJURY RECORDS LIST":LPRINT CHR$(255)
2780 LPRINT"FILE NAME = ";SN$
2790 FOR X=I8% TO I7%
2800 IF NI$(X)<>"NON" THEN 2810 ELSE 2850
2810 LPRINT"INJURY","BODY PART","EVENT","SKILL"
2820 LPRINT NI$(X),BP$(X),EV$(X),SK$(X)
2830 LPRINT"LIMITATIONS = ";LI$(X)
2840 LPRINT"TREATMENT = ";TR$(X)
2850 NEXT X
2860 GOTO 690
2870 END
2880 I9%=LOF(1)
2890 PRINT:PRINT"FILE NAME = ";SN$;"  HAS ";I9%;" RECORDS"
2900 PRINT"WHAT RECORD WOULD YOU LIKE TO BEGIN WITH"
2910 INPUT I8%
```

```
2920 PRINT:PRINT"WHAT RECORD WOULD YOU LIKE TO END WITH"
2930 INPUT I7%
2940 RETURN
3000 HOME:PRINT TAB(20)"DIETARY RECORDS":PRINT
3005 PRINT "FILE NAME = ";SN$
3010 FOR X=I8% TO I7%
3020 PRINT "DATE = ";DT$(X);"        DAY = ";DA$(X)
3030 PRINT "FOODS = ";FO$(X)
3040 PRINT
3050 NEXT X
3060 PRINT:PRINT"(L)PRINT OR (R)ETURN TO MENU":PRINT
3070 NH$=INKEY$:IF NH$="" THEN 3070
3080 IF NH$="L" THEN 3100
3090 IF NH$="R" THEN 690 ELSE 3080
3100 LPRINT CHR$(255):LPRINT"DIETARY INTAKE LIST":LPRINT CHR$(255)
3110 LPRINT"FILE NAME = ";SN$
3120 FOR X=I8% TO I7%
3130 LPRINT "DATE = ";DT$(X);"        DAY = ";DA$(X)
3140 LPRINT FO$(X)
3150 LPRINT CHR$(255)
3160 NEXT X
3170 LPRINT"NUMBER OF RECORDS = ";X-1
3180 GOTO 690
```

PROGRAM NUMBER 3

This program (Figure B-3) is titled "Compile" — it reads every gymnast's file and writes every gymnast's record to the line printer for each data factor. While this program compiles all the daily information records at once, it does not automatically compile the element records; this must be done by the element recording program. Compile can be selected from the menu in the Log.bas program by pushing "Z" or can be run independently. I use this program nearly every day after everyone has checked in on the computer. As the number of records gets large it takes several minutes for the computer to print them all out, but while this is happening I go back out to training and return to pick up the printout when I can't hear the printer anymore.

This program gives me a daily appraisal of the factors of sleep, health, heart rate, injury, a little information on diet, and other factors, so that I can scan the sheets to keep up with changes taking place in the athletes. If anyone looks sick, injured, or fatigued I can check to see if the printouts support my suspicion. If they do then I go to ask the gymnast how she feels or if she is hurt.

Figure B-3   Program 3: Compile.

```
100 CLEAR ,,10000
105 V=80:DIM DT$(V),DA$(V),TI$(V),TJ(V),AW$(V),AX(V),RE$(V),PA$(V),WG(V),HR
    (V),HE$(V),TE$(V),NI$(V),BP$(V),EV$(V),SK$(V),TR$(V),LI$(V),RT(V),RW(V),
    Y(V),FO$(V)
110 FOR BN=1 TO 15
120 RT=0:Q=0:N=0:JK=0:U=0:UI=0:MM=0:NN=0:X=0:GP=0:RQ=0:HR=0:I8%=0:I9%=0:RH=0
    :Y=0:RW=0:H=0:WG=0:V=0:IJ=0:HT=0
130 IF BN=1 THEN SN$="LEAFMAN":GOTO 400
140 IF BN=2 THEN SN$="LEDERER":GOTO 400
150 IF BN=3 THEN SN$="LINDHOLM":GOTO 400
160 IF BN=4 THEN SN$="MCDIVITT":GOTO 400
170 IF BN=5 THEN SN$="LABUY":GOTO 400
180 IF BN=6 THEN SN$="SCHAFFNER":GOTO 400
190 IF BN=7 THEN SN$="SOBOTKA":GOTO 400
200 IF BN=8 THEN SN$="KUROWSKI":GOTO 400
210 IF BN=9 THEN SN$="TREWITT":GOTO 400
220 IF BN=10 THEN SN$="KIPKA":GOTO 400
230 IF BN=11 THEN SN$="HAMILTON":GOTO 400
240 IF BN=12 THEN SN$="MILLS":GOTO 400
250 IF BN=13 THEN SN$="ROETHLISBERGER":GOTO 400
260 IF BN=14 THEN SN$="JAKOPIN":GOTO 400
270 IF BN=15 THEN SN$="TRAVLOS":GOTO 400
400 SN$=LEFT$(SN$,8):HOME:PRINT TAB(20)"WORKING"
410 OPEN "R", 1, "B:"+SN$+".DAT",128
420 GOSUB 15000
430 FIELD 1, 5 AS DT$,2 AS DA$,7 AS TI$,2 AS TJ$,7 AS AW$,2 AS AX$,1 AS RE$,
    1 AS PA$,7 AS WG$,6 AS HR$,10 AS HE$,6 AS TE$,3 AS NI$,9 AS BP$,2 AS EV$,
    9 AS SK$,9 AS TR$,15 AS LI$,25 AS FO$
440 FOR X=I8% TO I7%
450 GET 1,X
455 HOME:PRINT TAB(20)"READING RECORD NUMBER ";X;"   FILE NAME ==) ";SN$
460 DT$(X)=DT$
470 DA$(X)=DA$
480 TI$(X)=TI$
490 TJ(X)=VAL(TJ$)
500 AW$(X)=AW$
520 AX(X)=VAL(AX$)
530 RE$(X)=RE$
540 PA$(X)=PA$
550 WG(X)=VAL(WG$)
560 HR(X)=VAL(HR$)
570 HE$(X)=HE$
```

```
580 TE$(X)=TE$
590 NI$(X)=NI$
600 BP$(X)=BP$
610 EV$(X)=EV$
620 SK$(X)=SK$
630 TR$(X)=TR$
640 LI$(X)=LI$
645 FO$(X)=FO$
650 NEXT X
660 CLOSE 1
960 HOME:PRINT TAB(20)"GRAPH OF SLEEP RECORDS":PRINT
970 PRINT"FILE NAME = ";SN$
1140 LPRINT CHR$(255):LPRINT TAB(30)"SLEEP PERIOD GRAPH":LPRINT CHR$(255)
1150 LPRINT"FILE NAME = ";SN$
1160 LPRINT"7 8 9 1 1 1 1 1 2 3 4 5 6 7 8 9 1 1 1"
1170 LPRINT"        0 1 2                   0 1 2"
1180 FOR X=I8% TO I7%
1190 LPRINT CHR$(199);:LPRINT TAB(ABS(TJ(X)-46));STRING$(ABS(AX(X)-46)-(ABS
     (TJ(X)-46)),199);TAB(36)(TJ(X)-AX(X))/2;TAB(45)RE$(X);",";PA$(X);"
     ";DA$(X);"  ";DT$(X)
1200 NEXT X
1210 LPRINT CHR$(255)
1220 FOR T=I8% TO I7%
1230 RT(T)=(TJ(T)-AX(T))/2
1240 NEXT T
1250 FOR U=I8% TO I7%
1260 Q=N
1270 N=Q+RT(U)
1280 NEXT U
1290 JK=N/(U-1)
1295 LPRINT "AVERAGE SLEEP TIME = ";JK;" HOURS"
1300 FOR X=I8% TO I7%
1310 UI=MM
1320 MM=UI+WG(X)
1330 NEXT X
1340 MM=MM/(X-1)
1500 HOME:PRINT TAB(20)"WEIGHT RECORDS GRAPH":PRINT
1510 PRINT"FILE NAME ===)";SN$
1520 FOR H=I8% TO I7%
1530 RW(H)=WG(H)-MM
1540 Y(H)=25-RW(H)
1550 NEXT H
1600 LPRINT CHR$(255):LPRINT TAB(20)"WEIGHT RECORDS GRAPH":LPRINT CHR$(255)
1610 LPRINT "FILE NAME ==) ";SN$
```

```
1620 LPRINT CHR$(255)
1625 LPRINT "AVERAGE WEIGHT OVER RECORD PERIOD = ";NN
1630 LPRINT TAB(23)NN
1640 LPRINT TAB(10)"+5";TAB(13)"+4";TAB(16)"+3";TAB(19)"+2";TAB(22)"+1";TAB
     (25)"AV";TAB(28)"-1";TAB(31)"-2";TAB(34)"-3";TAB(37)"-4";TAB(40)"-5"
1645 FOR X=18% TO 17%
1650 LPRINT TAB(Y(X))CHR$(199);TAB(40)WG(X);"   ";DA$(X);"   ";DT$(X)
1660 NEXT X
1665 LPRINT CHR$(255)
1700 HOME:PRINT TAB(20)"HEART RATE GRAPH":PRINT
1710 PRINT"FILE NAME ==) ";SN$
1720 FOR X=18% TO 17%
1730 GP=RQ
1740 RQ=GP+HR(X)
1750 NEXT X
1760 GB=RQ/(X-1)
1780 FOR X=18% TO 17%
1790 RH=X:Y=ABS(HR(X)-50)
1800 NEXT X
2080 LPRINT CHR$(255):LPRINT TAB(20)"HEART RATE GRAPH":LPRINT CHR$(255)
2005 LPRINT"FILE NAME ==) ";SN$:LPRINT CHR$(255)
2010 LPRINT"1 1 1 1 1 1 1 1 1 1 2 2 2 2 2 2 2 2 2 2 3 3 3 3 3 3 3 3 3 4"
2015 LPRINT"0 1 2 3 4 5 6 7 8 9 0 1 2 3 4 5 6 7 8 9 0 1 2 3 4 5 6 7 8 9 0"
2020 FOR X=18% TO 17%
2030 IF HR(X))40 THEN 2034
2032 IF HR(X)(20 THEN HR(X)=HR(X)*10:GOTO 2034
2033 GOTO 2040
2034 HR(X)=HR(X)/4
2040 LPRINT TAB(2*HR(X)-20)"*";TAB(60)DA$(X);"   ";DT$(X);"   ";HR(X)
2050 NEXT X
2060 LPRINT CHR$(255)
2070 LPRINT"AVERAGE HEART RATE OVER RECORD PERIOD = ";GB
2080 LPRINT CHR$(255)
3000 HOME:PRINT TAB(20)"HEALTH RECORDS":PRINT
3010 PRINT"FILE NAME ==) ";SN$
3020 LPRINT TAB(20)"HEALTH RECORDS":LPRINT CHR$(255)
3030 LPRINT "FILE NAME ==) ";SN$:LPRINT CHR$(255)
3040 LPRINT "ILLNESS","TEMP","DATE","DAY"
3050 FOR X=18% TO 17%
3060 IF HE$(X)()"GOOD       " THEN 3070 ELSE 3100
3070 LPRINT HE$(X),TE$(X),DT$(X),DA$(X):HT=HT+1
3100 NEXT X
3105 LPRINT"NUMBER OF ILLNESS RECORDS = ";HT
3110 LPRINT CHR$(255)
```

```
3120 HOME:PRINT TAB(20)"INJURY RECORDS":PRINT
3130 PRINT "FILE NAME ==) ";SN$
3140 LPRINT TAB(20)"INJURY RECORDS":LPRINT CHR$(255)
3150 LPRINT"FILE NAME ==) ";SN$
3160 LPRINT CHR$(255)
3170 FOR X=I8% TO I7%
3180 IF NI$(X)="NEW" OR NI$(X)="OLD" THEN 3190 ELSE 3250
3190 LPRINT"INJURY","BODY PART","EVENT","SKILL","DATE":IJ=IJ+1
3200 LPRINT NI$(X),BP$(X),EV$(X),SK$(X),DT$(X)
3210 LPRINT"TREATMENT = ";TR$(X);"          DAY = ";DA$(X)
3220 LPRINT"LIMITATIONS = ";LI$(X)
3240 LPRINT CHR$(255)
3250 NEXT X
3260 LPRINT CHR$(255):LPRINT"TOTAL NUMBER OF INJURY RECORDS = ";IJ
3270 HOME:PRINT TAB(20)"DIETARY RECORDS":PRINT
3280 PRINT"FILE NAME ==) ";SN$
3290 LPRINT CHR$(255):LPRINT TAB(20)"DIETARY RECORDS":LPRINT CHR$(255)
3300 LPRINT "FILE NAME ==) ";SN$
3310 FOR X=I8% TO I7%
3320 LPRINT FO$(X)
3330 NEXT X
3340 NEXT BN
4000 RUN "LOG.BAS"
15000 HOME:PRINT"FILE NAME =";SN$:PRINT
15010 I9%=LOF(1)
15020 I8%=1
15030 I7%=I9%
15040 RETURN
```

PROGRAM NUMBER 4

This program (Figure B-4) is titled "Elements" — it is used for storage and analysis of the element data placed in the computer at the conclusion of practice by each gymnast. It can be selected from the main menu by typing "X." The gymnast again enters her own data and as I get the opportunity I go to the computer to get the printouts to see how everyone is doing. The number of elements shows me if we have neglected beam dismounts, done too much bars, and so forth.

Figure B-4 Program 4: Elements.

```
10 CLEAR ,,5000
20 HOME:PRINT TAB(20)"ELEMENT RECORDS":PRINT
30 PRINT "ARE YOU (S)TORING DATA OR (R)ETRIEVING ?"
```

```
40 X1$=INKEY$:IF X1$="" THEN 40
50 IF X1$="S" THEN XA=1:GOTO 90
60 IF X1$="R" THEN XA=2:GOTO 65
61 GOTO 40
65 HOME:PRINT TAB(20)"RETRIEVAL OF DATA":PRINT
70 XA=3:GOTO 100
90 GOTO 310
100 HOME:PRINT TAB(20)"ELEMENT RECORDS":PRINT
105 SN$="":VA=0:BA=0:BE=0:BD=0:FL=0:TU=0:TR=0:TT=0:M1=0:MN=0:BR=0:SR=0:FR=0
110 PRINT"A = LEAFMAN","B = LEDERER","C = SOBOTKA","D = HAMILTON":PRINT
120 PRINT"E = MCDIVITT","F = TREWITT","G = SCHAFFNER","H = JAKOPIN":PRINT
130 PRINT"I = MILLS","J = LINDHOLM","K = KUROWSKI","L = KIPKA":PRINT
140 PRINT"M = LABUY","N = TRAVLOS","O = ROETHLISBERGER"
145 PRINT
150 S$=INKEY$:IF S$="" THEN 150
160 IF S$="A" THEN SN$="LEAFMAN":GOTO 300
170 IF S$="B" THEN SN$="LEDERER":GOTO 300
180 IF S$="C" THEN SN$="SOBOTKA":GOTO 300
190 IF S$="D" THEN SN$="HAMILTON":GOTO 300
200 IF S$="E" THEN SN$="MCDIVITT":GOTO 300
210 IF S$="F" THEN SN$="TREWITT":GOTO 300
220 IF S$="G" THEN SN$="SCHAFFNER":GOTO 300
230 IF S$="H" THEN SN$="JAKOPIN":GOTO 300
240 IF S$="I" THEN SN$="MILLS":GOTO 300
250 IF S$="J" THEN SN$="LINDHOLM":GOTO 300
260 IF S$="K" THEN SN$="KUROWSKI":GOTO 300
270 IF S$="L" THEN SN$="KIPKA":GOTO 300
280 IF S$="M" THEN SN$="LABUY":GOTO 300
281 IF S$="N" THEN SN$="TRAVLOS":GOTO 300
282 IF S$="O" THEN SN$="ROETHLISBERGER":GOTO 300
290 GOTO 150
300 IF XA=1 THEN 400
301 IF XA=2 THEN 2000
302 IF XA=3 THEN 3000:REM SINGLE GYMNAST RETRIEVAL
310 HOME:PRINT"DATA ENTRY FOR INITIALIZATION":PRINT
320 LINE INPUT"ENTER THE DATE (MM/DD/YY) ";DT$
330 PRINT:INPUT"ENTER THE DAY ";DA$
340 PRINT:PRINT"ENTER (C)OMPULSORY OR (O)PTIONAL ";:INPUT FO$
345 PRINT:INPUT"ENTER NUMBER OF HOURS FOR TRAINING ";HR
346 PRINT:INPUT"OUTPUT TO LINEPRINTER (Y)ES OR (N)O ";LP$
350 GOTO 100
400 HOME:PRINT TAB(20)"DATA ENTRY FOR EVENTS ":PRINT
410 PRINT "DATA ENTRY FOR ***====)) ";SN$:PRINT
420 PRINT"DAY = ";DA$;"          DATE = ";DT$
```

```
430 IF FO$="C" THEN PRINT "COMPULSORY DAY"
435 IF FO$="O" THEN PRINT "OPTIONAL DAY"
436 PRINT
437 INPUT"VAULT ELEMENTS = ";VA
440 PRINT:INPUT"UNEVEN BARS ELEMENTS = ";BA
450 PRINT:INPUT"BALANCE BEAM ELEMENTS = ";BE
460 PRINT:INPUT"BALANCE BEAM DISMOUNTS = ";BD
470 PRINT:INPUT"FLOOR EXERCISE ELEMENTS = ";FL
471 PRINT:INPUT"TUMBLING ELEMENTS = ";TU
472 PRINT:INPUT"TRAMPOLINE ELEMENTS = ";TR
475 PRINT:PRINT"IS ALL THE DATA CORRECT (Y)ES OR (N)O ?"
476 R1$=INKEY$:IF R1$="" THEN 476
477 IF R1$="Y" THEN 480
478 IF R1$="N" THEN 400
479 GOTO 476
480 TT=VA+BA+BE+FL+TR+BD+TU
500 M1=HR*60
510 MN=TT/M1
520 PRINT:PRINT"TOTAL ELEMENTS = ";TT;"      ELEMENTS / MINUTE = ";MN
545 FOR X=1 TO 500:NEXT X
546 SN$=LEFT$(SN$,8)
550 GOSUB 10000
610 OPEN "R", 1, "B:"+SN$+".ELE",128
620 FIELD 1, 8 AS A$,3 AS B$,8 AS C$, 5 AS D$, 5 AS E$, 5 AS F$, 5 AS G$,5 AS
    H$,5 AS I$,5 AS J$,1 AS K$, 6 AS L$, 5 AS M$, 5 AS N$, 5 AS O$,52 AS P$
630 LSET A$=SN$
640 LSET B$=DA$
650 LSET C$=DT$
660 LSET D$=STR$(VA)
670 LSET E$=STR$(BA)
680 LSET F$=STR$(BE)
690 LSET G$=STR$(FL)
700 LSET H$=STR$(TR)
710 LSET I$=STR$(BD)
720 LSET J$=STR$(TU)
721 LSET K$=FO$
722 LSET L$=STR$(HR)
723 LSET M$=STR$(BR)
724 LSET N$=STR$(SR)
725 LSET O$=STR$(FR)
726 LSET P$=DU$
730 EN%=LOF(1)+1
740 PUT 1, EN%
750 CLOSE 1
```

```
755 IF LP$="Y" THEN GOSUB 11000
760 GOTO 100
3000 HOME:PRINT "NAME OF FILE = ";SN$
3010 PRINT:PRINT"WORKING":PRINT
3015 SN$=LEFT$(SN$,8)
3020 OPEN "R", 1, "B:"+SN$+".ELE", 128
3030 GOSUB 15000
3040 DIM SN$(I7%), DT$(I7%), DA$(I7%), FO$(I7%), HR(I7%), VA(I7%), BA(I7%),
     BE(I7%), FL(I7%), TR(I7%), T1(I7%), BD(I7%), TU(I7%), BR(I7%), SR(I7%),
     FR(I7%), T2(I7%), T3(I7%)
3050 FIELD 1, 8 AS A$, 3 AS B$, 8 AS C$, 5 AS D$, 5 AS E$, 5 AS F$, 5 AS G$,
     5 AS H$, 5 AS I$, 5 AS J$, 1 AS K$, 6 AS L$, 5 AS M$, 5 AS N$, 5 AS O$,
     52 AS P$
3060 FOR X=I8% TO I7%
3070 GET 1,X
3080 HOME:PRINT"READING RECORD NUMBER ";X;"  FILE ";SN$
3090 SN$(X)=A$
3100 DA$(X)=B$
3110 DT$(X)=C$
3120 VA(X)=VAL(D$)
3130 BA(X)=VAL(E$)
3140 BE(X)=VAL(F$)
3150 FL(X)=VAL(G$)
3160 TR(X)=VAL(H$)
3170 BD(X)=VAL(I$)
3180 TU(X)=VAL(J$)
3181 FO$(X)=K$
3182 HR(X)=VAL(L$)
3183 BR(X)=VAL(M$)
3184 SR(X)=VAL(N$)
3185 FR(X)=VAL(O$)
3186 DU$=P$
3200 NEXT X
3210 CLOSE 1
3220 HOME:PRINT"OUTPUT FORMAT":PRINT
3230 PRINT"    1 - SCREEN"
3240 PRINT"    2 - LINE PRINTER"
3250 G1$=INKEY$:IF G1$="" THEN 3250
3251 G1=VAL(G1$)
3252 ON G1 GOTO 4000, 4100, 3250
4000 HOME:PRINT TAB(20)"ELEMENT RECORDS FOR ";SN$
4010 PRINT"DATE";TAB(12)"VLT";TAB(19)"UPB";TAB(25)"BB";TAB(30)"FX";TAB(36)
     "BBDS";TAB(43)"TUM";TAB(48)"TOTAL";TAB(55);"L/M"
4020 FOR X=I8% TO I7%:S=S+1
```

```
4030 T1(X)=VA(X)+BA(X)+BE(X)+FL(X)+TR(X)+BD(X)+TU(X)
4035 T3(X)=T1(X)/(HR(X)*60)
4040 PRINT DT$(X);TAB(12)VA(X);TAB(19)BA(X);TAB(25)BE(X);TAB(30)FL(X);TAB
     (36)BD(X);TAB(43)TU(X);TAB(48)T1(X)
4041 T3(X)=T1(X)/(HR(X)*60)
4042 PRINT"    ROUTINES";TAB(19);BR(X);TAB(25)SR(X);TAB(30)FR(X);TAB(36)T2
     (X);TAB(55)T3(X)
4050 NEXT X
4055 GOSUB 12000
4056 GOSUB 13000
4060 PRINT:PRINT"(L)INE PRINT OR (R)ETURN TO MENU"
4070 A1$=INKEY$:IF A1$="" THEN 4070
4080 IF A1$="L" THEN 4100
4090 IF A1$="R" THEN 10
4095 GOTO 4070
4100 LPRINT CHR$(255):LPRINT TAB(20)"DATA - ELEMENTS IN DAILY TRAINING":
     LPRINT CHR$(255)
4110 LPRINT"FILE NAME =";SN$
4120 LPRINT CHR$(255):LPRINT "DATE";TAB(9)"VAULT";TAB(16)"BARS";TAB(23)
     "BEAM";TAB(31)"FLOOR";TAB(39)"BEDS";TAB(46)"TUMB";TAB(52)"TOTAL";TAB
     (60)"DAY";TAB(68)"EL/MIN"
4121 FOR X=18% TO 17%
4122 LPRINT DT$(X);TAB(9)VA(X);TAB(16)BA(X);TAB(23)BE(X);TAB(31)FL(X);TAB
     (39)BD(X);TAB(46)TU(X);TAB(52)T1(X);TAB(60)DA$(X)
4125 LPRINT"    ROUTINES";TAB(16)BR(X);TAB(23)SR(X);TAB(31)FR(X);TAB(52)T2
     (X);TAB(45)T3(X)
4130 NEXT X
4140 GOSUB 14000
4145 LPRINT CHR$(255):LPRINT TAB(20)"ELEMENT TOTALS FOR RECORD PERIOD":
     LPRINT CHR$(255)
4146 LPRINT "FILE NAME = ";SN$
4150 LPRINT"VAULT";TAB(9)"BARS";TAB(18)"BEAM";TAB(27)"FLOOR";TAB(36)"TRAMP";
     TAB(45)"BE DS";TAB(54)"TUMBL"
4160 LPRINT N1;TAB(9)B2;TAB(18)B3;TAB(27)F4;TAB(36)U1;TAB(45)N6;TAB(54)TJ
4170 LPRINT CHR$(255):LPRINT"AVERAGE ELEMENTS PER DAY":LPRINT CHR$(255)
4180 LPRINT"VAULT";TAB(12)"BARS";TAB(21)"BEAM";TAB(31)"FLOOR";TAB(40)"TRAMP"
     ;TAB(50)"BE DS";TAB(60)"TUMBL"
4190 LPRINT N1/S;TAB(12)B2/S;TAB(21)B3/S;TAB(31)F4/S;TAB(40)U1/S;TAB(50)N6/S
     ;TAB(60)TJ/S
4200 LPRINT CHR$(255):LPRINT"TOTAL NUMBER OF ELEMENTS = ";E1;" AVERAGE PER
     DAY = ";E1/S:LPRINT CHR$(255)
4210 LPRINT"TOTAL ROUTINES":LPRINT CHR$(255)
4220 LPRINT "BARS","BEAM","FLOOR","TOTAL ROUTINES"
4230 LPRINT Q2,Q4,Q6,Q2+Q4+Q6
```

```
4240 LPRINT "AVERAGE ROUTINES PER DAY"
4250 LPRINT "BARS","BEAM","FLOOR","ELEMENTS/MINUTE"
4260 LPRINT Q2/S,Q4/S,Q6/S,Q8
4265 LPRINT CHR$(255):LPRINT CHR$(255)
4270 GOTO 10
10000 HOME:PRINT TAB(20)"COMPLETE ROUTINES":PRINT
10010 PRINT"ENTER THE NUMBER OF COMPLETE ROUTINES":PRINT
10020 PRINT:INPUT"UNEVEN BARS = ";BR
10030 PRINT:INPUT"BALANCE BEAM = ";SR
10040 PRINT:INPUT"FLOOR EXERCISE = ";FR
10050 PRINT:PRINT"IS ALL YOUR DATA CORRECT (Y)ES OR (N)O"
10060 R2$=INKEY$:IF R2$="" THEN 10060
10070 IF R2$="Y" THEN RETURN
10080 IF R2$="N" THEN 10000 ELSE 10060
10090 RETURN
11000 LPRINT STRING$(80,199):LPRINT TAB(28)"DAILY ELEMENTS":LPRINT CHR$(255)
11005 LPRINT"FILE NAME = ";SN$;"     DATE = ";DT$;"          DAY = ";DA$
11010 LPRINT "VAULT","BARS","BEAM","FLOOR","BB DISM"
11020 LPRINT VA,BA,BE,FL,BD
11030 LPRINT "TUMBL","TRAMP","UPB ROUT","BB ROUT","FX ROUT"
11040 LPRINT TU,TR,BR,SR,FR
11050 LPRINT"TOT ELEMENTS","ELE / MIN":LPRINT TT,MN
11060 LPRINT CHR$(255)
11070 LPRINT STRING$(80,199)
11080 RETURN
12000 REM * TOTALLING ALL FACTORS
12005 N1=0:V1=0:N2=0:B2=0:N3=0:B3=0:N4=0:F4=0:N5=0:U1=0:B4=0:N6=0:TH=0:TJ=0:
      EV=0:E1=0:R1=0:R2=0:Q1=0:Q2=0:Q3=0:Q4=0:Q5=0:Q6=0:Q7=0:Q8=0
12010 FOR X=1 TO S
12020 V1=N1:N2=B2:N3=B3:N4=F4:N5=U1:B4=N6:TH=TJ:EV=E1:R1=R2:Q1=Q2:Q3=Q4:Q5=
      Q6:Q7=Q8
12030 N1=VA(X)+V1
12040 B2=BA(X)+N2
12050 B3=BE(X)+N3
12060 F4=FL(X)+N4
12070 U1=TR(X)+N5
12080 N6=BD(X)+B4
12090 TJ=TU(X)+TH
12100 E1=T1(X)+EV
12110 R2=T2(X)+R1
12120 Q2=BR(X)+Q1
12130 Q4=SR(X)+Q3
12140 Q6=FR(X)+Q5
12150 Q8=T3(X)+Q7
```

```
12160 NEXT I
12170 Q8=Q8/S
12180 RETURN
13000 PRINT:PRINT TAB(20)"TOTAL ELEMENTS FOR RECORD PERIOD"
13010 PRINT"VAULT";TAB(9)"BARS";TAB(18)"BEAM";TAB(27)"FLOOR";TAB(36)"TRAMP";
      TAB(45)"BE DS";TAB(54)"TUMBL"
13020 PRINT N1;TAB(9)B2;TAB(18)B3;TAB(27)F4;TAB(36)U1;TAB(45)N6;TAB(54)TJ
13030 PRINT"AVERAGE ELEMENTS PER DAY"
13035 PRINT"VAULT";TAB(12)"BARS";TAB(23)"BEAM";TAB(31)"FLOOR";TAB(40)"TRAMP"
      ;TAB(50)"BE DS";TAB(60)"TUMBL":PRINT N1/S;TAB(12)B2/S;TAB(23)B3/2;TAB
      (31)F4/S;TAB(40)U1/S;TAB(50)N6/S;TAB(60)TJ/S
13040 PRINT"TOTAL NUMBER OF ELEMENTS = ";E1;"    AVERAGE / DAY = ";E1/S
13050 PRINT"TOTAL ROUTINES"
13060 PRINT"BARS","BEAM","FLOOR","ELEM/MIN"
13070 PRINT Q2,Q4,Q6,Q8
13100 PRINT"AVERAGE ROUTINES PER DAY"
13110 PRINT"BARS","BEAM","FLOOR","ELEM/MIN"
13120 PRINT Q2/S,Q4/S,Q6/S,Q8
13200 RETURN
14000 REM * GRAPH OF DAILY ELEMENTS TOTAL
14010 LPRINT CHR$(255):LPRINT TAB(20)"GRAPH OF TOTAL DAILY ELEMENTS":LPRINT
      CHR$(255):LPRINT "FILE NAME = ";SN$
14020 LPRINT "TOTAL ELEMENTS"
14030 FOR I=18% TO I7%
14040 LPRINT STRING$(T1(I)/20,199);TAB(55)DT$(I);"   ";DA$(I);"   ";T1(I)
14050 NEXT I
14060 LPRINT CHR$(255)
14070 RETURN
14999 END
15000 I9%=LOF(1)
15010 PRINT:PRINT"FILE NAME = ";SN$;"    HAS ";I9%;" RECORDS"
15020 PRINT"WHAT RECORD TO BEGIN "
15030 INPUT I8%
15040 IF I8%<1 OR I8%>I9% THEN 15020
15050 PRINT"WHAT RECORD TO END"
15060 INPUT I7%
15070 IF I7%<I8% OR I7%>I9% THEN 15050
15080 RETURN
```

CHARTS OF PHYSIOLOGY AND ELEMENT RECORDS

The printouts shown as Figures B-5 through B-14 show the results of the programs listed previously and their treatment of the daily data of the gymnasts.

Figure B-5 is a sleep records list that displays time to bed, time awake, yes or no responses to questions regarding sleep disturbances, and date.

Figure B-5   Sleep Records List.

```
FILE NAME =KIPKA

IN BED     AWAKE      RESTLESS   PRE AWAKE  DAY  HOURSDATE
12:30AM    9:00AM     N          N          SU   8.5    02/06
10:30PM    6:00AM     Y          N          MO   7.5    02/07
9:30PM     6:00AM     Y          N          TU   8.5    02/08
10:30PM    6:45AM     N          N          TH   8      02/10
10:30PM    9:30AM     N          N          FR   11     02/11
11:00PM    8:30AM     N          N          SA   9.5    02/12
10:30PM    6:00AM     N          N          MO   7.5    02/14
10:30PM    6:00AM     N          N          TU   7.5    02/15
10:00PM    6:00AM     Y          N          TH   8      02/17
10:30PM    6:00AM     N          N          FR   7.5    02/18
10:30PM    5:30AM     Y          Y          MO   7      02/21
10:30PM    6:00AM     N          N          TU   7.5    02/22
10:30PM    7:00AM     Y          N          TH   8.5    02/24
12:30AM    7:00AM     N          N          FR   6.5    02/25
10:00PM    10:45AM    N          N          SU   12.5   02/27
11:30PM    7:00AM     N          N          TU   7.5    03/01
12:30AM    10:30AM    N          N          FR   10     03/04
12:30AM    8:30AM     Y          N          SA   8      03/05
10:00PM    10:30AM    Y          N          SU   12.5   03/06
11:00PM    6:30AM     Y          N          MO   7.5    03/07
10:00PM    7:30AM     N          N          TU   9.5    03/08
10:15PM    6:30AM     Y          N          TH   8.5    03/10
10:00PM    7:00AM     N          N          FR   9      03/11
10:00PM    6:30AM     N          N          MO   8.5    03/14
9:00PM     6:30AM     Y          N          TU   9.5    03/15
10:30PM    6:30AM     N          N          TH   8      03/17
10:00PM    7:00AM     N          N          FR   9      03/18
9:30PM     6:00AM     N          N          MO   8.5    03/21
9:45PM     6:30AM     Y          N          TU   9      03/22
10:45PM    6:30AM     N          N          TH   8      03/24
12:00AM    7:00AM     Y          N          TU   7      03/29
10:30PM    6:30AM     N          N          TH   8      03/31
12:00AM    7:30AM     N          N          FR   7.5    04/01
AVERAGE SLEEP TIME =  8.51515  HOURS
```

Figure B-6 displays the graphic representation of the daily sleep period along with the length of the sleep, sleep disturbances, date, and the average length of sleep over the entire record period. This can tell the coach quickly how the athlete has been sleeping.

Figure B-7 lists the weight records in pounds of the athlete, date, and the average weight over the record period at the bottom.

Figure B-6   Sleep Records Graph.

```
FILE NAME =KIPKA                        HOURS    SLEEP DISTURBANCES

7 8 9 1 1 1 1 2 3 4 5 6 7 8 9 1 1 1
    0 1 2                         0 1 2
```

	HOURS	SLEEP	DISTURBANCES	
	8.5	N,N	SU	02/06
	7.5	Y,N	MO	02/07
	8.5	Y,N	TU	02/08
	8	N,N	TH	02/10
	11	N,N	FR	02/11
	9.5	N,N	SA	02/12
	7.5	N,N	MO	02/14
	7.5	N,N	TU	02/15
	8	Y,N	TH	02/17
	7.5	N,N	FR	02/18
	7	Y,Y	MO	02/21
	7.5	N,N	TU	02/22
	8.5	Y,N	TH	02/24
	6.5	N,N	FR	02/25
	12.5	N,N	SU	02/27
	7.5	N,N	TU	03/01
	10	N,N	FR	03/04
	8	Y,N	SA	03/05
	12.5	Y,N	SU	03/06
	7.5	Y,N	MO	03/07
	9.5	N,N	TU	03/08
	8.5	Y,N	TH	03/10
	9	N,N	FR	03/11
	8.5	N,N	MO	03/14
	9.5	Y,N	TU	03/15
	8	N,N	TH	03/17
	9	N,N	FR	03/18
	8.5	N,N	MO	03/21
	9	Y,N	TU	03/22
	8	N,N	TH	03/24
	7	Y,N	TU	03/29
	8	N,N	TH	03/31
	7.5	N,N	FR	04/01

```
AVERAGE SLEEP TIME =  8.51515  HOURS
```

Figure B-7   Weight Records List.

```
FILE NAME =MCDIVITT
```

WEIGHT	DATE	DAY	107.8	03/06	SU
107.8	02/08	TU	107.36	03/08	TU
106.04	02/11	FR	107.36	03/10	TH
105.16	02/12	SA	106.04	03/11	FR
107.8	02/13	SU	107.8	03/12	SA
107.14	02/14	MO	107.8	03/13	SU
105.82	02/15	TU	107.8	03/15	TU
107.8	02/17	TH	106.48	03/17	TH
107.8	02/18	FR	105.6	03/18	FR
107.8	02/21	MO	105.16	03/19	SA
106.26	02/22	TU	104.72	03/20	SU
107.14	02/24	TH	104.5	03/21	MO
106.48	02/26	SA	103.84	03/22	TU
107.14	03/01	TU	104.28	03/24	TH
106.48	03/03	TH	107.8	03/31	TH
105.16	03/04	FR	107.36	04/01	FR

```
AVERAGE WEIGHT OVER RECORD PERIOD =  106.565
```

Figure B-8, the fourth chart, shows the weight records in graphic format. The average weight is displayed in the middle and the changes in weight above and below the average are shown for each day. In this chart the gymnast shows a gain in weight as the line moves to the left and a loss as it moves to the right. The small squares move as the gymnast's weight moves to the next highest integer.

Figure B-8   Weight Records Graph.

```
FILE NAME = MCDIVITT

                      106.565
          +5 +4 +3 +2 +1 AV -1 -2 -3 -4 -5
                           ■        107.8      TU 02/08
                            ■       106.04     FR 02/11
                            ■       105.16     SA 02/12
                           ■        107.8      SU 02/13
                           ■        107.14     MO 02/14
                            ■       105.82     TU 02/15
                           ■        107.8      TH 02/17
                           ■        107.8      FR 02/18
                           ■        107.8      MO 02/21
                          ■         106.26     TU 02/22
                           ■        107.14     TH 02/24
                           ■        106.48     SA 02/26
                           ■        107.14     TU 03/01
                           ■        106.48     TH 03/03
                            ■       105.16     FR 03/04
                           ■        107.8      SU 03/06
                           ■        107.36     TU 03/08
                           ■        107.36     TH 03/10
                            ■       106.04     FR 03/11
                           ■        107.8      SA 03/12
                           ■        107.8      SU 03/13
                           ■        107.8      TU 03/15
                            ■       106.48     TH 03/17
                            ■       105.6      FR 03/18
                            ■       105.16     SA 03/19
                             ■      104.72     SU 03/20
                             ■      104.5      MO 03/21
                              ■     103.84     TU 03/22
                             ■      104.28     TH 03/24
                           ■        107.8      TH 03/31
                           ■        107.36     FR 04/01
```

In Figure B-9 the resting heart rate is listed along with the day, date, and average heart rate at the bottom. The heart rate is checked by an electronic heart rate monitor when the gymnast enters the office.

Figure B-10, the sixth chart, is the resting heart rate graph. For ease of manipulation of the heart rate on a small piece of paper the heart rate is shown as if the pulse were taken for 15 seconds. The graph must be turned on its side to see the up and down fluctuations of the heart rate.

Figure B-9 Heart Rate List.

```
FILE NAME = MCDIVITT

HEART RATE     DATE      DAY
   60        02/08      TU              62       03/08     TU
   65        02/11      FR              88       03/10     TH
   90        02/12      SA              90       03/11     FR
   70        02/13      SU             105       03/12     SA
   64        02/14      MO              73       03/13     SU
   60        02/15      TU              65       03/15     TU
   60        02/17      TH              65       03/17     TH
   87        02/18      FR              63       03/18     FR
   87        02/21      MO              68       03/19     SA
   68        02/22      TU              58       03/20     SU
   60        02/24      TH              59       03/21     MO
   77        02/26      SA              70       03/22     TU
   85        03/01      TU              72       03/24     TH
   75        03/03      TH              94       03/31     TH
   72        03/04      FR              78       04/01     FR
   95        03/06      SU

         AVERAGE HEART RATE OVER RECORD PERIOD =  73.7097
```

Figure B-10 Heart Rate Graph.

```
FILE NAME = MCDIVITT

1 1 1 1 1 1 1 1 1 1 2 2 2 2 2 2 2 2 2 2 3 3 3 3 3 3 3 3 3 3 4
0 1 2 3 4 5 6 7 8 9 0 1 2 3 4 5 6 7 8 9 0 1 2 3 4 5 6 7 8 9 0
          *                                    TU 02/08   15
            *                                  FR 02/11   16.25
                  *                            SA 02/12   22.5
              *                                SU 02/13   17.5
             *                                 MO 02/14   16
          *                                    TU 02/15   15
          *                                    TH 02/17   15
                *                              FR 02/18   21.75
                *                              MO 02/21   21.75
             *                                 TU 02/22   17
           *                                   TH 02/24   15
               *                               SA 02/26   19.25
              *                                TU 03/01   21.25
             *                                 TH 03/03   18.75
            *                                  FR 03/04   18
                 *                             SU 03/06   23.75
           *                                   TU 03/08   15.5
                *                              TH 03/10   22
                *                              FR 03/11   22.5
                   *                           SA 03/12   26.25
             *                                 SU 03/13   18.25
           *                                   TU 03/15   16.25
           *                                   TH 03/17   16.25
           *                                   FR 03/18   15.75
               *                               SA 03/19   17
          *                                    SU 03/20   14.5
           *                                   MO 03/21   14.75
             *                                 TU 03/22   17.5
            *                                  TH 03/24   18
                 *                             TH 03/31   23.5
          *                                    FR 04/01   19.5
AVERAGE HEART RATE OVER RECORD PERIOD = 73.7097
```

The health records list, Figure B-11, shows only those days when the athlete records an illness. The temperature is included when appropriate. The total number of illness records and the day and date are also displayed.

Figure B-11   Health Records List.

```
FILE NAME = MCDIVITT
HEALTH          TEMP          DATE          DAY
HEADACHE        98.6          02/08         TU
HEADACHE        98.6          02/11         FR
GOOD            0             02/12         SA
GOOD            0             02/13         SU
GOOD            0             02/14         MO
GOOD            0             02/15         TU
STOMACH AC      98.6          02/17         TH
GOOD            0             02/18         FR
HEADACHE        98.6          02/21         MO
GOOD            0             02/22         TU
GOOD            0             02/24         TH
GOOD            0             02/26         SA
GOOD            0             03/01         TU
GOOD            0             03/03         TH
GOOD            0             03/04         FR
HEADACHE        98.6          03/06         SU
COLD            98.6          03/08         TU
COLD            98.6          03/10         TH
COLD            98.6          03/11         FR
COLD            98.6          03/12         SA
COLD            98.6          03/13         SU
GOOD            0             03/15         TU
GOOD            0             03/17         TH
GOOD            0             03/18         FR
GOOD            0             03/19         SA
GOOD            0             03/20         SU
GOOD            0             03/21         MO
GOOD            0             03/22         TU
GOOD            0             03/24         TH
HEADACHE        98.6          03/31         TH
GOOD            0             04/01         FR
NUMBER OF ILLNESS RECORDS =  11
```

Figure B-12   Dietary Information List.

```
FILE NAME = MCDIVITT
DATE = 02/08        DAY = TU      DATE = 02/18        DAY = FR
CHILI CORNBREAD MILK CHOC         STEAK RICE BEETS CAKE TAB

DATE = 02/11        DAY = FR      DATE = 02/21        DAY = MO
PIZZA ICE CREAM TAB 2 APP         TAB STEAK RICE YOGURT CER

DATE = 02/12        DAY = SA      DATE = 02/22        DAY = TU
PEANUTBUTTER/JELLY SAND.          CHICKEN CORN 3 APPLES CUC

DATE = 02/13        DAY = SU      DATE = 02/24        DAY = TH
EGGS CHIPS COOKIES POTATO         MEATLOAF JELLO BROCOLLI M

DATE = 02/14        DAY = MO      DATE = 02/26        DAY = SA
BEEF STEW POTATO CANDY 2A         HOT DOG POTATO CHIPS COOK

DATE = 02/15        DAY = TU      DATE = 03/01        DAY = TU
PEANUTBUTTER WAFER 3APPLE         PIZZA TAB CARAMELS GRANOL

DATE = 02/17        DAY = TH      DATE = 03/03        DAY = TH
TUNA CASSEROLE JELLO TOMA         HOT DOG FRIES COOKIE OATM
```

The coach can see how the athlete has been and the duration of any longstanding illnesses.

The dietary information, Figure B-12, is the most incomplete portion of the program; since the amount of storage space is limited, I have only allowed a small number of characters for storage of foods on the disk. The daily printouts of the athlete are saved so that when dietary analysis is made it is done from these printouts rather than totally from stored records. The addition of another disk drive would help solve my problem, but expense has prevented such an outlay.

The injury records in Figure B-13 give the coach useful information regarding incidence of injury, duration of injury, the event, the skill, treatment, and any limitations that may have occurred.

Figure B-13   Injury Records List.

```
FILE NAME = KUROWSKI
INJURY          BODY PART       EVENT           SKILL
OLD             ANKLE           TU              UNKNOWN
LIMITATIONS = WHEN IT HURTS.
TREATMENT = ICE
INJURY          BODY PART       EVENT           SKILL
OLD             ANKLE           TU              UNKNOWN
LIMITATIONS = WHEN IT HURTS.
TREATMENT = NONE
INJURY          BODY PART       EVENT           SKILL
OLD             ANKLE           TU              UNKNOWN
LIMITATIONS = VAULTING TUMBLI
TREATMENT = ICE
INJURY          BODY PART       EVENT           SKILL
OLD             ANKLE           TU              UNKNOWN
LIMITATIONS = WHEN IT HURTS.
TREATMENT = ICE
INJURY          BODY PART       EVENT           SKILL
OLD             ANKLE           TU              UNKNOWN
LIMITATIONS = WHEN IT HURTS.
TREATMENT = ICE
INJURY          BODY PART       EVENT           SKILL
OLD             ANKLE           TU              UNKNOWN
LIMITATIONS = WHEN IT HURTS.
TREATMENT = ICE
INJURY          BODY PART       EVENT           SKILL
NEW             THIGHS          BB              ALL KINDS
LIMITATIONS = WHEN I SWING DO
TREATMENT = ICE
INJURY          BODY PART       EVENT           SKILL
NEW             THIGHS          BB              SWING UPS
LIMITATIONS = RUBBING TOGETHE
TREATMENT = ICE
INJURY          BODY PART       EVENT           SKILL
NEW             THIGHS          BB              SWING UPS
LIMITATIONS = WHEN I SWING UP
TREATMENT = ICE
INJURY          BODY PART       EVENT           SKILL
OLD             THIGHS          BB              SWING UPS
LIMITATIONS = SWING UPS    RUB
TREATMENT = ICE
INJURY          BODY PART       EVENT           SKILL
OLD             THIGHS          BB              SWING UPS
LIMITATIONS = SWING UPS RUBBI
TREATMENT = ICE
INJURY          BODY PART       EVENT           SKILL
OLD             THIGHS          BB              SWING UPS
```

Figure B-14 shows the elements for the gymnast by giving the elements done on each day, a compilation of the elements done on each event through averaging. Figure B-15 is a graph of the number of total elements done on any particular training day.

Figure B-14   Element Records List.

FILE NAME =KUROWSKI

DATE	VAULT	BARS	BEAM	FLOOR	BEDS	TUMB	TOTAL	DAY	EL/MIN
02/08/83	7	161	497	311	0	0	976	TUE	
ROUTINES		8	13	3			0		3.25333
02/10/83	0	158	468	276	0	139	1041	THU	
ROUTINES		9	9	3			0		3.15455
02/11/83	32	0	312	71	0	0	415	FRI	
ROUTINES		0	10	0			0		2.30556
02/12/83	0	138	274	143	86	171	812	SAT	
ROUTINES		3	5	0			0		2.70667
02/15/83	15	112	306	422	0	0	855	TUE	
ROUTINES		5	0	3			0		2.85
02/17/83	0	132	412	0	0	147	691	THU	
ROUTINES		0	5	0			0		2.09394
02/27/83	22	114	277	0	0	175	588	SUN	
ROUTINES		4	9	0			0		2.45
03/04/83	26	166	283	100	0	0	575	FRI	
ROUTINES		8	8	2			0		3.19444
03/07/83	0	211	93	249	0	207	760	MON	
ROUTINES		8	0	3			0		2.30303
03/08/83	31	119	184	337	0	0	671	TUE	
ROUTINES		9	8	3			0		2.23667
03/10/83	0	121	214	564	0	10	909	THU	
ROUTINES		7	10	8			0		2.75455
03/11/83	12	84	216	69	0	0	381	FRI	
ROUTINES		4	6	0			0		2.11667
03/14/83	0	121	83	203	0	189	596	MON	
ROUTINES		0	0	3			0		1.80606
03/17/83	0	115	432	289	0	168	1004	THU	
ROUTINES		6	15	4			0		3.04242
03/19/83	30	201	376	258	53	0	918	SAT	
ROUTINES		9	12	3			0		3.06
03/20/83	0	182	467	123	0	248	1020	SUN	
ROUTINES		10	15	3			0		4.25
03/21/83	24	109	201	222	0	0	556	MON	
ROUTINES		5	10	2			0		1.68485
03/22/83	0	89	343	203	0	78	713	TUE	
ROUTINES		4	10	3			0		2.37667
03/24/83	17	101	272	179	0	0	569	THU	
ROUTINES		6	7	3			0		2.10741
03/29/83	35	77	130	24	0	0	266	TUE	
ROUTINES		0	0	0			0		.886667
04/01/83	0	57	495	0	0	207	759	FRI	
ROUTINES		0	15	0			0		3.1625

Figure B-15   Element Records Graph.

```
            GRAPH OF TOTAL DAILY ELEMENTS

FILE NAME = KUROWSKI
TOTAL ELEMENTS
██████████████████████████████████████    02/08/83    TUE     976
█████████████████████████████████████████ 02/10/83    THU    1041
███████████████████                        02/11/83    FRI     415
████████████████████████████████████       02/12/83    SAT     812
██████████████████████████████████████     02/15/83    TUE     855
█████████████████████████████              02/17/83    THU     691
███████████████████████                    02/27/83    SUN     588
██████████████████████                     03/04/83    FRI     575
██████████████████████████████             03/07/83    MON     760
██████████████████████████                 03/08/83    TUE     671
████████████████████████████████████       03/10/83    THU     909
███████████████                            03/11/83    FRI     381
████████████████████████                   03/14/83    MON     596
███████████████████████████████████████████ 03/17/83   THU    1004
████████████████████████████████████       03/19/83    SAT     918
████████████████████████████████████████   03/20/83    SUN    1020
██████████████████████                     03/21/83    MON     556
████████████████████████████               03/22/83    TUE     713
██████████████████████                     03/24/83    THU     569
███████████                                03/29/83    TUE     266
███████████████████████                    04/01/83    FRI     759


              ELEMENT TOTALS FOR RECORD PERIOD

FILE NAME = KUROWSKI
VAULT     BARS      BEAM      FLOOR     TRAMP     BE DS     TUMBL
 251      2568      6335      4043        0        139      1739

AVERAGE ELEMENTS PER DAY

VAULT       BARS       BEAM       FLOOR      TRAMP      BE DS       TUMBL
11.9524    122.286   301.667    192.524       0       6.61905    82.8095

TOTAL NUMBER OF ELEMENTS =   15075      AVERAGE PER DAY =   717.857

TOTAL ROUTINES

BARS          BEAM          FLOOR          TOTAL ROUTINES
 105           167            46             318
AVERAGE ROUTINES PER DAY
BARS          BEAM          FLOOR          ELEMENTS/MINUTE
 5            7.95238       2.19048         2.56171
```

C

Associations

Academy for the Psychology of Sports International
P.O. Box 200
Toledo, OH 43602
(419) 385-0044
Research in sport psychology and sport sociology.

Amateur Athletic Union of the U.S.
3400 W. 86th St.
Indianapolis, IN 46268
(317) 297-2900

American Alliance for Health, Physical Education, and Recreation
1201 16th St. NW
Washington, DC 20036
(202) 833-5530

American College of Sports Medicine
1440 Monroe St.
Madison, WI 53706
(608) 262-3632
This group is in the process of changing headquarters.

American Sokol
6426 West Cermak Rd.
Berwyn, IL 60402
(312) 795-6671

American Turners
1550 Clinton Ave. N.
Rochester, NY 14621
(716) 266-5800

Association of Intercollegiate Athletics for Women
1201 16th St. NW
Washington, DC 20036
(202) 833-5485

Athletic Institute
200 Castlewood Dr.
North Palm Beach, FL 33408
(305) 842-3600
Sponsors athletic competitions, educational programs, statistics, list of speakers.

International Association of Physical Education and Sports for Girls and Women
Department of Physical Education
University of Rhode Island
Kingston, RI 02881
(401) 792-2975
Women's sports and dance.

National Association for Girls' and Women's Sports
1201 16th St. NW
Washington, DC 20036
(202) 833-5540
Women's sports programs.

**National Association for Sports and
Physical Education**
1201 16th St. NW, Suite 627
Washington, DC 20036
(202) 833-5536

**National Association of Women's
Gymnastics Judges**
National Judges Training Chairman
Cheryl Grace
1401 Patricia 509
San Antonio, TX 78213
(512) 349-9298

National Athletic Trainers Association
C/O Philadelphia Eagles
Veterans Stadium
Philadelphia, PA 19148
(215) 874-8192

National Collegiate Athletic Association
U.S. 50 and Nall Ave.
P.O. Box 1906
Shawnee Mission, KS 66222
(913) 384-3220

**National Federation of State High
School Associations**
P.O. Box 98
Elgin, IL 60120
(312) 697-4100
Coordinates state associations.

**National High School Athletics
Coaches Association**
3423 E. Silver Springs Blvd., Suite 9
Ocala, FL 32670
(904) 622-3660

**National Junior College Athletic
Association**
George E. Killian, Executive Director
P.O. Box 1586
Hutchinson, KS 67501
(316) 663-5445

**North American Society for the
Psychology of Sport and
Physical Activity**
Dept. of Health, Recreation, and
Physical Education
Louisiana State University
Baton Rouge, LA 70803
(504) 388-2015
Scientific research in sport psychology.

People to People Sports Committee
98 Cutler Mill Rd.
Great Neck, NY 11021
(516) 482-5158
Promotes international sports exchanges
among those interested in sports.

**United States Association of
Independent Gymnastics Clubs**
Edgar M. Knepper
235 Pinehurst Rd.
Wilmington, DE 19803
(302) 656-3715
Represents the needs of the private
gymnastics school with a variety
of programs and activities.

**United States Elite Coaches Association
for Women's Gymnastics**
Jim Gault, Chairman
3511 Fiesta Del Sol East
Tucson, AZ 85715
(602) 886-3390
Coaches' organization for policies and
activities pertaining to elite-level
female gymnasts.

United States Gymnastics Federation
P.O. Box 1977
Indianapolis, IN 46204
(317) 638-8743
Governing body of gymnastics in the
United States.

**United States Gymnastics Safety
Association**
424 C Street NE
Capitol Hill
Washington, DC 20002
(202) 543-3403
Promotes safety in gymnastics.

United States Olympic Committee
1750 E. Boulder St.
Colorado Springs, CO 80908
(303) 632-5551

D

Magazines and Journals

AAU News
3400 W. 86th St.
Indianapolis, IN 46268
(317) 297-2900
Published monthly.

American Coaching Effectiveness Program
Human Kinetics Publishers
Box 5076
Champaign, IL 61820
(217) 351-5076
Coaching courses for all sports in a variety of levels for certification.

The American Journal of Sports Medicine
American Orthopaedic Society for Sports Medicine
Williams and Wilkins
428 East Preston St.
Baltimore, MD 21202
(800) 638-0672
Published bimonthly. $30.00/year.

American Turner Topics
1550 Clinton Ave. North
Rochester, NY 14621
(716) 832-3909
Published bimonthly.

Athletic Journal
1719 Howard St.
Evanston, IL 60202
(312) 328-8545
Published monthly.
General coaching, all sports.

Athletic Training
P.O. Box 1865
Greenville, NC 27834
(919) 752-1725
Published quarterly.

British Journal of Sports Medicine
Dr. Henry E. Robson, Editor
39 Linkfield Rd.
Mounstorrel, Loughborough
Leicestershire LE12 7DJ
Published quarterly. $30.00/year (U.S.)

Canadian Gymnastics Federation
11th Floor, 333 River Rd.
Vanier, Ontario
Canada K1L869
Publishes a variety of materials for its members.

Coaching: Women's Athletics
P.O. Box 867, 508 Main St.
Wallingford, CT 06492
(203) 265-0937
Published bimonthly.
General coaching, all sports.

*Institute for the Study of Athletic
Motivation*
P.O. Box 4109
San Jose, CA 95126
Provides a testing program to determine
a sports profile for any athlete.

International Gymnast Magazine
410 Broadway
Santa Monica, CA 90406
(213) 451-4330
Published monthly.

International Sport Sciences
The Franklin Institute Press
20th St. and the Parkway, Box 2266
Philadelphia, PA 19103
Published monthly. $95.00/year.
Wide variety of articles on all aspects
of sport science.

*The Journal of Orthopaedic and Sports
Physical Therapy*
See *American Journal of Sports
Medicine* (above)

The Journal of Sport Psychology
Human Kinetics Publishers
Box 5076
Champaign, IL 61820
(217) 351-5076
Published quarterly. $20.00/year

Medicine and Science in Sports
The American College of Sports
Medicine
1440 Monroe St.
Madison, WI 53706
(608) 262-2328
Published quarterly. $18.00/year
Medicine and exercise physiology for
all sports.

*National Directory of College Athletics
for Women*
4117 W. 49th St.
Amarillo, TX 79109
(806) 355-6417
Published annually.

The Physician and Sportsmedicine
Suite 200, 4530 West 77th St.
Minneapolis, MN 55435
(612) 835-3222
Published monthly. $32.00
General sports medicine information
for doctors, coaches, and
athletic trainers.

Scholastic Coach
50 West 44th St.
New York, NY 10036
(212) 867-7700
Published monthly.
General coaching, all sports.

USGF Gymnastics
P.O. Box 1977
Indianapolis, IN 46204
(317) 638-8743
General interest gymnastics for men
and women.

USGF Technical Journal
P.O. Box 1977
Indianapolis, IN 46204
(317) 638-8743
Technical information for coaches and
judges.

Women's Sports
1660 S. Amphlete Blvd.
San Mateo, CA 94402
(415) 574-4622
Published monthly.
All sports.

World Gymnastics
H-1553
Budapest Pf. 37
Hungary
Published quarterly.

E

Recommended Books

SPORTS MEDICINE

Arnheim, Daniel D. (1980). *Dance Injuries: Their Prevention and Care*. St. Louis, MO: The C.V. Mosby Co.

Cailliet, Rene (1973). *Knee Pain and Disability*. Philadelphia: F.A. Davis Co.

Dominguez, Richard H. (1979). *The Complete Book of Sports Medicine*. New York: Charles Scribner's Sons.

Krejci, Vladimir, and Koch, Peter (1979). *Muscle and Tendon Injuries in Athletes*. Chicago: Year Book Medical Publishers, Inc.

Larson, Leonard A. (Executive Ed.) (1971). *Encyclopedia of Sports Sciences and Medicine*. The American College of Sports Medicine. New York: Macmillan, Inc.

O'Donoghue, Don H., M.D. (1976). *Treatment of Injuries to Athletes*. Philadelphia: W.B. Saunders Co.

Sheehan, George (1972). *The Encyclopedia of Athletic Medicine*. Mountain View, CA: World Publications, Inc.

Subotnick, Steven I. (1979). *Cures for Common Running Injuries*. Mountain View, CA: World Publications, Inc.

Unitas, John, and Dintiman, George (1979). *Improving Health and Performance in the Athlete*. Englewood Cliffs, NJ: Prentice-Hall, Inc.

Vincent, L.M. (1978). *The Dancer's Book of Health*. Kansas City, KS: Sheed Andrews and McMeel, Inc.

Year Book of Sports Medicine (1981). Chicago: Year Book Medical Publishers, Inc. These books are published annually.

DANCE

Beaumont, Cyril W., and Idzikowski, Stanislas (1975). *A Manual of the Theory & Practice of Classical Theatrical Dancing.* New York: Dover Publications, Inc. (Originally published in 1922.)

Grant, Gail (1967). *Technical Manual and Dictionary of Classical Ballet.* New York: Dover Publications, Inc.

Vaganova, Agrippina (1969). *Basic Principles of Classical Ballet.* New York: Dover Publications, Inc.

PSYCHOLOGY

Eitzen, D. Stanley (1979). *Sport in Contemporary Society: An Anthology.* New York: St. Martin's Press, Inc.

Freudenberger, Herbert J. (1980). *Burn Out: The High Cost of High Achievement.* Garden City, NY: Doubleday/Anchor Press.

Gallwey, A. Timothy (1974). *The Inner Game of Tennis.* New York: Random House, Inc.

Gallwey, A. Timothy (1976). *Inner Tennis: Playing the Game.* New York: Random House, Inc.

Glasser, William (1976). *Positive Addiction.* New York: Harper & Row Publishers, Inc.

Murphy, Michael, and White, Rhea A. (1978). *The Psychic Side of Sports.* Reading, MA: Addison-Wesley Publishing Co., Inc.

Neal, Patsy E., and Tutko, Thomas A. (1975). *Coaching Girls and Women: Psychological Perspectives.* Boston: Allyn & Bacon, Inc.

Nideffer, Robert M. (1976). *The Inner Athlete.* New York: Thomas Y. Crowell.

Nierenberg, Gerard I., and Calero, Henry (1971). *How To Read A Person Like A Book.* New York: Hawthorne Books.

Ogilvie, Bruce, and Tutko, Thomas A. (1966). *Problem Athletes and How To Handle Them.* London: Pelham Books.

Ryan, Frank (1981). *Sports and Psychology.* Englewood Cliffs, NJ: Prentice-Hall, Inc.

Salmela, John H. (1980). *Competitive Behaviors of Olympic Gymnasts.* Springfield, IL: Charles C. Thomas, Publisher.

Tutko, Thomas, and Tosi, Umberto (1976). *Sports Psyching.* Los Angeles: J.P. Tarcher, Inc.

BIOMECHANICS

Dyson, Geoffrey (1970). *The Mechanics of Athletics.* New York: Dover Publications, Inc.

George, Gerald S. (1980). *Biomechanics of Women's Gymnastics.* Englewood Cliffs, NJ: Prentice-Hall, Inc.

Hay, James G. (1973). *The Biomechanics of Sports Techniques.* Englewood Cliffs, NJ: Prentice-Hall, Inc.

LeVeau, Barney (1977) *Biomechanics of Human Motion.* Philadelphia: W.B. Saunders Co.

PHYSIOLOGY AND NUTRITION

Astrand, Per-Olof, and Rodahl, Kaare (1977). *The Textbook of Work Physiology: Physiological Bases of Exercise.* New York: McGraw-Hill Book Co.

Bayrd, Ned, and Quilter, Chris (1982). *Food for Champions: How to Eat and Win.* Boston: Houghton Mifflin Co.

Benson, Herbert (1975). *The Relaxation Response.* New York: Avon Books.

de Vries, Herbert A. (1966). *Physiology of Exercise for Physical Education and Athletics.* Dubuque, IA: Wm. C. Brown Group.

Ellis, Audrey (1976). *The Kid Slimming Book.* South Bend, IN: Regnery/Gateway, Inc.

Fox, Edward L. (1979). *Sports Physiology.* Philadelphia: W.B. Saunders Co.

Morella, Joseph J., and Turchetti, Richard J. (1976). *Nutrition and the Athlete.* New York: Mason/Charter Publishers, Inc.

Smith, Nathan J. (1976). *Food for Sport.* Palo Alto, CA: Bull Publishing Co.

Taylor, Albert W. (Ed.) (1972). *Training: Scientific Basis and Application.* Springfield, IL: Charles C. Thomas, Publisher.

GENERAL

Appenzeller, Herb (1970). *From the Gym to the Jury.* Charlottesville, VA: The Michie Co.

Bowers, Carolyn, Fie, Jacquelyn Klein, and Schmid, Andrea Bodo (1981). *Judging and Coaching Women's Gymnastics.* Palo Alto, CA: Mayfield Publishing Co.

Carrasco, Roland (1976). *Essai de Systematique d'Enseignement de la Gymnastique aux Agres.* Paris: Editions Vigot.

Carrasco, Roland (1977). *Gymnastique aux Agres: l'Activite du Debutant. Programmes Pedagogiques.* Paris: Editions Vigot.

Carrasco, Roland (1978). *Gymnastique Pedagogie des Agres.* Paris: Editions Vigot.

Gault, Jim (1976). *The World of Women's Gymnastics.* Millbrae, CA: Celestial Arts.

Gilbert, Doug (1980). *The Miracle Machine.* New York: Coward, McCann, & Geoghegan, Inc.

Hartley, Sandra. *Training, Conditioning, and Flexibility Work for Women's Competitive Gymnastics.* Vanier, Ontario: Canadian Gymnastics Federation.

Hughes, Eric (Ed.) (1971). *Gymnastics for Girls: A Competitive Approach for Teacher and Coach.* New York: The Ronald Press Co.

Jerome, John (1980). *The Sweet Spot in Time.* New York: Summit Books.

Laptad, Richard Edd (1972). *A History of the Development of the United States Gymnastics Federation*. Fort Worth, TX: United States Gymnastics Federation.

Magakian, Arthur (1978). *La Gymnastique Artistique et Sportive Contemporaine Masculine et Feminine*. Paris: Chiron-Sports.

Martens, Rainer, Christina, Robert, Harvey, John, and Sharkey, Brian (1981). *Coaching Young Athletes*. Champaign, IL: Human Kinetics Publishers, Inc.

Peter, Laurence J., and Hull, Raymond (1969). *The Peter Principle: Why Things Always Go Wrong*. New York: Bantam Books.

Salmela, John H. (1976). *The Advanced Study of Gymnastics*. Springfield, IL: Charles C. Thomas, Publisher.

Sands, Bill (1981). *Beginning Gymnastics*. Chicago: Contemporary Books.

Sands, Bill (1982). *Modern Women's Gymnastics*. North Palm Beach, FL: Athletic Institute.

Taylor, Bryce, Bajin, Boris, and Zivic, Tom (1972). *Olympic Gymnastics for Men and Women*. Englewood Cliffs, NJ: Prentice-Hall, Inc.

Thomas, Vaughan (1970). *Science and Sport: How to Measure and Improve Athletic Performance*. Boston: Little, Brown & Co.

Wettstone, Eugene (Ed.) (1977). *Gymnastics Safety Manual*. University Park, PA: The Pennsylvania State University Press.

Wright, Russell (1976). *The Makings of an Olympic Champion: A New Approach to Weight Training and Weight Lifting*. Hicksville, NY: Exposition Press.

Bibliography

de Vries, Herbert (1966). *Physiology of Exercise for Physical Education and Athletics.* Dubuque, IA: William C. Brown.

Gallwey, W. Timothy (1974). *The Inner Game of Tennis.* New York: Random House.

Gilbert, Douglas (1980). *The Miracle Machine.* New York: Coward, McCann & Geoghegan.

Hartley, Sandra. *Training, Conditioning, and Flexibility Work for Women's Competitive Gymnastics.* Vanier, Ontario: Canadian Gymnastics Federation.

Jerome, John (1980). *The Sweet Spot in Time.* New York: Summit Books.

Karpovich, Peter V. (1971). Warm Up. *The Encyclopedia of Sport Sciences and Medicine.* New York: Macmillan.

Larson, Leonard A. (Executive Ed.) (1971). *The Encyclopedia of Sport Sciences and Medicine.* New York: Macmillan.

Lytle, Clyde Francis (Ed.) (1958). *Leaves of Gold.* Williamsport, PA: Coslett Publishing Co.

Peter, Laurence J., and Hull, Raymond (1969). *The Peter Principle.* New York: William Morrow.

Sands, W.A. (1981). Competition Injury Study: A Preliminary Report. *USGF Technical Journal,* 1 (3), 7.

Sharkey, Brian, J. (1979). *Physiology of Fitness.* Champaign, IL: Human Kinetics

Sheehan, George (1972). *The Encyclopedia of Athletic Medicine.* Mountain View, CA: World Publications.

Sheehan, George (1978). *Running and Being, The Total Experience.* New York: Simon and Schuster.

Wallis, Charles (Ed.) (1965). *The Treasure Chest.* New York: Harper & Row.